BETHANY
COLLEGE
LI

D1609326

796.079
W989b

The Book
of Sports Trophies

The Book
of Sports Trophies

Brian A. Wynne *and* Jerry Cotter Wynne

New York • Cornwall Books • London

© 1984 by Rosemont Publishing and Printing Corporation

Cornwall Books
440 Forsgate Drive
Cranbury, New Jersey 08512

Cornwall Books
25 Sicilian Avenue
London WC1A 2QH, England

Cornwall Books
2133 Royal Windsor Drive
Unit 1
Mississauga, Ontario
Canada L5J 1K5

Library of Congress Cataloging in Publication Data

Wynne, Brian A.
   The book of sports trophies.

   Bibliography: p.
   Includes index.
   1. Sports—History—Addresses, essays, lectures.
2. Sports—Awards—Addresses, essays, lectures.
I. Wynne, Jerry Cotter.   II. Title.
GV576.W95   1983   796′.079   82-71438
ISBN 0-8453-4746-2

Printed in the United States of America

For Jerry Cotter Wynne, *The Book of Sports Trophies* is the culmination of an idea that took root over twenty years ago in New York. He brought it with him to the West Coast where, with the help of his son, Brian, it began to take shape. Finally, his dream became a reality. However, in August of 1982, after a long battle with cancer, Jerry Wynne died in a Santa Barbara hospital. Although time cut short his life, it did not destroy his dream.

796.079
W89b

To my Dad,

> I wish fate had allowed you to see
> the fruits of our pride and faith in each other.

> B.W.

Contents

Acknowledgments

In any project of this size and nature, much assistance and cooperation are needed to make it a success. It is virtually impossible to repay all those who have graciously given of their time and effort and have asked nothing in return. It is our hope, however, that those special people know just how grateful we are and how much we value their contributions.

There is one person for whom thanks is not enough. Without the zest, energy, and artistic talent of Vicki Smart, this book would have less meaning and importance. Her love of sports, people, and life in general is an example to all of whose lives she has been a part. Tragically, prior to the publication of this book and before she could realize her goal and achievement, Vicki was killed in an automobile accident in Mexico. From those of us whose lives you have touched in such a special way, we say, "Thank you, Vicki."

Others to whom we are very thankful include Kellye DeVol, Julie Roberts, Laura Sorensen, Frank Cunningham, Carol Cunningham, Henry Goldy, Mike Goldy, Kay Duffy, Ken Williams, Cindy Brown, Phil Perry, Jr., Paul Rooney, T. W. Landis, Rich DeFrancesco, Tamar Gilfoil, Dave Hasemyer, Malcolm Tovey, Frank Kern, Scott Loveton, Pat Haggerty, Tom Gehrman, Tom Robertson, Dave Catherina, Steve Casad, Kevin Huska, Janice Berg, Joy Berg, John B. Williams, Tom Salyers, Bill Bowen, Bill Paznokas, Didi Paznokas, Arlanna Auzenne, Rita Peters, Bob Ward, and Peggy Brady.

Also, we would like to thank the many organizations that helped us with photographs, information, and other material. Those who were especially helpful include Claudia Starr (Churchill Downs), John Carroll (United Features Syndicates), Don Dunphy, Ray Nelson (American Bowling Congress), Joe Luppino (United Press International), Bert Sugar (Ring Magazine), Russ Adams (U.S. Tennis Association), Janet Seagle (U.S. Golf Association), Ron McQueenie (Indianapolis Speedway), Matt Winnick (National Basketball Association), Frank Kern (San Diego Hall of Champions), John Redding (Baseball Hall of Fame), Herbert Kramer (Special Olympics), JoAnn Evans (Special Olympics), Vernon Biever (Green Bay Packers), Susan McCann (National Football League), Joe Schwendeman (U.S. Golf Association), Edwin Broderick (New York Yankees), Steve Brener (Los Angeles Dodgers), Richard Rottkov (U.S. Soccer Federation), Mack Porter (Indianapolis Convention and Visitors Bureau), Louisa Raymond (XIII Olympic Winter Games), Kevin Kennedy (New York Knickerbockers), Leslie A. King (Amateur Athletic Union), Lefty Reid (Hockey Hall of Fame), the University of Southern California, Bill King II (Milwaukee Bucks), the Pittsburgh Steelers, the Boston Celtics, the Downtown Athletic Club, and the National Cowboy Hall of Fame.

Last, and certainly not least, we would like to thank the members of our family—John, Greg, Maryann, and Peggy—for their great help and support.

Introduction

The need for recognition has always been primary in man's life. In ancient times kings and noblemen displayed their elite status through the use of crowns, wreaths, and special garments. Prominent statesmen had buildings, or even entire cities, named after them. Great warriors had monuments dedicated to their achievements in battle. Though varying in form, these practices were all expressions of one underlying theme—man's continuing quest to be appreciated. Since the dawn of history the presentation of awards has been a common practice in virtually every culture. The Greeks and Romans were the first to construct trophies to commemorate great achievements. To them a trophy was "a structure erected (originally on the field of battle, later in any public place) as a memorial of a victory in war, consisting of arms or other spoils taken from the enemy, hung upon a tree or pillar, and dedicated to some divinity."[1]

Reference to the use of the trophy in war is found throughout the literature of the time. The *Aeneid*, for example, is very specific: "Around the posts hung helmets, darts and spears, and captive chariots, axes, shields and bars, and broken beaks of ships, the trophies of their wars."[2]

The brother of the warrior, the hunter, also incorporated the use of trophies into his rituals. Although his "enemies," chiefly of the animal kingdom, provided a different kind of challenge, his need to recognize his achievements still dominated. The hunter often brought home the skin of the conquered animal, or, as in modern times, he cut off its head and mounted it as a "trophy" in a place of observation.

The use of trophies has been an interesting one in the development of cultures. It often signifies the values held in highest esteem by the people of the time. The Romans made their trophies in the likeness of famous warriors. The Greeks sculptured theirs after philosophers. In medieval times great religious leaders or saints of the church were likewise honored. Rulers and other political figures have always been prime objects for such a practice.

A trophy can be considered to be "anything serving as a token or evidence of victory, valour, power, skill, etc."[3] In modern times, especially in the United States, trophies have fulfilled that basic role, but in a manner different from that of the past. While war has been in existence almost from the beginning of history—and its heroes revered—a new phenomenon has come along to surpass it on the mantle of human adulation. Sports, as we commonly refer to them, have become the new religion of our time and the vast and overwhelming stadiums and arenas in our cities, its temples.

While war heroes, politicians, and religious leaders still hold their place in modern man's heart, nothing can produce mass excitement as the success of a local sports figure. Local elections often struggle to produce a respectable turnout by the electorate, but on Super Bowl Sunday or Derby Day in Kentucky, fans pour into the area in overwhelming numbers.

The popularity of sports and recreation is neither

new nor regional. Man has always been obsessed with the need for physical activity and the stimulation of the body. War, of course, has always provided a means of fulfilling this need—and for some it still does. For others, games and recreation have provided the outlet. Organized sports in fact dates back at least to the ancient Greeks, with their famous Olympic Games. And in the Middle Ages, athletic competition was a popular form of entertainment among knights at festivals.

Whatever its origin, sports has played a central role in satisfying man's need for recognition. As in other facets of life, human beings need to prove who is the best, who is the most proficient at his specialty. For the athlete this need is fulfilled through the keeping of records, the setting of goals, the creation of championships, the scheduling of television appearances—and, ultimately, the presentation of trophies.

In professional basketball, the Boston Celtics can point to their numerous championship banners and remove any doubt as to whom is number one. Jack Nicklaus need only open the door to his trophy room to show who rules the golf circuit. And Mark Spitz, can let the seven gold medals draped neatly around his neck speak for his prowess in swimming.

For the professional athlete money is certainly one very desirable reward. But no matter what the sport or what the athlete's experience in it, there is something even more important. For most of his career with the Cincinnatti Royals of the National Basketball Association (NBA), the great Oscar Robertson had but one goal—to win the NBA championship, to be the best. His dream finally came true when he was traded to Milwaukee. In 1971 the Bucks won it all. Many athletes, despite their very big paychecks, endure a career of frustration for never being able to realize such a goal.

Amateur athletes are driven by a similar motivation—and they have no monetary recompense. Many train and practice for years for that one chance, that one moment to prove themselves against the best in the world. For a great number, the road ends in failure; for others there is that ultimate symbol of recognition—an Olympic Gold Medal.

Society today places a high value on being a winner, and the symbol of this success is the trophy. It is a reward, not just for the result, but for the effort it took to get there. Every year the Amateur Athletic Union presents the Sullivan Memorial Trophy to the "most outstanding amateur athlete of the year." The winners are outstanding, not only for the records broken or victories achieved, but for the dedication, hard work, and effort required to get to their respective plateaus. An athlete rarely

reaches the top of the sports world by an easy path.

Not uncommonly, an athlete, such as the great runner Wilma Rudolph, has had to overcome severe childhood illness and disease to go on to record-breaking careers. Such an achievement gives faith, hope, and optimism to millions of others around the world that they too can make it. Through the athlete's individual victories and defeats, he or she provides a sense of unification and pride to great numbers of people.

Nothing illustrates this point more than the accomplishment of the 1980 U.S. Olympic Hockey Team. Considered to be average at best, the American team entered the games as the underdog for even a third place medal. When it placed first, the nation rejoiced, and pride and patriotism were at a peak. From Maine to Maui, headlines proudly proclaimed the "miracle of Lake Placid."

For both the individual and the team, a trophy or medal can symbolize a lifetime of effort. Because of this, it seems that almost every sport, no matter how new, deems it appropriate to reward its participants with this type of recognition.

From the beginning of the practice of giving trophies, gold and silver were considered to be the most suitable material. As the monetary value of these precious metals has increased substantially over time, so has the price of trophies made of them. The solid gold Kentucky Derby Trophy, for example, is now worth $40,000, and the sterling silver Lombardi Trophy of the National Football League (NFL) is valued at $10,000.

One man who knew the value of a gold trophy was tennis star Arthur Ashe. In 1975 Ashe won the World Championship Tennis Finals in Dallas, Texas. The promoters, trying to be original, offered him a choice between $33,000 in prize money and a solid gold tennis ball. Ashe chose the ball. The next year, the talented Ashe won again and this time was offered even more prize money. But Ashe again chose the ball. While the cash he could have accepted adds up to a total of $78,000, the gold balls are now valued at over $105,000 each.

However important, the monetary value of the trophy is not the primary consideration. The prestige and symbolism surrounding it are of much more importance. In pro football, for example, the Pittsburgh Steelers will probably go down as one of the most famous teams in the history of the game—and not because in their early years they lived in the cellar. In the 1980 Super Bowl they won their fourth Lombardi Trophy, one of the most revered awards in sports. To say that it is a valued item would be an understatement. Chris Vecsey of the football commissioner's office knows just how valuable. He had to accompany the celebrated trophy on a flight to the Miami Super Bowl in 1969.

"I kept worrying that the plane would be hijacked to Cuba," young Vecsey said, "and when we got there, they'd leave everyone alone, but they'd take the trophy and melt it down like Cromwell did when he took over England. He melted down all the gold and silver and turned it into coins. How would I ever explain that?"

"The trophy got the window seat," Chris said with a note of disappointment, "I had to sit on the aisle."

In Florida Chris and the trophy were met by someone from the Commissioner's office and taken to a hotel with strict instructions not to let the trophy out of sight.

"They told me to sleep with it," Chris said. "But I think they were kidding."[4]

One of the more interesting moments in sports is the presentation of the trophy. For some awards, like the Sullivan Memorial Trophy and the Heisman Trophy, this comes at a dinner after the conclusion of the season. Such events, usually attended by dignitaries, businessmen, sports authorities, and past heroes of the sport are highlighted by the trophy winner's speech. Too often athletes are viewed as just uniformed figures on a field, and the human aspect is lost. But during these presentations they are seen as real people with their own individual personalities and with thoughts and feelings that the common man can understand and relate to.

Another context in which trophies are given— one that is used in most sports—is that of the postgame presentation. Usually occurring in the locker room of the winning team after a championship game, it often turns into a bottle-uncorking, champagne-drinking, toast-making, all-out celebration. After a season of very hard work and determination, the gates of emotion are opened, and victory is unabashedly enjoyed.

One of the most publicized and most awaited postgame presentations occurred in 1981 at the conclusion of the Super Bowl. All season long, Al Davis, the owner of the Oakland Raiders, and Pete Rozelle, the commissioner of the NFL, waged a personal battle in the media. The issue: whether or not Davis should be allowed to move his team to Los Angeles. It was no secret that there was very little love lost between the two. As fate would have it, the Raiders won the Super Bowl contest, and in the postgame ritual the commissioner of the league was called upon to present the Lombardi Trophy to the winning squad. For two weeks the media played up the possibility of such a confrontation. When it was about to occur, even the players readied themselves with cameras in the locker room. Perhaps they were expecting something along the lines of a Frazier-Ali rematch, but, unfortunately—or fortunately—they were disappointed. In a short but eloquent speech Rozelle congratulated Davis on his team's fine season and presented him with the trophy. Cameras flashed wildly in hopes of capturing a left hook or a jab to the throat. But Davis just graciously accepted the trophy, and that was that. Maybe they both knew that their day on the battlefield would come soon enough.

Since the beginning of man, whether expressed in the ancient Greek Olympics or in the wrestling of the cavemen in the dust, the need to determine who is the best has been prevalent. At one time, a fight to the death was the answer. Today, in a more civilized time, a loving cup has become more appropriate. Whether on the professional level or just on the level of the Sunday afternoon softballer, athletes everywhere deeply long for that mode of recognition—the trophy. After all, it is more than just something for the mantel.

The Book
of Sports Trophies

1
The Stanley Cup

On 18 March 1892 the Right Honourable Sir Frederick Arthur Stanley, Baron Stanley of Preston, in the County of Lancaster, in the Peerage of Great Britain, Knight Grand Cross of the Most Honourable Order of Bath, decided that it was time to introduce something new to the world of ice hockey:

> I have for some time been thinking it would be a good thing if there were a challenge cup, which could be held from year to year by the leading hockey club in Canada. There does not appear to be any outward or visible sign of the championship at present, and considering the interest that hockey matches now elicit, and the importance of having games fairly played under generally recognized rules, I am willing to give a cup that shall be annually held by the winning club.[1]

By this speech given to the Ottawa Club by Lord Kilcoursie on behalf of Lord Stanley, was born the most coveted award in the sport of ice hockey—the Stanley Cup.

An avid supporter of the game, Lord Stanley wanted there to be formal recognition for the sport, which had won the hearts of Canadian sports enthusiasts. At the time, ice hockey was primarily a Canadian sport, and controversies had arisen as to who truly was the national champion.

Though ice hockey was a relatively new sport, its history was as uncertain as its status at the time. There was evidence of a form of field hockey played in Greece as far back as 478 B.C. Comparable games were reported to have taken place in Holland, England, Scandanavia, and the Americas. But it was the Canadians who stubbornly claimed—and still do—that "hockey on ice" is strictly their creation.

Leagues were organized in Montreal, Ottawa, and Kingston, and in 1883 the Montreal Ice Carnival Committee held a world championship. The victor, McGill University, was awarded a $750 trophy.

In 1890 the Montreal AAA squad battled Quebec for the championship of the Canadian Amateur Hockey Association. The series of events that ensued proved once again the need for a professionally run, generally accepted championship tournament for the sport. Montreal and Quebec were set to square off at 8 P.M. for their league championship. Just two hours before game time, however, two of Quebec's best players were discovered missing. In a move of desperation, the Quebec squad grabbed a couple of friends from the stands, put them on the ice, and allowed them to play the match in their street clothes. Not surprisingly, Montreal won the match, 5–1.

As the game continued to grow, it spread into western Canada. Lord Stanley, realizing the need

The Stanley Cup Trophy. (NHL photo)

to solidify support for the sport, devised his proposal for the cup. He purchased a gold-lined silver bowl for ten guineas and set up trustees to manage the award. Appropriately, it was christened the Lord Stanley Cup.

Lord Stanley wanted his favorite team, the Ottawa Club, to be given the first cup. They were the 1892–93 champs. The trustees, however, decided that Ottawa had to play the Toronto Osgoode Hall Team for the award and to make matters worse, that the game was to be played in Toronto. Ottawa refused to go and threatened to resign from the Ontario Hockey Association. The trustees held fast, and neither party budged.

On 23 February 1894 a winner of the cup was finally declared. The Montreal Amateur Athletic Association team played at Montreal's Victoria Rink, with five-thousand people in attendance. Montreal won 3–1, and the first Stanley Cup was theirs.

Despite its early difficulties the Stanley Cup soon came to be revered by Canadian hockey enthusiasts. It was looked upon as a symbol of excellence by the club teams. But is was not just the players who became involved in its quest. Fans in both eastern and western Canada enthusiastically supported their local teams.

The first Stanley Cup final was sold out, and the precedent was set. Though their monetary rewards were little, players were treated royally—they were dined, entertained, and partied like kings. It was considered an honor just to be a part of the event. Referees often donated their services for the Final. By 1900, the Stanley Cup final had become a tradition.

Support for the game began to spread outside the

Playing like surgeons on ice, the Montreal Canadiens have won more Stanley Cups than any other National Hockey League team. (UPI photo)

borders of Canada, and in 1917 the fledgling National Hockey League (NHL) was born. In 1924 the first American team, from Boston, joined the league. It was not long before other cities—Pittsburgh, New York, Chicago, and Detroit—were also admitted.

Like all new leagues, the NHL went through a series of changes and modifications before it reached its present stable structure. In 1942 there were only six teams in the league, but expansion soon doubled its size. Rules were added, dropped, and changed, but for the most part the game remained the same.

Despite the difficulties, the Stanley Cup competition was not without its lighter moments. In the 1909 final between Ottawa and Montreal, the stage was set for a classic battle. Ottawa Arena was packed as both teams prepared for the struggle. The home team nervously awaited their chance to enter the ice and receive their ovation. Finally, their moment came. One by one, they moved out into the ice, and one by one they proceeded to fall flat on their backs! The crowd roared as three of their heroes lay sprawled on the ground. Stunned, the Ottawans picked themselves up only to discover that they had forgotten to take the leather covers off of their skate blades!

Another interesting aside concerns how some of the equipment originated. The puck, for example, was said to originally have been a solid rubber ball, like the ones used in lacrosse. Because of the physical damage caused by wild shots, however, a disgusted rink manager in the 1860s reportedly cut off the top and bottom sections. His innovation created a flattened "puck" that revolutionized the game—and prevented many a broken window.

Once it took its new efficient shape, the puck did not cease to be a center of controversy. In a game in Ontario the puck fell apart at a crucial moment. In those days pucks consisted of two halves cemented together. As the shot headed toward the goal, the puck split into two pieces—one going into the goal, the other missing. The offense celebrated, and the goalie protested. Perplexed, the referee checked his rulebook to try to come up with a decision. Finally, after intense deliberation he outlawed the goal, claiming that the puck that entered the goal was not regulation size, as it was only half an inch thick.

The Stanley Cup itself has been the object of some strange treatment. In 1905 the Ottawa Silver Seven team won the trophy and proceeded to set a precedent that must have had the trustees writhing in frustration. Following a hearty postgame celebration, several intoxicated members of the Silver Seven wandered home with the cup in hand. In a

One of the greatest players ever to step on the ice for Montreal was Maurice Richard. (UPI photo)

moment of craziness one of the players booted the coveted trophy into the nearby Rideau Canal. The next morning the players, realizing that the cup was missing, headed back to the canal equipped with a fishing rod. The cup was retrieved and was later given to a friend of the team, Harry Smith, for safekeeping.

The next year the cup was won by the Montreal Wanderers. When the time came for the presentation, the award was no where to be found. Officials frantically searched everywhere for it. Finally, an Ottawa player remembered—it was at Harry's place!

On another occasion the Montreal squad left the trophy at a photographer's studio after posing with it. It remained there for several months and was eventually used by the photographer's mother as a planter for some of her favorite greenery. Finally, the hockey world discovered once again that it was missing and, after some thorough backtracking, it was returned.

The Stanley Cup's prestige continued to be threatened. In 1910 the Montreal Wanderers won the award, and to show their gratitude they let one of the players use it to house chewing gum in his bowling alley as an advertising gimmick. Another insult to the dignity of the cup came in 1924, when the champion Montreal Canadiens, arriving at a postgame party, discovered that the trophy was no longer in their possession. Embarrassed, they quickly departed from the festivities and embarked on another infamous search for the trophy. Using the time-tested backtrack method, they eventually achieved success. In the middle of the night they found the coveted award sitting proudly by the roadside, exactly where they had earlier stopped to change a tire.

The trustees finally decided that enough was

enough. They gave Lord Stanley's bowl a permanent home—in the Hockey Hall of Fame in Toronto's National Exhibition Grounds. Despite the often reckless treatment afforded it, the cup still carried with it a mystique, a reverence, and a burning attraction to be owned. It is considered by fans and players alike to represent the pinnacle of achievement in ice hockey.

Like most sports trophies, the Stanley Cup has also been dominated by superstition. In 1947 the Toronto Maple Leafs were playing the Montreal Canadiens in the final. Toronto jumped out to a 3–2 lead in the games, and the sixth and potentially deciding contest was to be played on their home ice. Toronto manager Conn Smythe decided to leave the cup in Montreal, reasoning that to take it to the hometown would make his players overconfident and would provide the opponents with some extra motivation.

Similarly, the Detroit Red Wings opened up a lead against Toronto in the 1964 final. The two teams traveled to Detroit for what the Red Wings hoped would be the last game. But when Detroit Coach Sid Abel learned that the cup had been placed with the team's equipment on the trip, he quickly demanded that it be removed. The superstition seemed to hold true: in 1947, when the Maple Leafs left it behind, they won the final, and in 1964, when the Red Wings accidentally took it with them, they lost the series.

Players and coaches aren't the only ones who get caught up in Stanley Cup fever. Fans too have been known to catch it. In 1962, while a game was in progress in Chicago, a Blackhawk fan almost succeeded in walking off with the trophy. He was apprehended as he was heading toward the parking

From 1950 to 1967 the Toronto Maple Leafs became a powerful playoff contender. (UPI photo)

lot. The epidemic hit the city of Detroit in a much different way. Somehow, at each Stanley Cup contest an octopus was sneaked into the arena and flung onto the ice by a fan. Soon, the slimy visitor came to be expected, so the clever Detroit fans crossed them up one night and threw out an eel instead!

Despite the chicanery the Stanley Cup is considered to be serious business to fans throughout Canada and the United States. To the people of Montreal, it is very serious business. To them, heroes are easy to identify. They are the ones who have brought pride and prestige to their city via the Stanley Cup. They are Maurice Richard, Jean Beliveau, Bernie Geoffrion, Henri Richard, Yvan Cournoyer, Gilles Tremblay, Jacques Laperriere, and many more. The same is the case in Chicago with Bobby Hull and Stan Mikita. Likewise, in every other NHL city—only the names and the stories are different. The pride and enthusiasm are the same, as is the hope that maybe "next year" they will be able to say that the Stanley Cup is theirs.

But it is one team that has truly dominated the history of the cup competition. In fact, when one thinks of the Stanley Cup, one also automatically thinks of the Montreal Canadiens, who have won the cup a record twenty-two times. Their standard of excellence is unparalleled in the sport. They have dominated the game in the past, and they continue to dominate it today. Their names litter the Stanley Cup play-off record books. They also hold numerous team records, such as number of times named Stanley Cup champs, number of consecutive years in the Stanley Cup finals, amount of time taken to make five goals, number of goals scored in a shutout game, number of goals scored in a play-off game, and number of consecutive wins.

This is not to say that the Canadians have not had serious competition. Under the management of Conn Smythe, the Toronto Maple Leafs have enjoyed great success. In the thirties and forties Smythe led his Maple Leafs to seven cup championships. In the early sixties Punch Imlach, serving as both manager and coach, directed them to three straight championships.

For the most part ice hockey and the Stanley Cup have remained firmly in the hands of the Canadian people. Hockey, however, is rapidly spreading throughout North America, but on the professional level it is not a sport that is played all over the world. The need for a special medium—ice—and for specialized equipment has prevented its development in many areas of the globe. In his enthusiasm for the game, Lord Stanley attempted to develop a world championship. With the de-

The hard-hitting, aggressive style of the Philadelphia Flyers brought them success and the Stanley Cup. (UPI photo)

velopment of the Stanley Cup and the National Hockey League, the sport has grown by leaps and bounds. American teams have slowly but surely challenged the supremacy of the Canadians. Detroit, Chicago, Boston, New York, and Philadelphia have all achieved moderate success, but it is still the men from Montreal that are considered the team to beat.

Perhaps the only way to truly understand the enthusiasm and intensity that surrounds the world of ice hockey and the Stanley Cup is to relate a story that has undoubtedly made the rounds in Canadian hockey bars. The tale centers around a man who, in Montreal, makes a bigger hit than one of Mickey Mantle's line drives, who stands taller than a Wilt Chamberlain, and who packs more punch than a Muhammad Ali right hook. He is, of course, Maurice ("the Rocket") Richard, and the story centers on a 1952 Stanley Cup semi-final game between the Canadiens and the Boston Bruins. The score was tied in the second period when Richard was checked very heavily by an opposing defenseman. He crashed to the ice and was knocked unconscious. Blood poured down his face from a cut, which later required six stitches to close. Groggy and unstable, the stubborn Richard was back on the ice in the third period. The Montreal crowd roared as their hero returned to the game. He responded with one of the most sensational plays in the history of the game. In his book *The Stanley Cup Story*, Henry Roxborough describes the action:

In mid-ice, [Butch] Richards laid a flat pass right on the stick of the flying Rocket. In full flight, with body crouched and skates flashing, Richard swooped across the centre line, bobbled the puck for an instant, picked it up again, and swerved to the right as he crossed the blue line.

NHL President Clarence Campbell presents the coveted trophy to members of the championship Flyers squad. (UPI photo)

It appeared for a moment as though he would end in the corner. But he cut sharply toward the goal, decked a defender out of his boots, curved to the centre, and fired a bullet-like puck that the goalkeeper never saw until he turned around and fished it out of the net.[2]

Stanley Cup competition at its best!

Stanley Cup Winners

1893–94	Montreal AAA
1894–95	Montreal Victorias
1895–96	Winnipeg Victorias
1896–97	Montreal Victorias
1897–98	Montreal Victorias
1898–99 (Mar.)	Montreal Shamrocks
1898–99 (Feb.)	Montreal Victorias
1899–1900	Montreal Shamrocks
1900–1901	Winnipeg Victorias
1901–2	Montreal AAA
1902–3	Ottawa Silver Seven
1903–4	Ottawa Silver Seven
1904–5	Ottawa Silver Seven
1905–6	Montreal Wanderers
1906–7 (Mar.)	Montreal Wanderers
1906–7 (Jan.)	Kenora Thistles
1907–8	Montreal Wanderers
1908–9	Ottawa Senators
1909–10	Montreal Wanderers
1910–11	Ottawa Senators
1911–12	Quebec Bulldogs
1912–13	Quebec Bulldogs
1913–14	Toronto Ontarios
1914–15	Vancouver Millionaires
1915–16	Montreal Canadiens
1916–17	Seattle Metropolitans
1917–18	Toronto Arenas
1918–19	No decision
1919–20	Ottawa Senators
1920–21	Ottawa Senators
1921–22	Toronto St. Pats
1922–23	Ottawa Senators
1923–24	Montreal Canadiens
1924–25	Victoria Cougars
1925–26	Montreal Maroons
1926–27	Ottawa Senators
1927–28	New York Rangers
1928–29	Boston Bruins
1929–30	Montreal Canadiens
1930–31	Montreal Canadiens
1931–32	Toronto Maple Leafs
1932–33	New York Rangers
1933–34	Chicago Black Hawks

1934–35	Montreal Maroons	1959–60	Montreal Canadiens
1935–36	Detroit Red Wings	1960–61	Chicago Black Hawks
1936–37	Detroit Red Wings	1961–62	Toronto Maple Leafs
1937–38	Chicago Black Hawks	1962–63	Toronto Maple Leafs
1938–39	Boston Bruins	1963–64	Toronto Maple Leafs
1939–40	New York Rangers	1964–65	Montreal Canadiens
1940–41	Boston Bruins	1965–66	Montreal Canadiens
1941–42	Toronto Maple Leafs	1966–67	Toronto Maple Leafs
1942–43	Detroit Red Wings	1967–68	Montreal Canadiens
1943–44	Montreal Canadiens	1968–69	Montreal Canadiens
1944–45	Toronto Maple Leafs	1969–70	Boston Bruins
1945–46	Montreal Canadiens	1970–71	Montreal Canadiens
1946–47	Toronto Maple Leafs	1971–72	Boston Bruins
1947–48	Toronto Maple Leafs	1972–73	Montreal Canadiens
1948–49	Toronto Maple Leafs	1973–74	Philadelphia Flyers
1949–50	Detroit Red Wings	1974–75	Philadelphia Flyers
1950–51	Toronto Maple Leafs	1975–76	Montreal Canadiens
1951–52	Detroit Red Wings	1976–77	Montreal Canadiens
1952–53	Montreal Canadiens	1977–78	Montreal Canadiens
1953–54	Detroit Red Wings	1978–79	Montreal Canadiens
1954–55	Detroit Red Wings	1979–80	New York Islanders
1955–56	Montreal Canadiens	1980–81	New York Islanders
1956–57	Montreal Canadiens	1981–82	New York Islanders
1957–58	Montreal Canadiens	1982–83	New York Islanders
1958–59	Montreal Canadiens		

2
The Heisman Memorial Trophy

He had just received the most sought-after award in college football. A brilliant season for this Penn State running back had insured that his name would be forever etched in the record books of the game. But as John Cappelletti stood at the podium at the Downtown Athletic Club, his own achievements seemed minimal.

His voice choked a bit as he began his acceptance speech. He had come a long way in four years. But somehow, even though he was being given the Heisman Memorial Trophy in honor of his own accomplishments, there was someone he could not forget:

> The youngest member of my family, Joseph, is very ill. He has leukemia, and if I can dedicate this trophy to him tonight and give him a couple of days of happiness, it is worth everything. I think a lot of people think that I go through a lot on Saturdays, and during the week—as most athletes do—you get your bumps and bruises, and it is a terrific battle out there on the field. But for me it's on Saturdays, and it's only in the fall. For Joseph it's all year round, and it's a battle that's unending with him, and he puts up with much more than I'll ever put up with. I think that this trophy is more his than it is mine because he has been a great inspiration to me.[1]

When John Cappelletti finished his speech that day at the Downtown Athletic Club in New York, it was apparent to everyone present that the idea behind the trophy was truly being fulfilled. The intent of its founder, Bill Prince, a member of the club and editor of its journal, was to honor the most outstanding college football player in the United States every year. This was back in 1935. Little did Prince realize that his simple thought would take off the way it did and that the award would be held in such honor and prestige. Thousands of college football players have put forth herculean efforts every year toward the goal, the dream, of winning

Penn State's John Cappelletti presents his Heisman Trophy to his brother Joey. (UPI photo)

24

the Heisman Memorial Trophy. And when John Cappelletti walked away from the podium that December day in 1973, it was easy to see why he was so outstanding. Not only was he an extraordinary football player, he was an extraordinary human being. Had he been alive to see it, Bill Prince would have been proud.

As successful as Prince's idea proved to be, it was not at first easily accepted. When Prince first thought of the trophy, he presented the idea to the club's athletic director, John Heisman. No stranger to the sport of football, Heisman had devoted almost his entire life to the game. After gaining experience as a player, he served thirty-six years as a coach at eight different colleges. He was widely known for his various innovations. He helped invent the forward pass, the direct snap of the ball, and many other ideas that enlivened the game. He was one of the most influential men that the sport has known.

When Bill Prince approached him with the idea, Heisman was not overly receptive. He thought that since football is a team game, individual recognition would be neither practical nor beneficial to the sport. Heisman also thought that it was impossible to determine whether, for example, a quarterback was more valuable than a lineman—or an offensive player more valuable than a defensive player. Then, at a luncheon one day with some local reporters, Heisman mentioned the proposal for the trophy. To his surprise, it received enthusiastic support. Suddenly, the wheels were in motion.

Despite Heisman's initial skepticism the idea took root, and in time he too became amenable to the concept. Once it was decided that the club would annually present the award, the next hurdle was to decide on a design for the trophy. The man chosen to undertake the project was G. Gilson Terriberry, the chairman of publicity. Terriberry set out to find a sculptor for the award, but he soon

The Heisman Trophy. (Downtown Athletic Club Trophy)

found that most either overcharged or were not interested in football. His search finally brought him to a man named Frank Eliscu.

A graduate of Pratt Institute and a respected sculptor, Eliscu eagerly accepted the offer, hoping to promote his own name at the same time. Terriberry and the committee wanted a trophy that showed a football player, and that's exactly what Eliscu gave them. Using his friend Ed Smith (a football star at New York University) as a model, he soon finished the project. Wanting to make sure it was acceptable, he asked Coach Jimmy Crowley of Fordham University to look it over. One stormy afternoon Eliscu brought his clay model to the practice field where Crowley and his players were going through drills. While the rain poured down upon them, Coach Crowley and his players observed and criticized the piece of work. Eliscu took their words to heart, and as Crowley had his boys demonstrate the "side-step" position, he shaped and reshaped the model until a final product was reached.

Eliscu gave his model one more test. He took it to Elmer Layden, the head coach of the Notre Dame football team. Layden expressed enthusiastic approval. Eliscu then took it to the Downtown Athletic Club, where it was also accepted and sent out to be cast in bronze.

When the trophy itself was completed, the board pondered how to choose the nation's most outstanding player. After much deliberation and debate, they decided that the sportswriters and sportscasters of the country were the most qualified to decide the issue. The nation was then divided into various sections, each of which was given a specific number of votes. Originally, 908 electors were chosen, but the number has since increased. To make the election as fair as possible, the division was made on a geographically equal basis. This idea and method have stood the test of time for it is still being used today, over 45 years later.

In 1935 the first Downtown Athletic Club Trophy, as it was called, was given. The recipient was a young man named Jay Berwanger. A student at the University of Chicago, Berwanger was known as a one-man football team. In his career at Chicago he gained 1,839 yards rushing, passed for 926 yards, scored twenty-two touchdowns, kicked twenty extra points, averaged over 46 yards per kickoff return and 38 yards per punt return. He probably also sold programs at half-time to help keep the football program alive. The team itself, however—appropriately named the Maroons,—was not very successful. Berwanger carried them as long as he could, but eventually the program folded. An all-around player, he was one of the first

supermen in college football. To have been chosen the top player in the nation thrilled the young Chicagoan. He and his coach, Clark Shaughnessey, traveled to New York to receive the trophy. Where was the first place Berwanger wanted to go? Coney Island, of course. The reason—he'd never seen the ocean before!

In 1936 a tragedy hit the sports community. The great John Heisman died. He had helped revolutionize a game that was slowly but surely taking hold of the country itself. His renovations, inventiveness, and sheer enthusiasm would not be easily forgotten. To commemorate his accomplishments, the trophy was renamed the Heisman Memorial Trophy. The move was widely acclaimed. The winner that year was Larry Kelley, a very talented receiver from Yale University.

The following season another Yalie won the award. This time it was quarterback Clint Frank. He led Yale to an outstanding season and was consequently deemed the most outstanding player in the nation.

Eventually, many people started to complain that since the award was centered in the East, Eastern athletes received a disproportionate share of attention. The critics were mollified in 1938, however, when Davey O'Brien of Texas Christian University won the vote. The fiery little quarterback not only made his mark on college football but, when he arrived in the city to receive his award, he made it on the metropolis of New York itself. Because he was from Texas, where things are often done in a big fashion, it soon became apparent that the Big Apple would get a taste of the West. Colonel Amon Carter of Fort Worth, Texas, was chairman of the On-to–New-York Committee. Some of the festivities included a special motorcycle escort, a parade, uniformed riders, a stagecoach for the official party, and a dinner that included top-name entertainers. Everything had to be the best because, after all, that's how they do things in Texas.

The University of Iowa produced the 1939 winner, Nile Kinnick. The United States Navy flew the Heisman winner to his award presentation in New York. There was one catch, however. On his way there he had to put in a good word for Naval air training. He did it, and, true to his words, he served in Naval aviation during World War II. He soon found it was more demanding than any college football game could ever be. As he was about to land his plane on the deck of a carrier one day, Kinnick ran out of gas and crashed into the ocean. He died that day, a victim of an unfortunate accident. The country lost one of its first college football heroes.

The 1940 Heisman winner was Tom Harmon,

who was hailed as "one of the nation's all-time greats." The vote was very one-sided—and for a good reason. In his three years with the Michigan Wolverines, Harmon scored thirty-three touchdowns, threw sixteen touchdown passes, kicked two field goals, and gained 3,438 yards rushing and passing. It was quite a career for the versatile back, who played almost every minute in every game of his career.

The 1941 race for the Heisman was very close. Up until the day before the announcement, it was impossible to tell whether the winner would be Angelo Bertelli of Notre Dame or Bruce Smith of the University of Minnesota. Smith, the Gopher running back narrowly won. The captain of the all-American team, he led Minnesota to one of its most successful seasons ever. He received his award on 9 December 1941, two days after the famous attack on Pearl Harbor.

Frank Sinkwich—a running back from Georgia—Angelo Bertelli—a quarterback from Notre Dame—and Les Horvath—a quarterback from Ohio State University—were the next three winners of the coveted trophy. Sinkwich, who showed up to the award dinner in a Marine uniform, set a Southeastern Conference record for total offense with 2,187 yards and an Orange Bowl record for total offense with 332 yards (rushing and passing). Known as "the Springfield Rifle," Bertelli scored twenty-nine touchdowns and totalled over 2,500 yards in offense during his career with the Fighting Irish. Horvath, also a quarterback, had an outstanding senior year with the Buckeyes. He rushed for 924 yards, scored eight touchdowns, and passed for 344 yards.

By 1945 college football had taken a back seat to the devastating war. Bertelli, like Sinkwich, joined the military after his collegiate career. To say that the nation's mind was preoccupied with the war effort would be an understatement. An illustration of this point is that the next two Heisman winners, in 1945 and 1946, were both from West Point. They were Felix ("Doc") Blanchard and Glenn Davis. Known as "Mr. Outside," and "Mr. Inside," respectively, they led one of the most outstanding running games in college football history. Blanchard, a fullback, was all-American for three years, gained 1,908 yards rushing, and scored thirty-eight touchdowns. Davis scored an incredible fifty-one touchdowns and contributed 3,276 yards (rushing and passing) to the Army offense. They were two incredible football players.

Johnny Lujack continued what was becoming a fine tradition at the University of Notre Dame. By winning the Heisman in 1947, he helped set a standard that the school would maintain through the 1980s. In his three-year career the star quarterback gained over two thousand yards offensively and led the team to twenty-four victories.

Record-setting Ewell Doak Walker of Southern Methodist University (SMU) in Texas was the recipient in 1948. In his thirty-five–game football career at SMU he rewrote many Southwest Conference records. His accomplishments included forty touchdowns, 60 extra points, 303 points, and over thirty-four hundred yards total offense. After he graduated, Walker went on to play for the Detroit Lions of the National Football League. He soon entered the record books once again with his great ability to put points on the scoreboard.

Notre Dame produced another winner in 1949. This time it was their big end Leon Hart. The two-time all-American was one of the few linemen ever to receive the award. Also effective as a wide receiver, he made himself an even more valuable commodity.

From 1950 to 1955 the Heisman Trophy winners were all running backs. They came from different schools with different philosophies, but they were equally impressive. In 1950 Vic Janowicz from Ohio State won the award. Following in his footsteps were Dick Kazmaier of Ohio State (1951), Billy Vessels of Oklahoma (1952), John Lattner of

O. J. Simpson, the University of Southern California's record-setting tailback, stands with the coveted trophy. (USC photo)

Throughout the years college football's popularity has grown by great leaps. Every year over 100,000 fans pack Pasadena's Rose Bowl to watch the best in the game. (Rose Bowl photo)

Notre Dame (1953), Alan ("The Horse") Ameche of Wisconsin (1954), and Howard ("Hopalong") Cassady of Ohio State (1955). Janowicz, an all-around athlete, took a shot at professional baseball before going on to the Washington Redskins in the NFL. Both Vessels and Ameche went on to play pro ball also. In fact they ended up playing for the same team—the Baltimore Colts. Someone in Baltimore knew what he was doing! Cassady, who scored thirty-seven touchdowns in thirty-six games for Ohio State, was drafted by the Detroit Lions and went on to play for them. A gifted athlete, he was called "the greatest player of this century" by his coach, Woody Hayes.

Breaking the string of running backs was a young quarterback from Notre Dame. Having finished in third place behind Cassady the year before, Paul Hornung won the spotlight in 1956. And he made the most of it. Despite the fact that he played for a losing team (2–8 record), he showed the nation the depth of his skills. When the season ended, he led the squad in rushing, passing, scoring, kickoffs returned, punting, punts returned, and passes broken up. The only statistic in which he wasn't on top was receiving—and that's only because he was the one doing the passing!

Determination, guts, and spirit characterized Hornung's play for the Fighting Irish. In a game against Michigan State he tackled a player so hard he dislocated his left thumb. Later, against North Carolina, he repeated the effort, getting his right thumb caught in an opposing running back's belt. With two dislocated thumbs he could no longer function at quarterback. Consequently he was moved to fullback and halfback during the period of recuperation. Despite the fact that his team kept losing, Hornung continued to excel. "At no time during the season," Hornung related, "did we feel we were laying down as far as spirit is concerned. We were trying in every game . . . I am proud to have wound up my collegiate football career with

this team. We lost. But it was Notre Dame."[2]
The football writers of America, recognizing that, awarded him the Heisman for his outstanding effort. It was the first time since Jay Berwanger back in 1935 that a player for a losing team was elected to the Heisman Hall of Fame.

"I couldn't believe it when they told me I'd won it," Hornung said. "I did not think I was even up for consideration."[3] Upon completion of his college football career, the versatile young man from Notre Dame received offers from Hollywood to go into the world of acting. Opting for professional football, however, he was drafted by the Green Bay Packers. Under immortal coach Vince Lombardi, the Packers, with Hornung as their star halfback, went on to dominate the game and become one of the best teams in the history of the sport. The secret to his success, according to Hornung was Practice, Practice, Practice.

The 1957 winner, John David Crow of Texas A & M, was considered, "the greatest back I ever coached." The man quoted was no stranger to the game of football. He is Paul ("Bear") Bryant, Crow's coach at Texas A & M. Bryant went on to become the nation's most successful college coach ever, at the University of Alabama.

The six-foot, two-inch 217-pounder was used with great success on both offense and defense. It was on offense, however, as a halfback, that the hard-hitting Crow did most of his damage and received most of his recognition. In addition to winning his Heisman, he was voted Player of the Year in many polls, was an all-American, and was elected to many all-star teams. Crow was an intense player who loved one aspect of football above the rest—hitting. "We often had to hold him out of practice," said assistant coach Elmer Smith, "because he couldn't pull his punches and we were getting too many players hurt . . . Every time the ball is snapped, even in practice, he starts looking for somebody to hit."[4] To Crow, that was the only way he knew how to perform. "That is the way this game should be played," he said, "and that is what, in my opinion, a trophy like this stands for."[5]

Drafted by the Chicago Cardinals of the NFL, Crow was on top of the world by the end of his senior year in college. But the hard-working young man from Marion, Louisiana, was born with partial paralysis of the face, a condition that resulted in "a slight droop to the left side of the mouth and a dirt-catching left eye which never closes."[6] Instead of letting this deter him, the determined Crow pushed himself forward until he became the best college football player in the nation. When he received his trophy at the huge presentation dinner for the Heisman, Crow humbly stated, "It all seems like a wonderful dream. And just to make sure I don't wake up, I'm going to stop talking right now."[7]

The outstanding achievements of running backs continued to be highly regarded by the nation's Heisman voters. The following four trophy winners were all runners who led their squads with some dazzling moves. Pete Dawkins of Army won the trophy in 1958, Billy Cannon from Louisiana State University (LSU) won it in 1959, Joe Bellino of Navy took it in 1960, and it was Ernie Davis of Syracuse in 1961. Their achievements were instrumental to the success of their teams, and their athletic ability was unquestionable. Take Billy Cannon, for example. Some called him "the fastest strongman ever to play football." Others disagreed. They thought he was "the strongest fast man the game has known." Both parties were right. Cannon was indeed an impressive athlete. He ran the 100-yard dash in 9.4 seconds, and in weight lifting he was known to have dead-lifted 420 pounds and straight-arm pressed 285 pounds above his head. On the football field he was no less spectacular. His LSU team, ranked third in the nation, went on to the Gator Bowl against Mississippi. When Cannon won the Heisman, it was by a huge margin. In fact it was the largest victory in the history of the award.

The next ten years, 1962 to 1971, showed a change in the voting trend for the Heisman. Running backs, who had previously dominated the award, took a back seat. Quarterbacks became big news and began to make the headlines. Seven of the next ten Heisman winners were all signal callers.

The first of these star quarterbacks was a young man named Terry Baker from Oregon State University (OSU). Winning the Heisman in 1962, he set the tone. Baker was another of those all-around athletes who captured the hearts of local fans and the admiration of the nation. During his senior year he passed for 1,738 yards and ran for another 538, thereby earning the highest total offense in the nation. He led his OSU team to a very successful season, which culminated in a 6-0 win over Villanova in the Liberty Bowl. How did Oregon State score in that game? Terry Baker ran 99½ yards for a touchdown. Baker won every major award afforded college football players (Heisman Memorial Trophy, Maxwell Award, AP and UPI Player of the Year, *Sports Illustrated* Sportsman of the Year, All-American, Academic All-American, All-Pacific Coast, etc.) To top it off, he was also a star on the university's basketball squad. Many people recognized the amazing qualities the six-foot, three-inch 190-pounder possessed, but nobody knew of them more than the Los Angeles Rams of the NFL.

They drafted him as the first choice in the entire pro draft. "Baker is so outstanding that we couldn't afford not to take him,"[8] said Ram General Manager Elroy Hirsch. It was definitely a compliment to Baker, for the Rams, it must be noted, already had three quarterbacks on their roster!

The Naval Academy produced the next Heisman winner, a scrambling young thrower named Roger Staubach. "Jolly Roger," as he was called by his teammates, was only a junior when he won the award, and his future looked unlimited. But at the Heisman dinner, Staubach gave the press his feelings about playing pro football. "I have a year and a half to go at Annapolis and, after that, four years of navy service," he said. "Right now, I'm thinking along the lines of the Navy, rather than pro ball."[9] Fortunately for the world of pro football, Roger didn't read crystal balls for a living. He eventually went on to a pro career with the Dallas Cowboys, leading them to the Super Bowl and becoming one of the best quarterbacks that the game has ever known.

In 1964 the quarterback to take the honors was John Huarte of Notre Dame. He was the sixth player from the illustrious Indiana University to win the award. The clever ball-handling skills of the senior quarterback helped turn a two-game winner into a contender for the national championship, in just one year. Hampered by injuries, Huarte played little as a sophomore and junior, but in his senior year it all came together. Leading the Irish to a 9-0 record at one point, he accumulated 1,790 yards passing and fifteen touchdowns. It was quite an achievement for someone who played a total of only forty-five minutes during the entire previous season. "Without Huarte, we would have been three-yards-and-a-cloud-of-dust type of team," said his coach, Ara Parseghian. "We built our whole offense around him. I lived in constant dread of what we would do if anything happened to him."[10]

The other four quarterbacks to capture the Heisman in that ten-year period were Florida's Steve Spurrier (1966), UCLA's Gary Beban (1967), Stanford's Jim Plunkett (1970), and Auburn's Pat Sullivan (1971). Passing was becoming a vital aspect of the game, and no one was considered better than these four Heisman winners. Plunkett's passing heroics to speedy little receiver Randy Vataha won him the hearts of northern California football fans and a Rose Bowl game. He went on to play for the New England Patriots and in 1980–81, in one of the greatest comebacks in the game, he led the Oakland Raiders to the Super Bowl in what was supposed to be a rebuilding year!

Beban, of UCLA, faced a different sort of challenge when he won the Heisman. Drafted in the second round by the Los Angeles Rams, he was delighted to continue his career before the local fans. What the young signal caller didn't realize was that to be a Heisman trophy winner and to be drafted by the Rams didn't always result in overwhelming success. In fact, it never did. The Rams had previously drafted no less than seven Heisman winners, and only one, Terry Baker, lasted more than two years. Around the city of Los Angeles this phenomenon came to be known as "the Heisman jinx," and Beban seemed to be walking right into its mouth.

Ram Coach George Allen received the rights to Beban in a very unusual way. He had traded scouting information to the expanding New Orleans Saints for their pick in the second round of the draft. The result was Gary Beban. "He was simply the best football player on the board when our turn came around," Allen said. "We rated him among the top ten football players in the country."[11] Unfortunately, there was one who was better than he on the Los Angeles roster. His name was Roman Gabriel, the quarterback who led the Rams to one of their best seasons in the previous year with a 12–2–2 record. Despite Beban's happiness about being drafted by the Rams, the jinx won.

Following the ten-year "period of the passer,"

In 1967 UCLA's All-American quarterback, Gary Beban, won the Heisman. (San Diego Hall of Champions photo)

the running back emerged once again as the central figure in college football. From 1972 to 1980 not one quarterback won the trophy. Largely responsible for this change in the trends were the three running backs who won the Heisman in the late sixties. Steve Owens, the durable, hard-hitting runner from Oklahoma, ran off with the trophy in 1969. But it was a pair of speedsters from the University of Southern California (USC) who set the football world afire. In 1965 USC's Mike Garrett collected almost as many postseason awards as he did touchdown runs. Despite the fact that the Trojans didn't make it to the Rose Bowl, Garrett led the nation in rushing. The likable young man showed why he was so popular when he made his acceptance speech. A Los Angeles newspaper captured the moment:

"I thank my teammates . . . I thank my coaches . . . I thank everybody who has helped me."

But Mike Garrett, as he accepted the Heisman Award at USC yesterday, suddenly spotted a couple of teammates, Rod Sherman and Frank Lopez, among the newsmen and photographers, and looking at them, he said with emotion:

"Thank you, Rod. Thank you, Frankie." And then came the tears.

And as you saw him there, head bowed and speechless, you know just how sincerely and deeply grateful Mike Garrett was to win the most coveted award in football.

Dr. Norman Topping, the USC president, said afterward, "You can see why Mike Garrett is so dearly beloved on this campus."[12]

In 1968 a runner for the USC Trojans, considered by many football experts to be the greatest

Many of the Heisman winners went on to professional football careers, like USC's Mike Garrett, shown running the ball for the San Diego Chargers. (San Diego Hall of Champions photo)

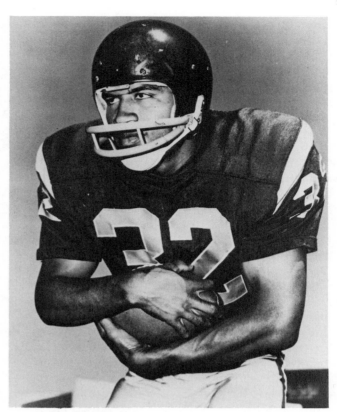

O. J. Simpson shows the determination that helped him become one of the best running backs in football history. (San Diego Hall of Champions photo)

running back in the history of college and professional football, hit the scene. His name is O. J. Simpson. The powerful, dashing young athlete set numerous records and helped his team to a national championship in 1967. His overwhelming strength and speed had professional scouts drooling over him. Simpson was drafted by the Buffalo Bills and almost single-handedly brought them up from mediocrity. Continuing the trends he set in college, he eclipsed many of the rushing records set by Cleveland's immortal Jim Brown. He gained over two thousand yards rushing one year, and when he eventually retired from the game to a career in acting, it became evident that his shoes would be hard to fill.

That didn't keep many runners from trying to fill them. All across the nation, running backs were smashing records and assaulting defenses. They were like a species possessed. For some reason they seemed bigger and quicker and more exciting than ever before. In the last decade running backs have won the award every year except 1972, when Nebraska's flashy flanker Johnny Rodgers claimed it. From that point on it was all runners. Penn State's stubborn John Cappelletti started the trend in 1973 with his relentless, never-say-die style.

Ohio State's agile speedster Archie Griffin continued the movement. Griffin was the first back ever to win the Heisman twice; he copped the award in 1974 and 1975. He was so elusive that only one team was ever able to capture the speedy runner—the Cincinnatti Bengals of the NFL, who drafted him in the first round.

As the years passed, the running backs continued to improve. The Pittsburgh Panthers produced the next Heisman winner, in 1976. He was Tony Dorsett, who possessed the speed of a sprinter and the agility of a cat. In his senior year he led his Panthers to their first national championship since 1937. Dorsett went on to play pro ball with the Dallas Cowboys. Following him through the gates of Heisman fame was a back who combined Dorsett's quickness with the power of a truck. Earl Campbell of the Texas Longhorns, one of the biggest backs ever to come along, left his mark on many a defense. Campbell didn't just go around or through defenses, he ran over them. When he turned pro with the Houston Oilers, he became a one-man offense. During the 1980 season he brought back memories of the great Simpson years, as he rushed for over nineteen hundred yards, led Houston to the play-offs, and generally dominated every team he came up against.

The next three Heisman winners were Billy Sims, Charles White, and George Rogers—from Oklahoma, USC, and South Carolina, respectively. For two straight years Sims and White battled it out for the coveted trophy. In 1978 Sims had an outstanding year and won the award while White finished a distant fourth. The competition for the 1979 Heisman became an interesting one for many reasons. If Sims had won it, he would have been the first to duplicate the feat since Archie Griffin. A highly respected pro prospect, he finished his senior year with two great games against Missouri and Nebraska, totalling 529 yards rushing (just 9 short of an NCAA record). White, on the other hand, was trying to fill some big shoes—shoes that he had placed in front of his own locker. As a cocky young freshman, White boldly predicted that he would win the Heisman—maybe even three or four of them. Confidence he didn't lack. But then something happened. "I'll never forget that first practice," White said, describing the one-on-one drill that is reserved for so-called hot-shots. "Gary Jeter welcomed me. Oh, how he welcomed me; I'll never forget it. After that, I didn't want any part of the Heisman."[13] Four years later White was a mature, motivated football player who gained over eighteen hundred yards rushing and helped his team to a tie for the national championship. His reward—the Heisman trophy. Sims, despite his

The only player ever to win the Heisman twice was Ohio State's talented running back Archie Griffin. (UPI photo)

strong finish, was a distant second in the voting. "It's something I'll cherish for a long time," White said.[14]

That's probably why so many college football players work so hard for so long toward such a single goal. It is something that will never be taken away from them. A national magazine helped put it in perspective:

Les Horvath, Ohio State quarterback, was the winner of the Heisman Trophy in 1944. Shortly after graduation, he married and moved to Los Angeles to practice dentistry. One day his bride asked what that big, ugly statuette was doing in their living room. "I'm very proud of it," Dr. Horvath told her. "It's a very exclusive trophy."

That week the Horvaths were invited to dinner twice: to the Tom Harmons' and [the] Glenn Davies', both Heisman winners. Shortly after, Horvath noticed his trophy was missing. "It's in the garbage, where it belongs," Mrs. Horvath said. "Exclusive trophy, my foot! Everyone in town has one!"[15]

Heisman Memorial Trophy Winners

1935	Jay Berwanger, Chicago, RB	
1936	Larry Kelley, Yale, E	
1937	Clint Frank, Yale, RB	
1938	Davey O'Brien, TCU, QB	
1939	Nile Kinnick, Iowa, RB	
1940	Tom Harmon, Michigan, RB	

1941	Bruce Smith, Minnesota, RB	1962	Terry Baker, Oregon State, QB
1942	Frank Sinkwich, Georgia, RB	1963	Roger Staubach, Navy, QB
1943	Angelo Bertelli, Notre Dame, QB	1964	John Huarte, Notre Dame, QB
1944	Lee Horvath, Ohio State, QB	1965	Mike Garrett, Southern California, RB
1945	Doc Blanchard, Army, FB	1966	Steve Spurrier, Florida, QB
1946	Glenn Davis, Army, RB	1967	Gary Beban, UCLA, QB
1947	John Lujack, Notre Dame, QB	1968	O. J. Simpson, Southern California, RB
1948	Doak Walker, SMU, RB	1969	Steve Owens, Oklahoma, RB
1949	Leon Hart, Notre Dame, E	1970	Jim Plunkett, Stanford, QB
1950	Vic Janowicz, Ohio State, RB	1971	Pat Sullivan, Auburn, QB
1951	Dick Kazmaier, Princeton, RB	1972	Johnny Rodgers, Nebraska, FL
1952	Billy Vessels, Oklahoma, RB	1973	John Cappelletti, Penn State, RB
1953	John Lattner, Notre Dame, RB	1974	Archie Griffin, Ohio State, RB
1954	Alan Ameche, Wisconsin, FB	1975	Archie Griffin, Ohio State, RB
1955	Howard Cassady, Ohio State, FB	1976	Tony Dorsett, Pittsburgh, RB
1956	Paul Hornung, Notre Dame, QB	1977	Earl Campbell, Texas, RB
1957	John Crow, Texas A&M, RB	1978	Billy Sims, Oklahoma, RB
1958	Pete Dawkins, Army, RB	1979	Charles White, Southern California, RB
1959	Billy Cannon, LSU, RB	1980	George Rogers, S. Carolina, RB
1960	Joe Bellino, Navy, RB	1981	Marcus Allen, Southern California, RB
1961	Ernie Davis, Syracuse, RB	1982	Herschel Walker, Georgia, RB
		1983	Mike Rozier, Nebraska, RB

3
The World Series Trophy

Why is baseball, you ask? Because it is like charity—it never faileth. It is always there, except on Mondays or wet grounds. And to the man who is too old to keep up with the attempt to civilize football, and too young to need so soothing a sedative as golf; who works hard when he works and wants to rest hard when he rests; who wants a drama that is full of surprises for the actors as it is for the audience; who wants a race that cannot be fixed like a horse race; who is so genuine an American that he wants something to kick about without meaning it, and something to yell about that everybody around him will think more of him for yelling about—to that man baseball is the one great life-saver in the good old summer-time.[1]

Los Angeles Times 1916

In a society where the people have been known to get more excited about local sporting events than local political elections, baseball has become a foundation. The "grand old game" has at times produced more heroes than world war. Mom, apple pie, and baseball—three symbols of the American way of life that no one dare desecrate.

Every year millions of fans across the country pour into local stadiums to support their hometown team. And every season, from April to October, these teams battle it out for the right to go to an October classic. At the end of each season preliminary play-offs take place. When they are com-

pleted, only two teams are left to decide who really is the champion of the sport. They face each other in a classic confrontation appropriately referred to as the World Series. What baseball is to the American culture, the World Series is to baseball. The winner is truly the champion of the world, and the country comes to a virtual standstill to watch the outcome.

Originally know as "rounders," baseball was introduced to the nation by English immigrants. The game quickly became popular. Around 1845 a New York surveyor named Alexander Cartwright helped to solidify it. Attempting to organize the sport, he developed a formal team with some of his fellow players.

In 1868 interest in baseball had grown to the point where a tournament was held in Detroit. Semiprofessional teams from Chicago, Detroit, Buffalo, Pittsburgh, Albany, Boston, New York, Brooklyn, Cleveland, Philadelphia, Quebec, Montreal, and Hamilton participated. At the end of the competition a champion was crowned. The team from Hamilton was the first "world champion."

Fourteen years later, in 1882, a similar tournament was held. By that time there were two professional leagues, the National League (NL), and the American Association (AA). In the championship series Chicago represented the National League and Cincinnati, the American Association. After each team won a game, the series was cancelled because of disputes between the two ball clubs. Two years later an NL squad from Providence swept by the New York Mets in three straight games.

In 1890 the American Association folded, and the championship series of the previous eight years ended. A Pittsburgh baseball enthusiast named Chase Temple renewed the idea four years later. He donated a cup to be given to the victor of a "world series" between the first- and second-place teams of the National League. Since the two ball clubs had played each other numerous times during the regular season, the outcome soon became anti-climactic. This so-called Temple Cup series was played four times, from 1894 to 1897.

In 1901 a new division came into operation. Composed of eight teams, it was called the American League (AL). The older National League resented the newcomers, and three years of conflict followed. Finally, in 1903 the two leagues reconciled their differences, and a postseason match was scheduled. The National League sent Pittsburgh to the contest, and the American League countered with Boston in a best-of-nine series. A test of superiority, pitting the two best professional teams in American baseball, the event was billed as "the World Series."

Pittsburgh came out of the gates quickly, winning three of the first four games. But Boston refused to fold, and behind the pitching of Bill Dinneen and Cy Young, the New Englanders came back to win four straight and capture the series, five games to three. Jimmy Collins, Boston's player-manager, said afterward, "I should not be surprised to see postseason games each fall as long as there are two big leagues. There is no reason, when the games are played on their own merits, as they were in this case, why they should not be successful."[2]

In 1904, however, a feud between Ban Johnson, president of the American League and John Brush, the New York Giants manager, caused the series to be cancelled. The next year a national commission was set up to organize the postseason series. New rules were devised and the contest was changed to a "best-of-seven" competition.

The next championship games were played by the Giants and the Philadelphia Athletics. In this famous "Shutout Series," the loser failed to score even a single run in all five games. New York's Christy Mathewson, a thirty-one–game winner during the year, pitched a record three shutouts and the Giants won four games to one.

The 1906 series featured the Chicago Cubs and the Chicago White Sox. The first crosstown series in history, it pitted two very dissimilar teams. The powerful Cubs had posted 116 wins, a league record, and were led by their famous Tinkers-to-Evers-to-Chance double play combination. The White Sox, on the other hand, finished last in the American League in hitting with a meek .228 average. Both teams, however, fielded strong pitching staffs. The White Sox won, four games to two. The series was not without its controversial moments. Because this was a crosstown series, fan interest was at a peak, and in the last game policemen were hired to keep spectators outside the ropes that bordered the outfield. The lawmen's presence was not always enough. In one play Cub outfielder Frank Schulte drifted back toward the ropes to catch a fly ball. Just as he got to the ropes, a fan pushed him. The ball went past him and fell to the ground for a double. The White Sox took full advantage of the event, scoring three runs in the inning en route to an 8-3 triumph.

The Cubs got revenge the following year as they swept the Detroit Tigers, four games to none. One game, called because of darkness, ended in a tie, 3-3. In the series, Chicago proved fleet-footed on the base paths, stealing eighteen bases in all. Tiger catcher Charlie Schmidt had a rough time, and after the series one writer said "Schmidt went under a doctor's care to get his nerves back into condition."[3]

The 1908 series was a rematch between the same two clubs. This time Detroit's Ty Cobb got his potent bat on track as he clubbed the ball for a .368 batting average. One strong man, however, was not enough, as once again Chicago's balance and power prevailed, four games to one. The Tigers tried again the next year against the Pittsburgh Pirates, but their frustration continued. The series came down to a final seventh game, and the Pirates, behind the hard-hitting Honus Wagner, trounced the Tigers by a score of 8–0.

In 1910 Connie Mack's Philadelphia Athletics took on the persistent Chicago Cubs. Mack had recruited some quick, agile college athletes, and the move paid off. The A's won the first two games, played in Philadelphia, and coasted on to a 4–1 series victory. The 1911 World Series was a rematch between the A's and the Giants. Both were powerful teams and had managers considered to be the best in baseball—Mack for the A's and John McGraw for the Giants. The A's were out to avenge their loss in 1905. A key to Philadelphia's success was to be their ability to stop New York's lightning-quick runners on the bases. When the series ended, the Giants had collected only four stolen bases, and the A's were the world champs.

The 1912 world championship is considered to be one of the most exciting series in history. It

Strong defensive play has helped make many a World Series Champion. In 1931 the St. Louis Cardinals won it all, largely because of the infield play of people like Frankie Frisch, shown here turning a double play. (United Press photo)

pitted the Boston Red Sox against the New York Giants. After each team won three games and tied one, a deciding contest was played. At the end of nine innings of intense play the score was tied 1–1. Both squads had their ace on the mound—Christy Mathewson for the Giants and Smoky Joe Wood for the Red Sox. In the top of the tenth the Giants scored a run to take a 2–1 lead. But in the bottom of the inning they made two glaring errors that proved very costly. Fred Snodgrass dropped a pop fly in the outfield, and first baseman Fred Markle misplayed a foul ball down the line. The errors prolonged a Boston rally, which enabled them to go on to a 3–2 win and the series championship.

From 1912 to 1918 a Boston team won five of the seven World Series played. The Red Sox captured the title again in 1915, 1916, and 1918 by defeating the Philadelphia Phillies, Brooklyn Dodgers, and

Chicago Cubs, respectively. The other Boston team, the Braves, won the series in 1914 by sweeping Philadelphia's Athletics in four straight games. Such stars as Babe Ruth, Casey Stengel, Carl Mays, and Dutch Leonard emerged during these years.

Among the lighter moments of this period was "Zim's boner" in the 1917 series between the Chicago White Sox and the New York Giants. In the fourth inning of the sixth game, the score was tied 0–0. Eddie Collins of the Sox hit a grounder to Giant third baseman Heinie Zimmerman, who proceeded to throw wildly to first, allowing Collins to advance to second. The next batter, Joe Jackson, hit a fly ball to right field, which was dropped. The following hitter knocked one back to the pitcher, Rube Benton, who noticed that Collins was standing a bit too far off third base. He turned and threw the ball to Zimmerman, who ran at Collins. At the same time Giant catcher Bill Rariden crept up to the runner, who quickly dashed by him. Zimmerman then found himself with no one to throw the ball to. The play soon came to be labeled "Zim's boner." Commented the frustrated third baseman in self-defense, "Who was I supposed to throw the ball to—myself?" The Sox went on to score three runs in that error-filled inning and eventually won, 4–2. They took the series.

"The Miracle Braves," the other Boston team to win the championship in that six-year period, earned the nickname by knocking off the heavily favored Philadelphia A's in the 1914 series. Composed mainly of cast-off players, the Braves went out and defeated the team that was on top of the baseball world. Not only did Boston win, but it swept the powerful opponent in four straight games! It was the biggest upset in baseball history.

The 1919 World Series will best be known as the one bought by the gamblers. The Chicago White Sox, favored to win, played against the Cincinnati Reds. After the Reds took the first game, 9–1, scores of gamblers placed huge wagers on Cincinnati. Word went out that Chicago players had accepted bribes to throw the series. The Reds did win, and scandal rumors persisted. A Chicago grand jury later indicted eight White Sox players for taking bribes. Although they were eventually acquitted, baseball's new commissioner, Kenesaw Mountain Landis, banned all eight of them from the sport. This so-called Black Sox scandal greatly harmed the integrity of the sport.

The 1920 championship, between the Brooklyn Dodgers and the Cleveland Indians, featured the first grand slam—by Cleveland's Elmer Smith in game five—and the first unassisted triple play—by Cleveland's Billy Wambsganns—in series history. The Dodgers failed to score a run in the last eighteen innings, and the Indians won five games to two. During the series one of the Dodger pitchers, Rube Marquard, was arrested for scalping tickets.

The New York Yankees got a taste of a real rivalry when they faced a crosstown opponent, the New York Giants, in the 1921 series. An exciting championship, it was characterized by a number of firsts. It was the first series (1) viewed by the new commissioner, Judge Landis; (2) lost by a team that won the first two games; (3) played entirely in one ballpark (both the Yankees and the Giants played in the Polo Grounds); (4) delighted by a Babe Ruth home run; (5) featured by the Yankees, who appeared in twenty-nine of the next forty-three postseason championships; and (6) won by Giant manager John McGraw since 1905. The Giants went on to pull it out in eight games. They repeated the victory against the same Yankees the following year.

For the third straight year the Giants and the Yanks locked horns in 1923. This time, however, the result was somewhat different. The Giants' cen-

The New York Yankees soon became one of the dominant teams in Series play. One of the main reasons was the bat of the great Babe Ruth. (UPI photo)

ter fielder captured the hearts of the fans with his antics on the field. But the Yankees, behind the hitting of their superstar Babe Ruth, captured the series, four games to two.

Unusual plays became common in the 1925 World Series. The Washington Senators were playing the Pittsburgh Pirates. In the third game, played in Washington, Senator Sam Rice made a spectacular play. Closing in on a fly ball in the far outfield, he jumped in the air, landed in the seats, and disappeared. He emerged moments later, grasping the ball triumphantly in his glove. "It's an

Led by Jackie Robinson the Brooklyn Dodgers often found themselves still active when World Series time came around. (Dodger photo)

out!" the umpire ruled—in the face of loud protest from the visiting team. The Pirates had the last laugh, however, as they went on to win the series.

In 1927 New York unleashed one of the most powerful teams in the history of the sport. The Yankees won the American League pennant by a whopping nineteen games, and when the Pirates came to town for the World Series, it was clearly a mismatch. "The Bronx Bombers," as the Yanks were known, were led by their famous "Murderers' Row"—Babe Ruth, Lou Gehrig, Bob Muesel, and Tony Lazzeri. Ruth had hit a record sixty homers that year. New York defeated the Pirates in four straight games to complete an awesome year.

The men in pinstripes continued to dominate baseball. From 1932 to 1962 the Yankees competed in an incredible twenty-one of the thirty postseason championships, winning seventeen of them. In 1932 Ruth provided one of the most dramatic moments in series history. New York was playing the Cubs, who won the first two games. Chicago fans had been very abusive to the great Babe throughout the series, going so far as to throw lemons at him before game three. Cub players derided Ruth and his ancestry. Despite it all, he played some great baseball. But in the fifth inning of one of the games, he decided to put his belligerent opponents in their place. As Babe stepped to the plate to bat

Another reason New York dominated the baseball world for so long was the all-around play of slugger Joe DiMaggio. (UPI photo)

against Chicago's Charley Root, the Cub bench threw barbs and rolled a lemon at him. Ruth retaliated with some uncomplimentary remarks of his own. Root followed by throwing two strikes to him. At that point Ruth responded with a gesture to the outfield. He pointed to centerfield, where he intended to hit the next pitch. Root fired the ball to the waiting Babe, who hit a long fly ball right in the direction he had pointed. The ball sailed high into the air and landed in the bleachers. "Our bench was yelling awful things," Cub catcher Zack Taylor later recalled. "I don't even want to talk about them. . . . about Babe's personal life. Anyway, he turned to us. He put up two fingers. Two strikes. Then he put up one finger, saying 'I got one left.' And then he pointed to direct center field. He hit that pitch right into what must have been a sixty-mile-an-hour wind coming off that lake, and I don't know how he did it."[4] Not many people did.

Despite the long period of Yankee domination, superstars and super moments did emerge from other squads during some World Series play. For example, there was "the Gashouse Gang," of the St. Louis Cardinals, led by Dizzy and Daffy Dean (the pitching brothers), Stan Musial, Enos Slaughter, and Whitey Kurowski. In 1934 the Cards defeated Detroit in seven games and followed it up with victories in 1942 (over New York 4–1), 1944 (over the St. Louis Browns, 4–2) and 1946 (over Boston, 4–3). In the 1946 win Slaughter executed one of the most outstanding single efforts ever made in the series. In the seventh and deciding game, played in St. Louis, the Cards came up to bat in the botton of the eighth with the score tied at 3-3. Slaughter led off the inning with a single. The next two batters were retired easily, and then Harry ("the Hat") Walker stepped into the batter's box to pinch-hit. He ripped a single to center field. Slaughter streaked to second base, raced toward third, rounded the bag, and headed for home. Red Sox shortstop John Pesky fielded the throw from the outfield, turned, and looked in amazement as Slaughter headed home. Hesitating for a moment, he pulled the ball from his glove and fired it to the plate, where Slaughter slid past catcher Roy Partee with the winning run and a World Series championship. "I had never done that, go all the way from first to home on a hit like that, ever before in my career," Slaughter said later. "And I never did it after, either."[5]

Yankee pitcher Don Larsen throws the last pitch of his perfect game in the World Series. Second baseman Billy Martin looks on. (San Diego Hall of Champions photo)

In most of the following years, the Yankees continued to be in the news. The names were different, but the results were the same. Behind manager Casey Stengel and his players like Joe DiMaggio, Mickey Mantle, Whitey Ford, Allie Reynolds, Billy Martin, Don Larsen (who threw a perfect game against the Dodgers in 1956), and Roger Maris, New York dominated. When someone else won a series, it took a spectacular play to do it. In 1960 the Pittsburgh Pirates battled the Yankees to the seventh and deciding game. Pittsburgh's Bill Mazeroski stepped up to the plate late in the game against Ralph Terry. The Yankee pitcher fired an inside pitch to the strong second baseman, who swung and lofted the ball to the deep outfield. The ball, along with Yankee hopes, fell into the bleachers. After hitting the series-winning homer, Mazeroski was submerged by jubilant Pirate fans as he tried to make his way around the bases. When later asked what pitch he had thrown, Terry simply replied, "The wrong one!"[6]

From 1963 to 1971 no single team dominated the World Series. In fact, in that span no ball club was able to produce consecutive victories. The Los Angeles Dodgers and their southpaw ace, Sandy Koufax, won in 1963 and 1965. The St. Louis Cardinals flew high with wins in 1964 and 1967. Clutch hitting by catcher Tim McCarver, great pitching by Bob Gibson, and the all-around performance of Lou Brock were largely responsible. The Baltimore Orioles also came up with a pair of World Series victories, in 1966 and 1970. In the former year the Dodgers failed to score a run in the last three games as the O's swept by them, four games to none. The Orioles were a powerful squad—with Frank Robinson, Boog Powell, Brooks Robinson, and an awesome pitching staff of Dave McNally, Jim Palmer, and Mike Cuellar. In 1969 their opponent was the lowly New York Mets. Of course, Baltimore was the heavy favorite. The Mets, considered baseball's joke team, had never finished higher than ninth. But this year, behind some acrobatic catches and clutch hitting, "the Miracle Mets" went on to win in five games. The impossible dream had come true.

In 1972 a new kid came to town. His name was Charlie O. Finley, and he owned the Oakland Athletics. The upstart A's beat the Detroit Tigers in the American League play-offs and went on to face the hard-slugging Cincinnati Reds in the series. Though the Reds were heavily favored to win, the

The 1927 World Champion New York Yankees. (NY Yankee photo)

40

When the Dodgers moved to Los Angeles, the powerful left arm of Sandy Koufax kept their World Series habits going. (Dodger photo)

series turned out to be very close. The sixth and seventh games were decided by a single run. It was the play of a reserve outfielder-catcher that proved to make the difference. The seldom-used Gene Tenace knocked in nine of the A's sixteen runs, hit four home runs, and led Oakland to the World Series championship.

Under Finley the A's were a controversial team, to say the least. Clubhouse squabbles between players, public criticism by Finley, and general lack of harmony were the rule. But no matter how bad the problem, the A's continued to win. Such was the case in 1973, when once again those incredible Mets were the opponent. In the twelfth inning of the second game Oakland utility infielder Mike Andrews made two crucial errors that enabled the decisive run to score. The Mets won the game 10–7, and Finley was furious. He reportedly coerced Andrews into signing a letter, "for the good of the team," stating falsely that he was physically unfit to continue playing. Players, fans, and baseball management erupted in disgust and anger. Oakland players taped Andrews's number, seventeen, to their sleeves in protest. Commissioner Bowie Kuhn ordered Finley to reinstate Andrews, and the second baseman was back in uniform for the fourth game in New York. As Andrews was sent in to pinch-hit late in the game, over fifty thousand Met fans stood up and gave him a thunderous ovation.

Despite the controversy surrounding the team, the A's defeated the Mets in seven games. Behind the fielding of Joe Rudi, the hitting of Reggie Jackson, and the pitching of Rollie Fingers, Oakland was unbeatable. In fact, the following year, in 1974, the team went on to win its third straight World Series trophy, whipping the Los Angeles Dodgers,

four games to one. For three consecutive seasons Oakland was the king of baseball.

In 1975 a new powerhouse, the Cincinnati Reds, stepped into the batter's box. The team had all the qualities of a winner—fielding (Dave Concepcion, Cesar Geronimo), speed (Ken Griffey, Joe Morgan), power hitting (Tony Perez, George Foster, Johnny Bench), hustle (Pete Rose), and great pitching (Fred Norman, Don Gullett, and Pedro Borbon). Added to that was an intelligent and crafty manager, Sparky Anderson. The result was two straight World Series trophies. In 1975 the Reds defeated the Boston Red Sox in seven games, in one of the most exciting play-offs in years. They followed it up in 1976 with a 4-0 whitewash of the rebuilding New York Yankees.

Even though the Yanks were humiliated in four straight games in 1976, the writing was on the wall. They were back. New York returned in 1977 and 1978 with consecutive 4–2 wins over the Los Angeles Dodgers. Reggie Jackson, now with New York, put on an incredible hitting display, and Craig Nettles, the rangy third baseman, made some unbelievable plays in the field. Making diving catches to his left and to his right, he single-handedly took the air out of several Dodger rallies. Through the free agent market the Yankees had erected a powerful club, and their future looked even brighter.

Considered one of the best Yankee pitchers ever was southpaw Whitey Ford. (NY Yankee photo)

41

But in 1979 a team of high-flying youngsters in Baltimore took the baseball world by surprise. They finished the season with the best record in the league and went on to defeat another Cinderella team, the California Angels, in the American League play-offs. Their abilities now recognized and appreciated, they went into the World Series as the favorite against Pittsburgh. Winning three of the first four games, Baltimore looked forward to clear sailing. But there was one problem. His name was Willie Stargell, the heart and soul of the Pittsburgh ball club. To be losing three games to one in the World Series is definitely a bad position, and that's when Stargell began to pour it on. The Pirates clawed back to tie the series at three games apiece and then flew to Baltimore for the seventh and final contest. Stargell got four hits in five times at bat, including a two-run homer in the sixth inning, and Pittsburgh became the world champion. It was truly one of the great comebacks of all time.

Like many others before them, the people of the city of Pittsburgh went wild. They were proud, for their team was the best, and no one could take that fact away from them. To most Americans the capital of the United States is Washington, D.C. In 1979 it would have been hard to convince anyone in Pittsburgh of that.

World Series Results

1903	Boston (AL) 5, Pittsburgh (NL) 3
1904	no series
1905	New York (NL) 4, Philadelphia (AL) 1
1906	Chicago (AL) 4, Chicago (NL) 2
1907	Chicago (NL) 4, Detroit (AL) 0, 1 tie
1908	Chicago (NL) 4, Detroit (AL) 1
1909	Pittsburgh (NL) 4, Detroit (AL) 3
1910	Philadelphia (AL) 4, Chicago (NL) 1
1911	Philadelphia (AL) 4, New York (NL) 2
1912	Boston AL (4), New York (NL) 3, 1 tie
1913	Philadelphia (AL) 4, New York (NL) 1
1914	Boston (NL) 4, Philadelphia (AL) 0
1915	Boston (AL) 4, Philadelphia (NL) 1
1916	Boston (AL) 4, Brooklyn (NL) 1
1917	Chicago (AL) 4, New York (NL) 2
1918	Boston (AL) 4, Chicago (NL) 2
1919	Cincinnati (NL) 5, Chicago (AL) 3
1920	Cleveland (AL) 5, Brooklyn (NL) 2
1921	New York (NL) 5, New York (AL) 3
1922	New York (NL) 4, New York (AL) 0, 1 tie
1923	New York (AL) 4, New York (NL) 2
1924	Washington (AL) 4, New York (NL) 3
1925	Pittsburgh (NL) 4, Washington (AL) 3
1926	St. Louis (NL) 4, New York (AL) 3
1927	New York (AL) 4, Pittsburgh (NL) 0
1928	New York (AL) 4, St. Louis (NL) 0
1929	Philadelphia (AL) 4, Chicago (NL) 1
1930	Philadelphia (AL) 4, St. Louis (NL) 2
1931	St. Louis (NL) 4, Philadelphia (AL) 3
1932	New York (AL) 4, Chicago (NL) 0
1933	New York (NL) 4, Washington (AL) 1
1934	St. Louis (NL) 4, Detroit (AL) 3
1935	Detroit (AL) 4, Chicago (NL) 2
1936	New York (AL) 4, New York (NL) 2
1937	New York (AL) 4, New York (NL) 1
1938	New York (AL) 4, Chicago (NL) 0
1939	New York (AL) 4, Cincinnati (NL) 0
1940	Cincinnati (NL) 4, Detroit (AL) 3
1941	New York (AL) 4, Brooklyn (NL) 1
1942	St. Louis (NL) 4, New York (AL) 1
1943	New York (AL) 4, St. Louis (NL) 1
1944	St. Louis (NL) 4, St. Louis (AL) 2
1945	Detroit (AL) 4, Chicago (NL) 3
1946	St. Louis (NL) 4, Boston (AL) 3
1947	New York (AL) 4, Brooklyn (NL) 3
1948	Cleveland (AL) 4, Boston (NL) 2
1949	New York (AL) 4, Brooklyn (NL) 1
1950	New York (AL) 4, Philadelphia (NL) 0
1951	New York (AL) 4, New York (NL) 2
1952	New York (AL) 4, Brooklyn (NL) 3
1953	New York (AL) 4, Brooklyn (NL) 2
1954	New York (NL) 4, Cleveland (AL) 0
1955	Brooklyn (NL) 4, New York (AL) 3
1956	New York (AL) 4, Brooklyn (NL) 3
1957	Milwaukee (NL) 4, New York (AL) 3
1958	New York (AL) 4, Milwaukee (NL) 3
1959	Los Angeles (NL) 4, Chicago (AL) 2
1960	Pittsburgh (NL) 4, New York (AL) 3
1961	New York (AL) 4, Cincinnati (NL) 1
1962	New York (AL) 4, San Francisco (NL) 3
1963	Los Angeles (NL) 4, New York (AL) 0
1964	St. Louis (NL) 4, New York (AL) 3
1965	Los Angeles (NL) 4, Minnesota (AL) 3
1966	Baltimore (AL) 4, Los Angeles (NL) 0
1967	St. Louis (NL) 4, Boston (AL) 3
1968	Detroit (AL) 4, St. Louis (NL) 3
1969	New York (NL) 4, Baltimore (AL) 1
1970	Baltimore (AL) 4, Cincinnati (NL) 1
1971	Pittsburgh (NL) 4, Baltimore (AL) 3
1972	Oakland (AL) 4, Cincinnati (NL) 3
1973	Oakland (AL) 4, New York (NL) 3
1974	Oakland (AL) 4, Los Angeles (NL) 1
1975	Cincinnati (NL) 4, Boston (AL) 3
1976	Cincinnati (NL) 4, New York (AL) 0
1977	New York (AL) 4, Los Angeles (NL) 2
1978	New York (AL) 4, Los Angeles (NL) 2
1979	Pittsburgh (NL) 4, Baltimore (AL) 3
1980	Philadelphia (NL) 4, Kansas City (AL) 2
1981	Los Angeles (NL) 4, New York (AL) 2
1982	St. Louis (NL) 4, Milwaukee (AL) 3
1983	Baltimore (AL) 4, Philadelphia (NL) 1

4
The Olympic Medals

In Kenya a middle-aged man heads wearily up a jagged mountainside trying to keep pace and fight the exhaustion that often defeats many aspiring runners much younger than he. Having one thing in mind, he pushes on.

In Brazil a young boy crosses a busy intersection but pays no attention. His mind is riveted on the black and white ball that he is skillfully bouncing from the top of one knee to the top of the other. He occasionally knocks it up a little higher and taps it off his chest or pops it with his head. What is going on around him is of little significance. He has a dream, a dream that he hopes will someday become a reality.

In Switzerland a skier crashes wildly down the slopes of a tricky mountain slalom course. She is young by most standards, but in the world of skiing she is a veteran. In fact to some she is already overage. But she continues to take the runs, to practice, to prove herself.

In the United States a sturdy young California girl pushes aimlessly through the chlorinated water of her high school swimming pool. Her arms feel numb and lifeless as she completes a turn, pushes off the wall, and heads back across the water for another lap. She keeps going and going, stroking and kicking with almost mindless determination. But there is a reason behind it all, a purpose for the pain.

Here are four different people in four different parts of the globe participating in four different activities, but all striving for the same purpose. Theirs is not just a goal; it is an obsession. Athletes throughout the world spend their whole lives practicing, enduring, and preparing for that one moment, that one brief second when success can be within their grasp. What is at stake is more than a symbol of recognition, it is *the* symbol of recognition. No championship, no title, no trophy in the world of sports can come close to providing the thrill that an athlete receives when he walks up to that three-tiered podium and stands proudly before a packed arena, listens to his national anthem, and receives his due recognition. It is a golden moment that thousands of athletes would give their right arm to experience. But only an elite few, the best in the world, are allowed to take part and shoot for it—an Olympic medal.

Whether it's the gold, silver, or bronze, no single medal or trophy can cause so many to spend so much effort. The Olympic Gold Medal is not big in size, but in status it is unparalleled. It symbolizes the best, not just in a town, state, or country, but in the entire world. When an athlete wins a medal in the Olympic Games, he knows he is not just good; he knows he is the best there is—anywhere!

The history of these prestigious games is a long and complex one, dating back to ancient Greece.

The Olympic Medal. (Lake Placid Olympic Organizing Committee photo)

The first recorded Olympics took place in 776 B.C., although the competition is believed to have begun much earlier. To the Greeks, the Olympics were not just games; they were a test of manhood. Nothing, not even a war, could stop the Olympics from taking place. In Greece athletes were highly revered. Thousands of spectators crowded the stadium to observe them compete.

No heroes were ever glorified as were the Olympic champions, not even victorious generals returning from war. From the moment an athlete was crowned with a wreath of wild olive, which was the symbol of victory, his name was proclaimed throughout the nation. Odes were written in his honor by the greatest poets of the age and were sung by choirs of youths. His deeds were chiseled on stone pillars, and sculptors shaped his likeness in life-size statues. A whole city would turn out to welcome home a victorious son and escort him in triumph through the streets.[1]

Since athletics at that time was used mainly as a mode of training young boys for war, the Olympics contained many events dealing with combat. For example, there was the hoplite, a footrace in which the participants, wearing only a helmet and carrying a shield, ran a distance of two *stades*. Other events included the javelin throw, the pentathlon (five different events), wrestling, and the anything-goes pancratium—a combination of punching, wrestling, kicking, and whatever else the combatants could think of.

It was a preoccupation with physical perfection that motivated the Greeks to originate the Olympics.

For many years the games flourished as one of the highlights of Greek culture. Throughout the fifth and fourth centuries B.C. they were regarded as an example of Greek superiority. Not surprisingly when this superiority began to wane and the civilization in Rome became recognized as the new world power, the games lost their prominence. Greek youths no longer desired to spend hours training in the gymnasium. To be an Olympic champion was not worth the effort. In response to this change in attitude, foreign athletes were brought in, nationalized, and allowed to compete in the games.

The writing was on the wall. After Greece was conquered by Rome and made into a province, the Olympics faded into insignificance. In A.D. 67 the Roman emperor Nero made a mockery of the competition. Bringing with him a modest group of supporters, numbering around five thousand, Nero entered himself in some of the events, and, whether or not he won, he was awarded first place. The proud tradition of the past was gone.

Around A.D. 390 Theodosius I, the Christian emperor of Rome, banned the games on the grounds that they were a pagan festival. The once highly revered games of the Olympiad thus ended.

The Olympics were not forgotten; their spirit and memory lived on through the centuries. Finally, in April 1896, they were revived through the diligent efforts of a French baron named Pierre de Coubertin. Interested in "improving the youth of France through competitive sports and thus strengthen[ing] the manhood of the nation,"[2] the baron worked tirelessly to promote the ideas. Though he received little response to his proposals at first, the tide eventually turned. It was decided that the games would be held and that they would take place in Athens, the capital of Greece.

Though the United States as a whole showed little interest in the revived Olympics, some dedicated and spirited American athletes wanted very badly to participate. One such person was Robert Garrett, the captain of the Princeton track team.

Paying all their expenses, he persuaded three other members of the squad to go with him. Another dedicated athlete was James Connolly of Harvard University. Connolly desperately wanted to compete but was not allowed a leave of absence from the school. So what did he do? He dropped out of the prestigious university in order to go. The Boston Athletic Association also decided to take part, sending five athletes. These athletes, combined with swimmer Gardner Williams and the pistol-shooting brothers John and Sumner Paine, formed a squad. It was the first unofficial United States Olympic Team—a group of fourteen dedicated athletes. At that time there was no U.S. Olympic Committee, and no funds were raised to aid them.

When the Americans arrived in Greece, they were welcomed heartily. The Greeks, proud of the Olympic tradition and happy to see American participants, were gracious hosts. Because of their great sports heritage, the local athletes and fans assumed that they would do well and that the twelve other competing nations wouldn't have much of a chance. For the most part they were right. But they did underestimate the spirited young men from the United States. The American upstarts ended up winning nine of the twelve track-and-field events, took two firsts in the shooting competition, and walked away with eleven gold medals—more than was won by any other nation. The Americans thus started a winning tradition that would be carried on for years to come. In an effort to contribute a piece of their own culture and return some of the hospitality shown them, the Yanks introduced the game of baseball to the Greeks. One of the people whom they coaxed into taking part was none other than the king of Greece himself!

The games took place again four years later, in 1900. Feeling that it was vital to rotate the site of the competition, Baron de Coubertin decided to stage them in his home country of France. Unfortunately, the French could not duplicate the marvelous reception given the games by the Greeks. The World's Fair was also held in France at the time, and the Olympics were greatly overshadowed. The fields and facilities were poor, and the fan attendance was less than expected. Despite the obstacles over fifteen hundred athletes, representing sixteen nations, took part.

The most interesting story of the 1900 Olympics concerned the pairs-with-coxswain rowing finals. It was billed to be a battle between the strong French team and the pair from the Netherlands. Just before the race, however, the Dutch coxswain, a doctor, was found to be over the officially allowed weight and was disqualified. It appeared that the Netherlands would be forced to drop out of the

competition. At the last minute the Dutch squad appeared at the starting line with a brand new coxswain. Very new and very small, he was estimated to be from eight to twelve years old. Where he came from, nobody know. As the race began, the French grew more confident by the moment. Despite the pressure of the situation the young boy performed capably and helped the Dutch take the event at a time of 2:34.2—just two tenths of a second ahead of their French rival!

In that same year, three American track athletes stole the show in their respective events. Roommates and close friends in college, Alvin Kraenzlein, Irving Baxter, and J. Walter Tewksbury dominated the track-and-field competition. Collectively, they won fourteen Olympic medals—eight gold (four for Kraenzlein), five silver, and a bronze. That was more than was was earned by any *nation* that year in track and field.

Another impressive athlete who emerged in 1900 was Ray Ewry. His specialties were the standing high jump, long jump, and the triple jump. At the age of twenty-six he won gold medals in all three events. He followed up that performance with three golds in 1904, two in 1906 (the only Olympics ever held in an off-year) and two in 1908, at the age of 34. His was a grand total of ten gold medals—an achievement that would be hard to match.

The 1908 Games, held in London, were marked by controversy. All during the competition the Americans and the British argued over various rules and their interpretation. The confrontation reached a climax in the 400-meter run. The final featured four runners—three Americans and an Englishman. As the race progressed two of the Americans, J. C. Carpenter and W. C. Robbins, were in the lead, the Englishman, Lt. Wyndham Halswelle, was third, and the other American, J. B. Taylor, was in last place. Robbins was in first place as they headed down the stretch. But then Carpenter and Halswelle simultaneously made a move to the outside and bumped into each other. The British judges screamed foul, and the race was declared invalid. American officials Amos Alonzo Stagg and James Sullivan vigorously protested the move. Their efforts went for naught, however, as the race was scheduled to be rerun two days later, when the Olympics were to close. The dash took place as arranged, and this time Halswelle sprinted on to victory unmolested. There was only one catch—he was the only runner in the field. Sullivan ordered the Americans not to take part.

The early years of the revived games saw Germany's G. E. Fuchs scored ten goals in the 1912 soccer competition. To the amazement of everyone, he scored them all in one game! Also that year,

Ralph Craig of Michigan won the 100- and 200-meter dashes—a double victory, not uncommon in track and field. Craig reappeared in the competition thirty-six years later as a crewman for *Rhythm* in the yachting competition.

Sports, and especially the Olympics, are commonly thought to be for the young. Oscar Swahn would never have agreed. In 1908, at the age of sixty-one, Swahn won a gold medal in the shooting event called Running Deer. In 1920, at the age of seventy-three, Swahn picked up another medal—this time a silver—in the same event at Antwerp. He is the oldest Olympic medal winner in history.

There have been many courageous performers in the Olympics, and one who must be listed at the top of this class is Eddie Eagan. In 1920 Eagan won the light-heavyweight boxing championship. Though this was no mean achievement, Eagan was not content. He decided that he needed to do more. His chance came eight years later, in 1928, in the winter games. An all-around athlete, Eagan decided to try his hand at the bobsled event. He quickly found out that it was more than a game. In return for being admitted to the four-man team, he had to sign a form releasing his teammates from liability for anything that might happen to him. In his first few practice runs Eagan found out that the sport was not as simple as it seemed. He also quickly appreciated what the word *terror* means. Despite his initial fears he persisted until he became competent. In 1928 he helped guide the four-man team to a gold medal performance. It was the first time anyone had won a gold medal in both the Summer and Winter Olympics.

Sometimes athletes who make it to the Olympics find little competition. The night in 1924 when the Canadian ice hockey team squared off against the Czechoslovakian squad will be remembered by the Czechs as a night to be forgotten. Canada won the contest by an incredible score of 30–0. Harry Watson scored thirteen goals in the game—a record undoubtedly unequalled. For Finnish track star Paavo Nurmi, the competition was a little easier to find. During the 1920s the great long-distance runner collected nine gold medals and three silvers. It was an outstanding feat, on that no other runner from any other country could hope to match. But another runner from his own country came very close. He was Willie Ritola, who, during that same period, claimed five golds and four silvers.

In 1924 Bob Le Gendre of the United States found formidable opposition, but only from the record books. A participant in the pentathlon (which was discontinued after that year), Le Gendre set a world record in one of the events, the long jump. His leap of 25 feet, 5¾ inches was far better than that of any other competitor in Olympic history. Because his record jump was not made during the regular long-jump competition, however, it could not be registered as an Olympic record. The following day, DeHart Hubbard of the United States won the long jump with a leap of 24 feet, 5 inches.

Time certainly proved to be no obstacle to Aladar Gerevich of Hungary. In 1932, as a member of his nation's saber fencing team, he won a gold medal. In 1960, Gerevich was still in the running as he once again won the gold, to complete what was an incredible string. In between those two gold medal performances, he put together four others, for a total of six straight golds in six straight Olympics.

The 1936 games, held on the eve of the Second World War, were staged in Berlin, in the backyard of Nazi Germany's leader Adolf Hitler. Hitler tried to use the games to demonstrate to the world the strength of his nation and the superiority of the Aryan race. Hitler's contestants, however, did nothing to promote the point that the führer was trying to get across. One example was Germany's Dora Ratjin. The favorite in the women's high jump, Dora came in a dismal fourth. To make things worse, "Dora" was later discovered not even to be a woman. The athlete was actually Hermann Ratjin, a male waiter who was unable to make it in the men's competition. It was one of the biggest hoaxes ever perpetrated in the Olympics.

The rest of Hitler's athletes did not do much better than "Dora." One of the main reasons was the performance of the American track superstar Jesse Owens. His performances assaulted not only Hitler's philosophy, but the present competition, the record books, and, apparently, the laws of nature. Owens ran away with four gold medals—in the 100-meter dash, the 200-meter dash, the 400-meter relay, and the long jump. What was most galling to Hitler was that one of his own athletes aided Owens in his quest to win the long jump. Owens, experiencing difficulty with his technique, continued to foul. Then, Luz Long, Germany's respected long jumper, came along and told Owens to imagine a spot in front of the line and aim for it. Owens listened, thanked his new friend, followed his instructions, and went on to win the gold medal.

In 1936 a new sport was added to the games of the Olympiad. Basketball, an American invention, was placed on the agenda. It soon became apparent why the Americans wanted it to be part of the competition. Before the Russians finally stopped them in 1972, the United States piled up an overwhelming string of sixty-three straight victories. A total of eight golds have been captured by the Americans, seven before that defeat, and one after it in the

Jesse Owens stunned the world and Nazi leader Adolph Hitler with his outstanding performance at the Berlin Olympics. (UPI photo)

1976 games. No other Olympic sport has been so dominated by one nation. Anticipating the superiority of American players, the Japanese in 1936 proposed a rule to limit the height of participants. Fortunately for the United States, the proposal was not approved.

The list of players for the United States Olympic basketball team over the years contains the names of many players who later became stars of the National Basketball Association (NBA). In 1956 there was the great Bill Russell; in 1960 there was Adrian Smith, Jerry Lucas, Oscar Robertson, Jerry West, Terry Dischinger, Walt Bellamy, and Bob Boozer; in 1964 there was Joe Caldwell, Lucius Jackson, Jim Barnes, and Bill Bradley; in 1968 there was little known Spencer Haywood and Jo Jo White; in 1972 there was Tom Henderson, Doug Collins, Jim Brewer, Dwight Jones, Mike Bantom, Bobby Jones, Tom Burleson, and Tom McMillen. The talent of these individuals seemed almost endless. In one 1960 game against Japan, for example, Jerry

Lucas of Ohio State scored fourteen baskets in fourteen attempts!

Despite the overwhelming success nothing will be remembered with as much pain and anger by American basketball enthusiasts as the controversial final game of the 1972 Olympics. As the Americans and the Russians were facing each other, more was at stake than just a basketball game. Each team was fighting for national pride and political ideology. From the opening whistle the Russians proved that they would not just roll over and play dead. They held the lead for over thirty-five minutes in the forty-minute contest. But with three seconds remaining they found themselves behind their American opponents by one point. What occurred from that stage until the end of the game has to be considered the most bizarre string of events in Olympic history.

Down by a point, the Russians inbounded the ball and made an attempt at the winning basket. It failed, and the Americans celebrated wildly. But then the officials suddenly ruled that the three seconds had to be played over. The reason—the Rus-

47

The United States and Russia have staged some of the most exciting and controversial games in Olympic basketball competition. (UPI photo)

sian coach had called an illegal time-out during the previous play. The officials not only decided to give him the time-out, but they gave it to him after the contest should rightfully have been over. The three seconds were replayed, and once again the Russians failed to score the winning basket. Again, to the shock of the Americans the officials ruled that the three seconds had to be played over. For a third time the game's final seconds were replayed. This time, however, when the Russians lobbed the ball over the length of the court in desperation, the result was different. The big Russian center, knocking over the two Americans guarding him, caught the ball and laid it in the goal for the winning basket. Once again the Americans protested but to no avail. The Russians were awarded the victory and the American's glorious string of victories ended.

When the 1976 Olympics rolled around in Montreal, the United States was ready to win back the gold medal they felt was rightfully theirs. Having refused to accept the silver medal in 1972, they wanted to show the world that they belonged on top. And that's exactly what they did as they swept their way through the competition and won the coveted gold.

Aside from basketball, there have been many other events in the summer games at which the Americans have excelled. An example is the decathlon. From 1932 to 1976 the United States failed to win it only twice. Some of the greatest athletes in the nation's history have emerged from this grueling ten-event competition. In 1948, seventeen-year-old Bob Mathias captured the gold medal and the hearts of the country, stunning the rest of the field with his performance. Four years later he repeated the feat at Helsinki, winning the gold by the biggest margin in the history of the decathlon. The trend that Mathias set was capably followed by other superb American athletes. In 1956 Milton Campbell won the gold; in 1960 Rafer Johnson won it; in 1968 it was Bill Toomey; and in 1976, one of the greatest of them all, Bruce Jenner, set the Montreal stadium crowd on fire with his record-breaking gold-medal performance.

In the winter games the Americans have not been as successful, but their performances have improved. One of the first Americans to hit it big was ice skater Dick Button. In 1948 he easily outclassed the rest of the competition on his way to a gold medal. When the 1952 games arrived, Button was not just content to win; he wanted to do something that no one had ever done before. It was a risky idea—if he failed, he would have probably lost the gold—but he pressed on anyway. Heading out onto the ice for the free-skating portion of the program, he awed the crowd with one of the most difficult maneuvers in the event. Never before had anyone completed a triple loop jump, but Button did it and did it well. Without a doubt the gold medal belonged on Button's lapel.

Of the winter events, figure skating has proven to be one of the more successful for the Americans, especially for the women. In 1956 Tenley Albright won the gold, and four years later Carol Heiss proved equal to the task. Peggy Fleming's grace and beauty enabled her to skate home with the gold in 1968, as did Dorothy Hamill (inventor of the Hamill camel) in 1976. Linda Fratianne continued the string of impressive performances as she captured the silver medal before the home crowd at Lake Placid in 1980.

Although they were not on the level of excellence of the summer Olympians, the winter athletes continued to improve. Nothing epitomized the American will to excel and enthusiasm for sports as did the ice hockey teams of 1960 and 1980. In those two Olympics the United States squads pulled off unbelievable upsets, stunning the world as they won the gold medal.

In 1960 a team was fielded that had very little, if any, international experience. But they didn't let that stop them. Behind the outstanding goalkeep-

American figure skaters soon made their mark on the ice. Peggy Fleming shows why. (UPI photo)

The 1980 United States Hockey Team captured the heart and soul of a nation by defeating the powerful Russians and winning the gold. (UPI photo)

ing of Jack McCartan and the offensive firepower of the Christian and Cleary brothers, the Americans pulled off some incredible victories. Most notable among them were their 2–1 victory over the experienced Canadian team and their 3–2 win over the powerful Russians. In the final against Czechoslovakia, the Americans trailed 4–3 after two periods. Their backs were against the wall. But then into their locker room came the captain of the Russian team, Nik Sologubov, offering some friendly words of encouragement and some advice about taking oxygen to get back their energy. The Americans listened, and, after the game resumed, scored six goals to win the gold, 9–4.

1980 was a repeat of the 1960 "Miracle of Squaw Valley." Once again, the Olympics were held in the United States, this time in Lake Placid, New York. Once again, the Americans were not expected to do very well. They were not even expected to come close to winning a medal. They were too young, too inexperienced. But the Americans turned what people thought would be a handicap into an advantage. They turned their youth into boundless enthusiasm and their inexperience into a burning desire and a never-say-die attitude. They just didn't know any better. Their upset win over Russia stunned the world and, when they defeated Finland 4–2 in the final, the nation went into a state of ecstatic shock. Reported one major newspaper:

> The United States hockey team won its first gold medal since 1960 yesterday, getting third period goals from Phil Verchota, Rob McClanahan, and Mark Johnson to beat Finland 4-2 and complete a storybook journey into the hearts of the nation.
>
> "You are watching a group of people who startled the athletic world—not the hockey world, but the athletic world," said coach Herb Brooks (who, ironically, was the last man cut from the 1960 team). . . .
>
> "If there's anybody in here that thought we'd win a gold medal, I'd like to meet him," said [goalie Jim] Craig, who gave up only fifteen goals in seven games. "I wouldn't want to go through this tournament again next week—it might have a different result."[3]

Many top-notch American athletes have emerged from obscurity in the Winter Olympics. Very few true superstars, however, have come forth. In 1980 one such athlete did. His achievement was so outstanding that it was recognized throughout the world as the greatest in the history of the sport. Even the media in Russia hailed his effort and publicized his victories. His name was Eric Heiden, and his accomplishment was winning all five gold

Following their win over the Russians, the young Americans wildly celebrated. (UPI photo)

medals in the speed skating competition. The twenty-one-year-old resident of Wisconsin skated his way into the record books with a truly unprecedented effort.

To a lot of people, what Heiden did came as no surprise. In a nation as sports-oriented as America, fans have almost become accustomed to athletes doing the impossible. It has been almost commonplace to see an athlete go beyond what seems to be human limitations.

Expectations can often be a major factor in determining the outcome of a competition. For the U.S. team in the 1984 Winter Games in Sarajevo, Yugoslavia, the expectations were not only there, but wins were boldly predicted. By some accounts the Americans could have won up to seventeen medals. But when it was all said and done, they could manage only four gold and four silver medals.

Following the "Miracle of Lake Placid" in 1980, the ice hockey team, a young and talented group, had probably the biggest skates to fill. Pregame analysts had them winning a silver medal if they played badly. Unfortunately it was not to be, as the competition proved stiffer than expected and they didn't even make it to the medal round.

As the games progressed many of the American athletes stressed the importance of the fun of just competing. Brothers Phil and Steve Mahre of the ski team claimed winning a medal was not that important, that they had made their fortunes already. Downhiller Bill Johnson, on the other hand, boldly asserted that he would win the gold—easily. Figure skaters Rosalyn Sumners and Scott Hamilton should have won gold medals too, it was said.

Hamilton did win the gold and Sumners skated away with a silver medal. To everyone's surprise but his own, Johnson did exactly what he said he would do and won the downhill. And Phil and Steve Mahre swept to first and second place finishes in the slalom. Despite the predictions and expectations, and maybe because of them, it was one of the most interesting and exciting Winter Olympic Teams the U.S. has ever fielded. The history of the Olympics is just one big catalog of sports excellence. There have also been the failures and the disappointments, but it is the successes and the Herculean efforts that will always be remembered.

In 1952 a seventeen-year-old Brooklyn boy traveled to Helsinki as a member of the U.S. boxing team. The little-known middle-weight battled some very stiff competition and some very biased referees on his way to the gold medal. But then, for Floyd Patterson, it was just the beginning.

Diving has always been a strong area for the United States in Olympic competition. In 1952 at

Rafer Johnson won the Olympic gold in the decathlon, and the respect and admiration of thousands of sports fans. (San Diego Hall of Champions photo)

the age of twenty-two, Pat McCormick of California captured the gold in both the springboard and platform events. Four years later, at the Melbourne games, she decided to give it another try. During most of the year before she had been unable to train due to a pregnancy. The five months that she did have she utilized to the most. Having been coached by her husband, she easily won the springboard gold. In the platform event, however, with only one dive remaining, she found herself in fourth place. Executing a near-perfect forward one-and-a-half somersault with full twist, she bolted past the competition and won her fourth Olympic gold. Back home, she was also awarded the coveted Sullivan Award that year.

When most people think of the Olympic discus throw, one name immediately comes to mind—Al Oerter. And when they think of Al Oerter, two adjectives immediately pop up—*underdog* and *clutch*. Though Oerter won the gold medal in the discus from 1956 to 1968, it would be deceptive to say that he dominated the event, for the way he won them was most unusual. In 1956 he was an unknown nineteen-year-old sophomore from the University of Kansas. On his first throw he shocked his competitors by heaving the disc 184 feet, 10 ½ inches—well over the Olympic record. Unable to catch the upstart, the rest of the field struggled through the competition. In the next two Olympiads, at Rome and Tokyo, Oerter fell behind early and was all but counted out. On both occasions, however, he put forth herculean efforts on his final throw, stunning his opponents and winning the gold. His last Olympics, in 1968 at Mexico City,

was no different. Now a thirty-two-year-old veteran, he was assumed to have had his day in the sun. But he proved himself once again, as he psyched out the favorites with three outstanding throws and again walked away with the gold.

At times athletes have managed outstanding performances despite physical illness. In 1960 American swimmer Jeff Farrell, expected to do well in the freestyle event, was hospitalized for an emergency appendectomy just before the Olympic trials. Twenty-four hours after the surgery he was out of the hospital, and three days later, his abdomen heavily taped, he was back in the water practicing. To say the operation lessened his chances would be an understatement. But Farrell didn't let it dampen his enthusiasm, and he qualified for the squad as a member of the 400-meter and 800-meter relay teams. By the time the Olympics arrived he was back in shape and turned in a couple of outstanding performances that resulted in gold medals.

A similar story concerned sixteen-year-old Dick Roth of California in the 1964 games at Tokyo. Three days before his 400-meter individual medley race, he got appendicitis. Like Farrell, he wouldn't let the misfortune stop him, and he participated in pain. To the disbelief of everyone, he was able to defeat his respected opponent, Gerhard Hetz of Germany. Roth did have one thing going for him, though. On the day of the event, Hetz, too, was not feeling very well. He had pneumonia!

To break a world record at the Olympic Games is an achievement of which many athletes dream and few achieve. In 1968 at Mexico City, Bob Beamon of the United States not only broke the long-jump record, but shattered it. In what is considered to be the greatest single performance in the history of the sport, Beamon smashed the record books with his jump of 29 feet, 2½ inches. This was 16 inches over the current world record!

In those same games at Mexico City, a cocky young swimmer named Mark Spitz was making waves both in and out of the water. The confident

Swimmer Mark Spitz set an unbeatable record, collecting seven gold medals in one Olympic competition. (UPI photo)

young Californian boldly predicted that six gold medals were within his grasp. At the end of the competition he took home with him two golds, a silver, a bronze, a case of tonsillitis, diarrhea, and a deflated ego. The two golds he did win were from his participation on the powerful U.S. relay teams.

Four years later a more experienced and humbled Spitz traveled to Munich, West Germany, to try to atone for what he had taken to be a dismal performance. Spitz handled the pressure quite well, as he dominated the games and collected a record seven gold medals.

When the Olympic Games were revitalized in the nineteenth century, they were intended to be solely a sporting event designed to bring the people of the world together. Unfortunately, however, politics have become a part of the event. The United States, although dedicated to the Olympic philosophy, has been touched by this trend. In 1968 black members of the track-and-field team protested what they felt were injustices perpetrated against their race. Sprinters Tommie Smith and John Carlos defiantly held black-gloved fists in the air as they received their medals and listened to the national anthem. Others protested in a similar manner—Vince Matthews, Lee Evans, and Larry James wore black berets on the victory stand, and the long jumpers wore black socks. It was a period of political turmoil, and the black athletes reflected it.

In 1980 the United States government protested military moves made by the Soviet Union into Afghanistan. President Jimmy Carter decided that the only viable option was to disallow his nation to send a team to the summer games, which were to be held in Moscow. Hundreds of athletes, who had been training for years, were not allowed to participate. Once again, politics had a profound effect on the Olympics.

Despite the interruptions and distractions the Olympics remain the most important athletic event in the world. Every four years, when athletes from nations all over the globe get together for sporting competition, almost everything else takes on lesser importance. Having put in years and years of training, amateur athletes everywhere aim for that one moment in the spotlight. For some, like Mark Spitz, that moment can become very financially profitable. Following the Olympics, he signed a million-dollar contract, which truly made his efforts worth their weight in gold. For others, like Jim Thorpe of Carlisle, who won both the pentathlon and the decathlon in 1912, it can end in bitter disappointment. When Thorpe returned to the United States, it was discovered that he had earlier accepted money to play baseball. An honest man,

Thorpe admitted the charge, and the Amateur Athletic Union declared his Olympic victories void. His name was stricken from the record book, and his great achievement was wiped out.

There are numerous reasons why so many people hold the Olympic Games in such high regard. For sheer effort, drama, and emotion, they are unsurpassed. Maybe that is why they can virtually make the world stand still every four years when the competition gets underway. Who could forget the effort put forth by the young girl from Tennessee named Wilma Rudolph? In the 1960 Olympiad in Rome she won an unprecedented three gold medals for the American team. What was most incredible about the trackster was that earlier in her life she had been crippled by a childhood illness and bedridden for about four years. Or what about the drama encircling the 1976 U.S. boxing team? An underdog throughout, they set the stage with some incredible performances and some gold medal efforts. To boxing fans, the names of Sugar Ray Leonard, Leon Spinks, John Tate, Michael Spinks, Clint Jackson, and Davey Armstrong will always be remembered. Or for sheer emotion, nothing could top the exciting performance of the 1980 U.S. hockey team. For these and many other reasons, the Olympic Games are held by athletes and fans throughout the world as the most important sporting even in the world. And in sports there is a lot to choose from.

Olympic Games Champions, 1896–1980 (*Indicates Olympic Records)

Track and Field—Men

60-METER RUN

1900	Alvin Kraenzdein, United States	7s*
1904	Archie Hahn, United States	7s*

100-METER RUN

1896	Thomas Burke, United States	12s
1900	Francis W. Jarvis, United States	10.8s
1904	Archie Hahn, United States	11s
1908	Reginald Walker, South Africa	10.8s
1912	Ralph Craig, United States	10.8s
1920	Charles Paddock, United States	10.8s
1924	Harold Abrahams, Great Britain	10.6s
1928	Percy Williams, Canada	10.8s
1932	Eddie Tolan, United States	10.3s
1936	Jesse Owens, United States	10.3s
1948	Harrison Dillard, United States	10.3s
1952	Lindy Remigino, United States	10.4s
1956	Bobby Morrow, United States	10.5s
1960	Armin Hary, Germany	10.2s
1964	Bob Hayes, United States	10.0s
1968	Jim Hines, United States	9.9s*

1972	Valeri Borzov, USSR	10.14s
1976	Hasely Crawford, Trinidad	10.06s
1980	Allan Wells, Great Britain	10.25s

200-METER RUN

1900	Walter Tewksbury, United States	22.2s
1904	Archie Hahn, United States	21.6s
1908	Robert Kerr, Canada	22.4s
1912	Ralph Craig, United States	21.7s
1920	Allan Woodring, United States	22s
1924	Jackson Scholz, United States	21.6s
1928	Percy Williams, Canada	21.8s
1932	Eddie Tolan, United States	21.2s
1936	Jesse Owens, United States	20.7s
1948	Mel Patton, United States	21.1s
1952	Andrew Stanfield, United States	20.7s
1956	Bobby Morrow, United States	20.6s
1960	Livio Bérruti, Italy	20.5s
1964	Henry Carr, United States	20.3s
1968	Tommie Smith, United States	19.6s*
1972	Valeri Borzov, USSR	20.00s
1976	Donald Quarrie, Jamaica	20.23s
1980	Pietro Mannea, Italy	20.19s

400-METER RUN

1896	Thomas Burke, United States	54.2s
1900	Maxey Long, United States	49.4s
1904	Harry Hillman, United States	49.2s
1908	Wyndham Halswelle, Great Britain, walkover	50s
1912	Charles Reidpath, United States	48.2s
1920	Bevil Rudd, South Africa	49.6s
1924	Eric Liddell, Great Britain	47.6s
1928	Ray Barbuti, United States	47.8s
1932	William Carr, United States	46.2s
1936	Archie Williams, United States	46.5s
1948	Arthur Wint, Jamaica, B W I	46.2s
1952	George Rhoden, Jamaica B W I	45.9s
1956	Charles Jenkins, United States	46.7s
1960	Otis Davis, United States	44.9s
1964	Michael Larrabee, United States	45.1s
1968	Lee Evans, United States	43.8s*
1972	Vincent Matthews, United States	44.66s
1976	Alberto Juantorena, Cuba	44.26s
1980	Viktor Markin, USSR	44.60s

800-METER RUN

1896	Edwin Flack, Great Britain	2m. 11s
1900	Alfred Tysoe, Great Britain	2m. 1.4s
1904	James Lightbody, United States	1m. 56s
1908	Mel Sheppard, United States	1m. 52.8s
1912	James Meredith, United States	1m. 51.9s
1920	Albert Hill, Great Britain	1m. 53.4s
1924	Douglas Lowe, Great Britain	1m. 52.4s
1928	Douglas Lowe, Great Briain	1m. 51.8s
1932	Thomas Hampson, Great Britain	1m. 49.8s
1936	John Woodruff, United States	1m. 52.9s
1948	Mal Whitfield, United States	m. 49.2s
1952	Mal Whitfield, United States	1m. 49.2s
1956	Thomas Courtney, United States	1m. 47.7s
1960	Peter Snell, New Zealand	1m. 46.3s

1964	Peter Snell, New Zealand	1m. 45.1s
1968	Ralph Doubell, Australia	1m. 44.3s
1972	Dave Wottle, United States	1m. 45.9s
1976	Alberto Juantorena, Cuba	1m. 43.50s*
1980	Steve Ovett, Great Britain	1m. 45.40s

1,500-METER RUN

1896	Edwin Flack, Great Britain	4m. 33.2s
1900	Charles Bennett, Great Britain	4m. 6s
1904	James Lightbody, United States	4m. 5.4s
1908	Mel Sheppard, United States	4m. 3.4s
1912	Arnold Jackson, Great Britain	3m. 56.8s
1920	Albert Hill, Great Britain	4m. 1.8s
1924	Paavo Numi, Finland	3m. 53.6s
1928	Harry Larva, Finland	3m. 53.2s
1932	Luigi Becali, Italy	3m. 51.2s
1936	Jack Lovelock, New Zealand	3m. 47.8s
1948	Henri Eriksson, Sweden	3m. 49.8s
1952	Joseph Barthel, Luxemburg	3m. 45.2s
1956	Ron Delany, Ireland	3m. 41.2s
1960	Herb Elliott, Australia	3m. 35.6s
1964	Peter Snell, New Zealand	3m. 38.1s
1968	Kipchoge Keino, Kenya	3m. 34.9s*
1972	Pekka Vasala, Finland	3m. 36.3s
1976	John Walker, New Zealand	3m. 39.17s
1980	Sebastian Coe, Great Britain	3m. 38.4s

3,000-METER STEEPLECHASE

1920	Percy Hodge, Great Britain	10m. 0.4s
1924	Willie Ritola, Finland	9m. 33.6s
1928	Tolvo Loukola, Finland	9m. 21.8s
1932	Volmari Iso-Hollo, Finland	10m. 33.4s
	(About 3,450 mtrs. extra lap by error)	
1936	Volmari Iso-Hollo, Finland	9m. 3.8s
1948	Thure Sjoestrand, Sweden	9m. 4.6s
1952	Horace Ashefelter, United States	8m. 45.4s
1956	Chris Brasher, Great Britain	8m. 41.2s
1960	Zdzislaw Krzyszkowiak, Poland	8m. 34.2s
1964	Gaston Roelants, Belgium	8m. 30.8s
1968	Amos Biwott, Kenya	8m. 51s
1972	Kipchoge Keino, Kenya	8m. 23.6s
1976	Anders Garderud, Sweden	8m. 08.2s*
1980	Bronislaw Malinowski, Poland	8m. 09.7s

5,000-METER RUN

1912	Hannes Kolehmainen, Finland	14m. 36.6s
1920	Joseph Gulliemot, France	14m. 55.6s
1924	Paavo Numi, Finland	14m. 31.2s
1928	Willie Ritola, Finland	14m. 38s
1932	Lauri Lehtinen, Finland	14m. 30s
1936	Gunnar Hockert, Finland	14m. 22.2s
1948	Gaston Reiff, Belgium	14m. 17.6s
1952	Emil Zatopek, Czechoslovakia	14m. 6.6s
1956	Vladimir Kuts, USSR	13m. 39.6s
1960	Murray Halberg, New Zealand	13m. 43.4s
1964	Bob Schul, United States	13m. 48.8s
1968	Mohamed Gammoudi, Tunisia	14m. 05.0s
1972	Lasse Viren, Finland	13m. 26.4s
1976	Lasse Viren, Finland	13m. 24.76s
1980	Miruts Yifter, Ethiopia	13m. 21.0s*

10,000-METER RUN

1912	Hannes Kolehmainen, Finland	31m. 20.8s
1920	Paavo Nurmi, Finland	31m. 45.8s
1924	Willie Ritola, Finland	30m. 23.2s
1928	Vaavo Nurmi, Finland	30m. 18.8s
1932	Janusz Kusocinski, Poland	30m. 11.4s
1936	Llmari Salminen, Finland	30m. 15.4s
1948	Emil Zatopek, Czechoslovakia	29m. 59.6s
1952	Emil Zatopek, Czechoslovakia	29m. 17.0s
1956	Vladimir Kuts, USSR	28m. 45.6s
1960	Pytor Bolotrikov, USSR	28m. 32.2s
1964	Billy Mills, United States	28m. 24.4s
1968	Naltali Temu, Kenya	29m. 27.4s
1972	Lasse Viren, Finland	27m. 38.4s*
1976	Lasse Viren, Finland	27m. 40.38s
1980	Miruts Yifter, Ethiopia	27m. 42.7s

MARATHON

1896	Spiridon Loues, Greece	2h. 58m. 50s
1900	Michel Teato, France	2h. 59m. 45s
1904	Thomas Hicks, United States	3h. 28m. 53s
1908	John J. Hayes, United States	2h. 55m. 18.4s
1912	Kenneth McArthur, South Africa	2h. 36m. 54.8s
1920	Hannes Kolehmainen, Finland	2h. 32m. 35.8s
1924	Albin Stenroos, Finland	2h. 41m. 22.6s
1928	A. B. El Quafi, France	2h. 32m. 57s
1832	Juan Zabala, Argentina	2h. 31m. 36s
1936	Kitei Son, Japan	2h. 29m. 19.2s
1948	Delfo Cabrera, Argentina	2h. 34m. 51.6s
1952	Emil Zatopek, Czechoslovakia	2h. 23m. 03.2s
1956	Alain Mimoun, France	2h. 25m.
1960	Abebe Bikila, Ethiopia	2h. 15m. 16.2s
1964	Abebe Bikila, Ethiopia	2h. 12m. 11.2s
1968	Mamo Wolde, Ethiopia	2h. 20m. 26.4s
1972	Frank Shorter, United States	2h. 12m. 19.8s
1976	Waldemar Cierpinski, E. Germany	2h. 09m. 55s*
1980	Waldemar Cierpinski, E. Germany	2h. 11m. 03s

10,000-METER CROSS-COUNTRY

1920	Paavo Nurmi, Finland	27m. 15s*
1924	Paavo Nurmi, Finland	32m. 54.8s

20-KILOMETER WALK

1956	Leonid Spirine, USSR	1h. 31m. 27.4s
1960	Vladimir Golubnichy, USSR	1h. 34m. 7.2s
1964	Kenneth Mathews, Great Britain	1h. 29m. 34.0s
1968	Vladimir Golubnichy, USSR	1h. 35m. 58.4s
1972	Peter Frenkel, E. Germany	1h. 26m. 42.4s
1976	Daniel Bautista, Mexico	1h. 24m. 40.6s
1980	Maurizio Damilano, Italy	1h. 23m. 35.5s*

50-KILOMETER WALK

1932	Thomas W. Green, Great Britain	4h. 50m. 10s
1936	Harold Whitlock, Great Britain	4h. 30m 41.4s
1948	John Ljunggren, Sweden	4h. 41m. 52s
1952	Giuseppe Dordoni, Italy	4h. 28m. 07.8s
1956	Norman Read, New Zealand	4h. 30m. 42.8s
1960	Donald Thompson, Great Britain	4h. 25m. 30s
1964	Abdon Pàmich, Italy	4h. 11m. 11.4s
1968	Christoph Hohne, E. Germany	4h. 20m. 13.6s
1972	Bern Kannenberg, W. Germany	3h. 56m. 11.6s
1980	Hartwig Gauter, E. Germany	3h. 49m. 24.0s*

110-METER HURDLES

1896	Thomas Curtis, United States	17.6s
1900	Alvin Kraenzlein, United States	15.4s
1904	Frederick Schule, United States	16s
1908	Forrest Smithson, United States	15s
1912	Frederick Kelly, United States	15.1s
1920	Earl Thomson, Canada	14.8s
1924	Daniel Kinsey, United States	15s
1928	Sydney Atkinson, South Africa	14.8s
1932	George Saling, United States	14.6s
1936	Forrest Towns, United States	14.2s
1948	William Porter, United States	13.9s
1952	Harrison Dillard, United States	13.7s
1956	Lee Calhoun, United States	13.5s
1960	Lee Calhoun, United States	13.8s
1964	Hayes Jones, United States	13.6s
1968	Willie Davenport, United States	13.3s
1972	Rod Milburn, United States	13.24s*
1976	Guy Drut, France	13.30s
1980	Thomas Munkelt, E. Germany	13.39s

200-METER HURDLES

1900	Alvin Kraenzlein, United States	25.4s
1904	Harry Hillman, United States	24.6s*

400-METER HURDLES

1900	J. W. B. Tewksbury, United States	57.6s
1904	Harry Hillman, United States	53s
1908	Charles Bacon, United States	55s
1920	Frank Loomis, United States	54s
1924	F. Morgan Taylor, United States	52.6s
1928	Lord Burghley, Great Britain	53.4s
1932	Robert Tisdall, Ireland	51.8s
1936	Glenn Hardin, United States	52.4s
1948	Roy Cochran, United States	51.1s
1952	Charles Moore, United States	50.8s
1956	Glenn Davis, United States	50.1s
1960	Glenn Davis, United States	49.3s
1964	Rex Cawley, United States	49.6s
1968	Dave Hemery, Great Britain	48.1s
1972	John Akii-Bua, Uganda	47.82s
1976	Edwin Moses, United States	47.64s*
1980	Volker Beck, E. Germany	48.70s

STANDING HIGH JUMP

1900	Ray Ewry, United States	5ft. 5 in.
1904	Ray Ewry, United States	4ft. 11 in.
1908	Ray Ewry, United States	5ft. 2 in.
1912	Platt Adams, United States	5ft. 4¼ in.*

RUNNING HIGH JUMP

1896	Ellery Clark, United States	5ft. 11¼ in.
1900	Irving Baxter, United States	6ft. 2⅖ in.

1904	Samuel Jones, United States.......	5ft. 11 in.
1908	Harry Porter, United States........	6ft. 3 in.
1912	Alma Richards, United States.......	6ft. 4 in.
1920	Richard Landon, United States.....	6ft. 4¼ in.
1924	Harld Osborn, United States.......	6ft. 6 in.
1928	Robert W. King, United States.....	6ft. 4⅜ in.
1932	Duncan McNaughton, Canada.....	6ft 5⅝ in.
1936	Cornelius Johnson, United States..	6ft. 7¹⁵⁄₁₆ in.
1948	John L. Winter, Australia...........	6ft. 6 in.
1952	Walter Davis, United States......	6ft. 8.32 in.
1956	Charles Dumas, United States....	6ft. 11¼ in.
1960	Robert Shaviakadze, USSR..........	7ft. 1 in.
1964	Valery Brumel, USSR.............	7ft. 1¾ in.
1968	Dick Fosbury, United States.......	7ft. 4¼ in.
1972	Yuri Tarmak, USSR	7ft. 3¾ in.
1976	Jacek Wiszola, Poland	7ft. 4½ in.
1980	Gerd Wessig, E. Germany.......	7 ft. 8¾ in.*

STANDING BROAD JUMP
1900	Ray Ewry, United States.........	10ft. 6⅖ in.
1904	Ray Ewry, United States	11 ft. 7⅞ in.*
1908	Ray Ewry, United States	10ft. 11¼ in.
1912	Constantin Tsicilitras, Greece	11ft. ¾ in.

LONG JUMP
1896	Ellery Clark, United States	20ft. 9¾ in.
1900	Alvin Kraenzlein, United States ...	23ft. 6⅞ in.
1904	Myer Prinstein, United States	24ft. 1 in.
1908	Frank Irons, United States........	24ft. 6½ in.
1912	Albert Gutterson, United States ..	24ft. 11¼ in.
1920	William Petterssen, Sweden	23ft. 5½ in.
1924	DeHart Hubbard, United States...	24ft. 5⅛ in.
1928	Edward B. Hamm, United States ..	25ft. 4¾ in.
1932	Edward Gordon, United States	25ft. ¾ in.
1936	Jesse Owens, United States	26ft. 5⁵⁄₁₆ in.
1948	William Steele, United States......	25ft. 8 in.
1952	Jerome Biffle, United States........	24ft 10 in.
1956	Gregory Bell, United States	25ft. 8¼ in.
1960	Ralph Boston, United States	26ft. 7¾ in.
1964	Lynn Davies, Great Britain	26ft. 5¾ in.
1968	Bob Bearmon, United States	29ft. 2½ in.
1972	Randy Williams, United States	27ft. ½ in.
1976	Arnie Robinson, United States	27ft. 4½ in.
1980	Lutz Dombrowski, E. Germany	28ft. ¼ in.

400-METER RELAY
1912	Great Britain........................	42.4s
1920	United States	42.2s
1924	United States.......................	41s
1928	United States.......................	41s
1932	United States.......................	40s
1936	United States	239.8s
1948	United States	40.6s
1952	United States	40.1s
1958	United States	39.5s
1960	Germany (U.S. disqualified)...........	39.5s
1964	United States	39.0s
1968	United States	38.2s
1972	United States	38.19s
1976	United States	38.33s

| 1980 | USSR............................ | 38.26s |

1,600-METER RELAY
1908	United States	3m. 27.2s
1912	United States	3m. 16.6s
1920	Great Britain.....................	3m. 22.2s
1924	United States	3m. 16s
1928	United States	3m. 14.2s
1932	United States	3m. 8.2s
1936	Great Britain	3m. 9s
1948	United States	3m. 10.4s
1952	Jamaica, B.W.I....................	3m. 03.9s
1956	United States	3m. 04.8s
1960	United States	3m. 02.2s
1964	United States	3m. 00.7s
1968	United States	2m. 56.1s*
1972	Kenya............................	2m. 59.8s
1976	United States	2m. 59.52s
1980	USSR............................	3m 01.1s

POLE VAULT
1896	William Hoyt, United States......	10ft. 9¾ in.
1900	Irving Baxter, United States	10ft. 9⅞ in.
1904	Charles Dvorak, United States......	11ft. 6 in.
1908	A. C. Gilbert, United States	
	Edward Cook, Jr., United States	12ft. 2 in.
1912	Harry Babcock, United States....	12ft. 11½ in.
1920	Frank Foss, United States.........'..	13ft. 5 in.
1924	Lee Barnes, United States.......	12ft. 11½ in.
1928	Sabin W. Carr, United States	13ft. 9⅜ in.
1932	William Miller, United States.....	14ft. 1⅞ in.
1936	Earle Meadows, United States	14ft. 3¼ in.
1948	Guinn Smith, United States	14ft. 1¼ in.
1952	Robert Richards, United States...	14ft. 11⅛ in.
1956	Robert Richards, United States...	14ft. 11½ in.
1960	Don Bragg, United States	15ft. 5⅛ in.
1964	Fred Hansen, United States	16ft. 8¾ in.
1968	Bob Seagren, United States.......	17ft. 8½ in.
1972	Wolfgang Nordwig, E. Germany ...	18ft. ½ in.
1976	Tadeusz Slusarsid, Poland	18ft. ½ in.
1980	Wladysiaw Kozakiewicz, Poland	
		18ft. 11½ in.*

16-LB. HAMMER THROW
1900	John Flanagan, United States......	167ft. 4 in.
1904	John Flanagan, United States......	168ft. 1 in.
1908	John Flanagan, United States	170ft. 4¼ in.
1912	Matt McGrath, United States....	179ft 7⅛ in.
1920	Pat Ryan, United States.........	179ft. 5⅝ in.
1924	Fred Tootell, United States.....	174ft. 10⅛ in.
1928	Patrick O'Callaghan, Ireland.....	168ft. 7½ in.
1932	Patrick O'Callaghan, Ireland....	176ft. 11⅛ in.
1936	Karl Hein, Germany	185ft. 4 in.
1948	Imre Nemeth, Hungary........	183ft. 11½ in.
1952	Jozsef Csemak, Hungary.......	197ft. 11⁹⁄₁₆ in.
1956	Harold Connolly, United States ..	207ft. 3½ in.
1960	Vasily Rudenkov, USSR.........	220ft. 1⅝ in.
1964	Romuald Klim, USSR..........	228ft. 9½ in.
1968	Gyula Zsivotsky, Hungary........	240ft. 8 in.
1972	Anatoli Bondarchuk, USSR........	248ft. 8 in.

55

| 1976 | Yuri Syedykh, USSR | 254ft. 4 in. |
| 1980 | Yuri Syedykh, USSR | 268ft. 4½ in.* |

DISCUS THROW

1896	Robert Garrett, United States	95ft. 7½ in.
1900	Rudolf Bauer, Hungary	118ft. 2.9⁄10in.
1904	Martin Sheridan, United States	128ft. 10½ in.
1908	Martin Sheridan, United States	134ft. 2 in.
1912	Armas Taipale, Finland	148ft. 4 in.
	Both hands—Armas Taipele, Finland	271ft. 10¼ in.
1920	Elmer Niklander, Finland	146ft. 7¼ in.
1924	Clarence Houser, United States	151ft. 5⅛ in.
1928	Clarence Houser, United States	155 ft. 3 in.
1932	John Anderson, United States	162ft. 4⅞ in.
1936	Ken Carpenter, United States	165ft. 7⅜ in.
1948	Adolfo Consolini, Italy	173ft. 2 in.
1952	Sim Iness, United States	180ft. 6.85 in.
1956	Al Oerter, United States	184ft. 10½ in.
1960	Al Oerter, United States	194ft. 2 in.
1964	Al Oerter, United States	200ft. 1½ in.
1968	Al Oerter, United States	212ft. 6½ in.
1972	Ludvik Danek, Czechoslovakia	211ft. 3 in.
1976	Mac Wilkins, United States	221ft 5.4 in.*
1980	Viktor Rashchupkin, USSR	218ft. 8 in.

STANDING HOP, STEP AND JUMP

| 1890 | Ray Ewry, United States | 34ft. 8½ in. |
| 1904 | Ray Ewry, United States | 34ft. 7¼ in. |

TRIPLE JUMP

1896	James Connolly, United States	45ft.
1900	Myer Prinstein, United States	47ft. 4¼ in.
1904	Myer Prinstein, United States	47 ft.
1908	Timothy Aheame, Great Britain	48ft. 11¼ in.
1912	Gustaf Lindblom, Sweden	48ft. 5⅛ in.
1920	Viho Tuulos, Finland	47ft. 6⅞ in.
1924	Archie Winter, Australia	50ft. 11¼ in.
1928	Mikio Oda, Japan	49ft. 11 in.
1932	Chulhei Nambu, Japan	51ft. 7 in.
1936	Naoto Tajima, Japan	52ft, 5⅞ in.
1948	Arne Ahman, Sweden	50ft. 6¼ in.
1952	Adhemar de Silva, Brazil	53ft. 2⁹⁄16in.
1956	Adhemar de Silva, Brazil	53ft. 7½ in.
1960	Jozef Schmidt, Poland	55ft. 1¾ in.
1964	Jozef Schmidt, Poland	55ft. 3¼ in.
1968	Viktor Saneev, USSR	57ft ¾ in.
1972	Viktor Saneev, USSR	56ft. 11 in.
1976	Viktor Saneev, USSR	56ft. 8¾ in.
1980	Jaak Uudmae, USSR	56ft. 11⅛ in.

16-LB. SHOT PUT

1896	Robert Garrett, United States	36ft. 9¾ in.
1900	Robert Sheldon, United States	46ft. 3⅛ in.
1904	Ralph Rose, United States	48 ft. 7 in.
1908	Ralph Rose, United States	46ft. 7½ in.
1912	Pat McDonald, United States	40ft. 4 in.
	Both hands—Ralph Rose, United States	90ft. 5½ in.

1920	Ville Porhola, Finland	48ft. 7⅛ in.
1924	Clarence Houser, United States	49ft. 2½ in.
1928	John Kuck, United States	52ft. ¾ in.
1932	Leo Sexton, United States	52ft. 6³⁄16 in.
1936	Hans Woelike, Germany	53ft. 1¾ in.
1948	Wilbur Thompson, United States	56ft. 2 in.
1952	Parry O'Brien, United States	57ft. 1¹⁄16 in.
1956	Parry O'Brien, United States	60ft. 11 in.
1960	William Nieder, United States	64ft. 6¾ in.
1964	Dallas Long, United States	66ft. 8¼ in.
1968	Randy Matson, United States	67ft. 4¾ in.
1972	Wladyslaw Komar, Poland	69ft. 8 in.
1976	Udo Beyer, E. Germany	69ft. ¾ in.
1980	Vladmir Kiselyov, USSR	70ft. ½ in.*

JAVELIN THROW

1908	Erik Lemming, Sweden	178ft. 7½ in.
	Held in middle—Erik Lemming, Sweden	179ft. 10½ in.
1912	Erik Lemming, Sweden	198ft. 11¼ in.
	Both hands, Julius Saaristo, Finland	358ft. 11⅞ in.
1920	Jonni Myrra, Finland	215ft. 9¾ in.
1924	Jonni Myrra, Finland	206ft. 6¾ in.
1928	Eric Lundquist, Sweden	218ft. 6⅛ in.
1932	Matt Jarvinen, Finland	238ft. 7 in.
1936	Gerhard Sloeck, Germany	235ft. 8⁵⁄16 in.
1948	Kaj Rautavaara, Finland	228ft. 10½ in.
1952	Cy Young, United States	242ft. 0.79 in.
1956	Egil Danielsen, Norway	281ft. 2¼ in.
1960	Viktor Tsibulenko, USSR	277ft 8⅜ in.
1964	Pauli Nevala, Finland	271ft. 2½ in.
1968	Janis Lusis, USSR	295ft. 7¼ in.
1972	Klaus Wolfemann, W. Germany	296ft. 10 in.
1976	Mikios Nameth, Hungary	310ft. 4 in.*
1980	Dainis Kula, USSR	299ft. 2⅜ in.

DECATHLON

1912	Hugo Wieslander, Sweden	7,724.49 pts.
1920	Helge Lovland, Norway	6,804.35 pts.
1924	Harold Osborn, United States	7,710.77 pts.
1928	Paavo Yrjola, Finland	8,053.29 pts.
1932	James Bausch, United States	8,462.23 pts.
1936	Glenn Morris, United States	7,900 pts.
1948	Robert Mathias, United States	7,139 pts.
1952	Robert Mathias, United States	7,887 pts.
1956	Milton Campbell, United States	7,937 pts.
1960	Rafer Johnson, United States	8,392 pts.
1964	Will Holdorf, Germany	7,887 pts.
1968	Bill Toomey, United States	8,193 pts.
1972	Nikota Avilov, USSR	8,454 pts.
1976	Bruce Jenner, United States	8,618 pts.*
1980	Daley Thompson, Great Britain	8,495 pts.

Former point systems used prior to 1964

Track and Field—Women

100-METER RUN

| 1928 | Elizabeth Robinson, United States | 12.2s |
| 1932 | Stella Walsh, Poland | 11.9s |

1936	Helen Stephens, United States	11.5s
1948	Francina Blankers-Koen, Netherlands	11.9s
1952	Majorie Jackson, Australia	11.5s
1956	Betty Cuthbert, Australia	11.5a
1960	Wilma Rudolph, United States	11.0s*
1964	Wyomia Tyus, United States	11.4s
1968	Wyomia Tyus, United States	11.0s*
1972	Renate Stacher, E. Germany	11.07s
1976	Annegret Richter, W. Germany	11.08s*
1980	Ludmita Kondratyeva, USSR	11.6s

200-METER RUN

1948	Francina Blankers-Koen, Netherlands	24.4s
1952	Marjorie Jackson, Australia	23.7s
1956	Betty Cuthbert, Australia	23.4s
1960	Wilma Rudolph, United States	24.0s
1964	Edith McGuire, United States	23.0s
1968	Irena Szewinska, Poland	22.5s
1972	Renate Stecher, E. Germany	22.40s
1976	Barbel Eckert, E. Germany	22.37s
1980	Barbel Wockel, E. Germany	22.03*

400-METER RUN

1964	Betty Cuthbert, Australia	52s
1968	Colette Besson, France	52s
1972	Monika Zehrt, E. Germany	51.08s
1976	Irena Szewinska, Poland	49.29s
1980	Marita Koch, E. Germany	48.88s*

800-METER RUN

1928	Lina Radke, Germany	2m. 16.8s
1960	Ludmila Shevcova, USSR	2m. 4.3s
1964	Ann Packer, Great Britain	2m. 1.1s
1968	Madeline Manning, United States	2m. 0.9s
1972	Hildegard Flack, W. Germany	1m. 58.6s
1976	Tatyana Kazankina, USSR	1m. 54.94
1980	Nadezhda Olizayrenko, USSR	1m. 53.5s*

1,500-METER RUN

1972	Ludmila Bragina, USSR	4m. 01.4s
1976	Tatyana Kazankina, USSR	4m. 05.48s
1980	Tatyana Kazankina, USSR	3m. 56.6s*

400-METER RELAY

1928	Canada	48.4s
1932	United States	47.0s
1936	United States	46.9s
1948	Netherlands	47.5s
1952	United States	45.9s
1956	Australia	44.5s
1960	United States	44.5s
1964	Poland	43.6s
1958	United States	42.8s
1972	West Germany	42.81s
1976	East Germany	42.55s
1980	East Germany	41.60s*

1,600-METER RELAY

1972	East Germany	3m. 23s
1976	East Germany	3m. 19.23s*
1980	USSR	3m. 30.02s

80-METER HURDLES

1932	Mildred Didrikson, United States	11.7s
1936	Trebisonda Vila, Italy	11.7s
1948	Francina Blankers-Koen, Netherlands	11.2s
1952	Shirley Strickland de la Hunty, Australia	10.9s
1956	Shirley Strickland de la Hunty, Australia	10.7s
1960	Irina Press, USSR	10.8s
1964	Karen Balzer, Germany	10.5s
1968	Maureen Caird, Australia	10.3s*

100-METER HURDLES

1972	Annette Ehrhardt, E. Germany	12.59
1976	Johanna Schaller, E. Germany	12.77s
1980	Vera Komisova, USSR	12.56s*

HIGH JUMP

1928	Ethel Catherwood, Canada	5ft. 3 in.
1932	Jean Shiley, United States	5ft. 5¼ in.
1936	Ibolya Csak, Hungary	5ft. 3 in.
1948	Alice Coachman, United States	5ft. 6⅛ in.
1952	Esther Brand, South Africa	5ft. 5¾ in.
1956	Mildred L. McDaniel, United States	5ft. 9¼ in.
1960	Iolanda Bales, Romania	6ft. ¾ in.
1964	Iolanda Balas, Romania	6ft. 2¾ in.
1968	Miloslava Reskova, Czechoslovakia	5ft. 11¾ in.
1972	Ulrike Meyfarth, W. Germany	6ft. 3¼ in.
1978	Rosemarie Ackermann, E. Germany	6ft. 3¾ in.
1980	Sara Simeroni, Italy	6ft. 5½ in.*

DISCUS THROW

1928	Helena Konopacka, Poland	129ft. 11⅞ in.
1932	Lillian Copeland, United States	133ft. 2 in.
1936	Giseta Mauermayer, Germany	156ft. 3³⁄₁₆ in.
1948	Micheline Ostermeyer, France	137ft. 6½ in.
1952	Nina Romaschikova, USSR	168ft. 8½ in.
1956	Olga Fikotova, Czechoslovakia	176ft. 1½ in.
1960	Nina Ponomareva, USSR	180ft. 8¼ in.
1964	Tamara Press, USSR	187ft. 10½ in.
1968	Lia Manoliu, Romania	191ft. 2½ in.
1972	Faina Melnik, USSR	218ft. 7 in.
1976	Evelin Schlaak, E. Germany	226ft. 4½ in.
1980	Evelin Jahl, E. Germany	229ft. 6¼ in.*

JAVELIN THROW

1932	Mildred Didrikson, United States	143ft. 4 in.
1936	Tilly Fleischer, Germany	148ft. 2¾ in.
1948	Herma Bauma, Austria	149ft. 6 in.
1952	Dana Zatopkova, Czechoslovakia	165ft. 7 in.
1956	Inessa Janzeme, USSR	176ft. 8 in.
1960	Elvira Ozolina, USSR	183ft. 8 in.
1964	Mihaela Penes, Romania	198ft. 7½ in.
1968	Angela Nemeth, Hungary	198ft. ½ in.
1972	Ruth Fuchs, E. Germany	209ft. 7 in.
1976	Ruth Fuchs. E. Germany	216ft. 4 in.
1980	Maria Colon, Cuba	224ft. 5 in*

SHOT PUT (8 LB., 13OZ.)

1948	Micheline Ostemeyer, France	45ft. 1½ in.

1952	Galina Zybina, USSR	50ft. 1½ in.
1956	Tamara Tishkyevich, USSR	54ft. 5 in.
1960	Tamara Press, USR	58ft. 9⅞ in.
1964	Tamara Press, USSR	59ft. 6¼ in.
1968	Margita Gummel, E. Germany	64ft. 4 in.
1972	Nadezhda Chizova, USSR	69ft.
5976	Ivanka Christova, Bulgaria	69ft. 5 in.
1980	Liona Sluplanek, E. Germany	73ft. 6¼ in.

LONG JUMP

1948	Olga Gyamati, Hungary	18ft. 8¼ in.
1952	Yvette Williams, New Zealand	20ft. 5¾ in.
1956	Elzibieta Krzeskinska, Poland	20ft. 9¾ in.
1960	Vyera Krepkina, USSR	20ft. 10¾ in.
1964	Mary Rand, Great Britain	22ft. 2¼ in.
1968	Viorica Viscopoleanu, Romania	22ft. 4½ in.
1972	Heidemarie Rosendahl, W. Germany	22ft. 3 in.
1976	Angela Voigt, E. Germany	22ft. 2½ in.
1980	Tatyana Kolpakova, USSR	23ft. 2 in.*

PENTATHLON

1964	Irina Press, USSR	5,246 pts.
1968	Ingrid Becker, W. Germany	5,098 pts.
1972	Mary Peters, England	4,801 pts.
1976	Sigrun Siegl, E. Germany	4,745 pts.
1980	Nadyezhda Tkachenko, USSR	5,083 pts.*

Former point system, 1964–1968

Swimming—Men

100-METER FREESTYLE

1896	Alfred Hajos, Hungary	1:22.2
1904	Zoltan de Halmay, Hungary (100 yards)	1:02.8
1908	Charles Daniels, U.S.	1:05.6
1912	Duke P. Kahanamoku, U.S.	1:03.4
1920	Duke P. Kahanamoku, U.S.	1:01.4
1924	John Weissmuller, U.S.	59.0
1928	John Weissmuller, U.S.	58.6
1932	Yasuji Miyazakd, Japan	58.2
1936	Ferenc Csik, Hungary	57.6
1948	Wally Ris, U.S.	57.3
1952	Clark Scholes, U.S.	57.4
1956	Jon Henricks, Australia	56.4
1960	John Devitt, Australia	55.2
1964	Don Schollander, U.S.	53.4
1966	Mike Wenden, Australia	52.2
1972	Mark Spitz, U.S.	51.22
1976	Jim Montgomery, U.S.	49.99*
1980	Jorg Wotthe, E. Germany	50.40

200-METER FREESTYLE

1968	Mike Wenden, Australia	1:55.2
1972	Mark Spitz, U.S.	1:52.78
1976	Bruce Fumiss, U.S.	1:50.29
1980	Sergei Kopllakov, USSR	1:49.81*

400-METER FREESTYLE

1904	C. M. Daniels, U.S. (440 yards)	6:16.2
1908	Henry Taylor, Great Britain	5:36.8
1912	George Hodgson, Canada	5:24.4
1920	Norman Ross, U.S.	5:26.8
1924	John Weissmuller, U.S.	5:04.2
1928	Albert Zorilla, Argentina	5:01.6
1932	Clarence Crabbe, U.S.	4:48.4
1936	Jack Medica, U.S.	4:44.5
1948	William Smith, U.S.	4:41.0
1952	Jean Boiteux, France	4:30.7
1956	Murray Rose, Australia	4:27.3
1960	Murray Rose, Australia	4:18.3
1964	Don Schollander, U.S.	4:12.2
1968	Mike Burton, U.S.	4:09.0
1972	Brad Cooper, Australia	4:00.27
1976	Brian Goodell, U.S.	3:61.93
1980	Vladmir-Salnikov, USSR	3:51.31*

1,500-METER FREESTYLE

1908	Henry Taylor, Great Britain	22:48.4
1912	George Hodgson, Canada	22:00.0
1920	Norman Ross, U.S.	22:23.2
1924	Andrew Charlton, Australia	20:06.6
1928	Ame Borg, Sweden	19:51.8
1932	Kusuo Kitamura, Japan	19:12.4
1936	Noboru Terade, Japan	19:13.7
1948	James McLane, U.S.	19:18.5
1952	Ford Konno, U.S.	18:30.0
1956	Murray Rose, Australia	17:58.9
1960	Jon Konrads, Australia	17:19.6
1964	Robert Windle, Australia	17:01.7
1968	Mike Burton, U.S.	16:38.9
1972	Mike Burton, U.S.	15:52.58
1976	Brian Goodell, U.S.	15:02.40
1980	Vladimir Salnikov, USSR	14:58.27*

400-METER MEDLEY RELAY

1960	United States	4:05.4
1964	United States	3:58.4
1968	United States	3:54.9
1972	United States	3:48.16
1976	United States	3:42.22*
1980	Australia	3:45.70

400-METER FREESTYLE RELAY

1964	United States	3:33.2
1968	United States	3:31.7
1972	United States	3:26.42*

800-METER FREESTYLE RELAY

1908	Great Britain	10:55.6
1912	Australia	10:11.6
1920	United States	10:04.4
1924	United States	9:53.4
1928	United States	9:36.2
1932	Japan	8:58.4
1936	Japan	8:51.5
1948	United States	8:46.0
1952	United States	8:31.1
1956	Australia	8:23.6
1960	United States	8:10.2
1964	United States	7:52.1

1968	United States	7:52.3
1972	United States	7:35.78
1976	United States	7:23.22*
1980	USSR	7:23.50

100-METER BACKSTROKE

1904	Walter Brack, Germany (100 yds.)	1:16.8
1908	Amo Bieberstein, Germany............	1:24.6
1912	Harry Hebner, U.S.................	1:21.2
1920	Warren Kealoha, U.S.	1:15.2
1924	Warren Kealoha, U.S.	1:13.2
1928	George Kojack, U.S.	1:08.2
1932	Masaji Kryokawa, Japan.	1:08.6
1936	Adolph Kiefer, U.S.	1:05.9
1948	Allen Stack, U.S.	1:06.4
1952	Yoshi Oyakawa, U.S.	1:05.4
1956	David Thiele, Australia	1:02.2
1960	David Thiele, Australia	1:01.9
1968	Roland Matthes, E. Germany	58.7
1972	Roland Matthes, E. Germany	56.58
1976	John Naber, U.S.	55.49*
1980	Bengt Baron, Sweden	56.53

200-METER BACKSTROKE

1964	Jed Graef, U.S.	2:10.3
1968	Roland Matthes, E. Germany.	2:09.6
1972	Roland Matthes, E. Germany.	2:02.82
1976	John Naber, U.S.	1:59.19*
1980	Sandor Wladar, Hungary	2:01.93

100-METER BREASTSTROKE

1968	Don McKenzie, U.S.	1:07.7
1972	Nobutaka Taguchi, Japan.	1:04.94
1976	John Hencken, U.S.	1:03.11*
1980	Duncan Goodhew, Great Britain	1:03.34

200-METER BREASTSTROKE

1908	Frederick Holman, Great Britain	3:09.2
1912	Walter Bathe, Germany.	3:01.8
1920	Haken Malmroth, Sweden	3:04.4
1924	Robert Skelton, U.S.	1:56.6
1928	Yoshiyuki Tsuruta, Japan.	2:48.8
1932	Yoshiyuki Tsuruta, Japan.	2:45.4
1936	Tetsuo Hamuro, Japan.	2:42.5
1948	Joseph Verdeur, U.S.	2:39.3
1952	John Davies, Australia	2:34.4
1956	Masura Furukawa, Japan.	2:34.7
1960	William Muliken, U.S.	2:37.4
1964	Ian O'Brien, Australia	2:27.8
1968	Felipe Munoz, Mexico.	2:28.7
1972	John Hencken, U.S.	2:21.55
1976	David Wilkie, Great Britain	2:15.11*
1980	Robertas Zuipa,	2:15.85

100-METER BUTTERFLY

1968	Doug Russell, U.S.	55.9
1972	Mark Spitz, U.S.	54.27*
1976	Matt Vogel, U.S.	54.35
1980	Par Arvidsson, Sweden	54.92

200-METER BUTTERFLY

1956	William Yorzyk, U.S.	2:19.3
1960	Michael Troy, U.S.	2:12.8
1964	Kevin J. Berry, Australia	2:06.6
1968	Carl Robie, U.S.	2:08.7
1972	Mark Spitz, U.S.	2:00.70
1976	Mike Bruner, U.S.	1:59.23*
1980	Sergei Fesenko, USSR	1:59.76

200-METER INDIVIDUAL MEDLEY

1968	Charles Hickcox, U.S.	2:12.0
1972	Gunnar Larsson, Sweden	2:07.17*

400-METER INDIVIDUAL MEDLEY

1964	Dick Roth, U.S.	4:45.4
1968	Charles Hickcox, U.S.	4:48.4
1972	Gunnar Larsson, Sweden	4:31.98
1976	Rod Strachan, U.S.	4:23.68
1980	Ajeksandr Sidorenko, USSR	4:22.89*

SPRINGBOARD DIVING

1908	Albert Zumer, Germany.	85.5
1912	Paul Guenther, Germany.	79.23

Swimming—Women

100-METER FREESTYLE

1912	Fanny Durack, Australia	1:22.2
1920	Ethelda Blelbtrey, U.S.	1:13.6
1924	Ethel Lackie, U.S.	1:12.4
1928	Albina Osipowich, U.S.	1:11.0
1932	Helene Madison, U.S.	1:06.8
1936	Hendrika Mastenbroek, Holland	1:05.9
1948	Greta Anderson, Denmark	1:06.3
1952	Katalin Szoke, Hungary.	1:06.3
1956	Dawn Fraser, Australia	1:02.0
1960	Dawn Fraser, Australia	1:01.2
1964	Dawn Fraser, Australia	59.5
1968	Jan Henne, U.S.	1:00.0
1972	Sandra Neilson, U.S.	58.59
1976	Komelia Ender, E. Germany.	55.65
1980	Barbara Karuse, E. Germany.	54.79*

200-METER FREESTYLE

1968	Debbie Meyer, U.S.	2:10.5
1972	Shane Gould, Australia	2:03.56
1976	Komelia Ender, E. Germany	1:59.26
1980	Barbara Krause, E. Germany	1:58.33*

400-METER FREESTYLE

1924	Martha Norelius, U.S.	6:02.2
1928	Martha Norelius, U.S.	5:42.8
1932	Helene Madison, U.S.	5:28.5
1936	Hendrika Mastenbroek, Netherlands....	5:26.4
1948	Ann Curtis, U.S.	5:17.8
1952	Valerie Gyenge, Hungary	5:12.1
1956	Lorraine Crapp, Australia	4:54.6
1960	Susan Chris von Saltza, U.S.	4:50.6
1964	Virginia Duenkel, U.S.	4:43.3
1968	Debbie Meyer, U.S.	4:31.8

1972	Shane Gould, Australia	4:19.04
1976	Petra Thuemer, E. Germany	4:09.89
1980	Ines Diers, E. Germany	4:08.76*

800-METER FREESTYLE
1968	Debbie Meyer, U.S.	9:24.0
1972	Keena Rothhammer, U.S.	8:53.68
1976	Petra Thuemer, E. Germany	8:37.14
1980	Michelle Ford, Australia	8:28.90*

100-METER BACKSTROKE
1924	Sybil Bauer, U.S.	1:23.3
1928	Marie Braun, Netherlands	1:22.0
1932	Eleanor Holm, U.S.	1:19.4
1936	Dina Seniff, Netherlands	1:18.9
1948	Karen Harup, Denmark	1:14.4
1952	Joan Harrison, South Africa	1:14.3
1956	Judy Grinham, Great Britain	1:12.9
1960	Lynn Burke, U.S.	1:09.3
1964	Cathy Fergusson, U.S.	1:07.7
1968	Kaye Hall, U.S.	1:06.2
1972	Melissa Belote, U.S.	1:05.78
1976	Ulrike Richter, E. Germany	1:01.83
1980	Rica Reinisch, E. Germany	1:00.86*

200-METER BACKSTROKE
1968	Pokey Watson, U.S.	2:24.8
1972	Melissa Belote, U.S.	2:19.19
1976	Ulrike Richter, E. Germany	2:13.43
1980	Rica Reinisch, E. Germany	2:11.77*

100-METER BREASTSTROKE
1968	Djurdjica Bjedov, Yugoslavia	1:15.8
1972	Cathy Carr, U.S.	1:13.58
1976	Hannelore Anke, E. Germany	1:11.16
1980	Ute Geweniger, E. Germany	1:10.22*

200-METER BREASTSTROKE
1924	Lucy Morton, Great Britain	3:32.2
1928	Hilde Schrader, Germany	3:12.6
1932	Clare Dennis, Australia	3:06.3
1936	Hideko Maehata, Japan	3:03.6
1948	Nelly Van Vliet, Netherlands	2:57.2
1952	Eva Szekely, Hungary	2:51.7
1956	Ursula Happe, Germany	2:53.1
1960	Anita Lonsbrough, Great Britain	2:49.5
1964	Galina Prozumenschikova, USSR	2:46.4
1968	Sharon Wichman, U.S.	2:44.4
1972	Beverly Whitfield, Australia	2:41.71
1976	Marina Koshevaia, USSR	2:33.35
1980	Lina Kachushite, USSR	2:29.54*

200-METER INDIVIDUAL MEDLEY
| 1968 | Claudia Kolb, U.S. | 2:24.7 |
| 1972 | Shane Gould, Australia | 2:23.07* |

400-METER INDIVIDUAL MEDLEY
1964	Donna de Varona, U.S.	5:18.7
1968	Claudia Koib, U.S.	5:08.5
1972	Gall Neall, Australia	5:02.97

| 1976 | Ulrike Tauber, E. Germany | 4:42.77 |
| 1980 | Petra Schneider, E. Germany | 4:36.29* |

100-METER BUTTERFLY
1956	Shelley Mann, U.S.	1:1.0
1960	Carolyn Schuler, U.S.	1:09.5
1964	Sharon Stouder, U.S.	1:04.7
1968	Lynn McClements, Australia	1:05.5
1972	Mayumi Aoki, Japan	1:03.34
1976	Komelia Ender, E. Germany	1:00.13*
1980	Caren Metschuck, E. Germany	1:00.42

200-METER BUTTERFLY
1968	Ada Kok, Netherlands	2:24.7
1972	Karen Moe, U.S.	2:15.57
1976	Andrea Pollack, E. Germany	2:11.41
1980	Ines Geissler, E. Germany	2:10.44*

400-METER MEDLEY RELAY
1960	United States	4:41.1
1964	United States	4:33.9
1968	United States	4:28.3
1972	United States	4:20.75
1976	East Germany	4:07.95
1980	East Germany	4:06.67*

400-METER FREESTYLE RELAY
1912	Great Britain	5:52.8
1920	United States	5:11.6
1924	United States	4:58.8
1928	United States	4:47.6
1932	United States	4:38.0
1936	Netherlands	4:36.0
1948	United States	4:29.2
1952	Hungary	4:24.4
1956	Australia	4:17.1
1960	United States	4:08.9
1964	United States	4:03.8
1968	United States	4:02.5
1972	United States	3:55.19
1976	United States	3:44.82
1980	East Germany	3:42.71*

SPRINGBOARD DIVING   POINTS
1920	Aileen Riggin, U.S.	539.90
1924	Elizabeth Becker, U.S.	474.50
1928	Helen Meany, U.S.	78.62
1932	Georgia Coleman, U.S.	87.52
1936	Marjorie Gestring, U.S.	89.27
1948	Victoria M. Draves, U.S.	108.74
1952	Patricia McCormick, U.S.	147.30
1956	Patricia McCormick, U.S.	142.36
1960	Ingrid Kramer, Germany	155.81
1964	Ingrid Engel-Kramer, Germany	145.00
1968	Sue Gossick, U.S.	150.77
1972	Micki King, U.S.	450.03
1976	Jenni Chandler, U.S.	506.19
1980	Inna Kalinina, USSR	725.91

PLATFORM DIVING   POINTS
| 1912 | Greta Johansson, Sweden | 39.90 |

1920	Stefani Fryland-Clausen, Denmark	34.60
1924	Caroline Smith, U.S.	166.00
1928	Elizabeth B. Pinkston, U.S.	31.60
1932	Dorothy Poynton, U.S.	40.26
1936	Dorothy Poynton Hill, U.S.	33.93
1948	Victoria M. Draves, U.S.	68.87
1952	Patricia McCormick, U.S.	79.37
1956	Patricia McCormick, U.S.	84.85
1960	Ingrid Kramer, Germany	91.28
1964	Lesley Bush, U.S.	99.80
1968	Mllena Duchkova, Czech.	109.50
1972	Ulrika Knape, Sweden	390.00
1976	Elena Vaytsekhouskaya, USSR	406.59
1980	Martina Jaschke, E. Germany	596.25

Winter Olympic Games Champions, 1924–1984

Biathlon

10 KILOMETERS

		TIME
1980	Frank Ulrich, E. Germany	32:10.69
1984	Eirik Kvalfoss, Norway	30:53.8

20 KILOMETERS

		TIME
1960	Klas Lestander, Sweden	1:33:21.6
1964	Vladmir Melanin, USSR	1:20:26.8
1968	Magnar Solberg, Norway	1:13:45.9
1972	Magnar Solberg, Norway	1:15:55.50
1976	Nikolai Kruglov, USSR	;14:12.26
1980	Anatoly Alabyev, USSR	1:08:16.31
1984	Peter Angerer, W. Germany	1:11:52.7

40-KILOMETER RELAY

		TIME
1968	USSR, Norway, Sweden	2:13:02
1972	USSR, Finland, E. Germany	1:51:44
1976	USSR, Finland, E. Germany	1:57:55.64
1980	USSR, E. Germany, W. Germany (30 km.)	1:34:03.27
1984	USSR, Norway, W. Germany (30 km.)	1:38:51.70

Bobsledding

4-MAN BOB

(Driver in parentheses)		TIME
1924	Switzerland (Edward Scherrer)	5:45.54
1928	United States (William Fiske) 5-man	3:20.50
1932	United States (William Fiske)	7:53.68
1938	Switzerland (Pierre Musy)	5:19.85
1948	United States (Edward Rimkus)	5:20.10
1952	Germany (Andreas Ostier)	5:07.84
1956	Switzerland (Frank Kapus)	5:10.44
1964	Canada (Victor Emery)	4:14.46
1968	Italy (Eugenio Monti) (2 races)	2:17.39
1972	Switzerland (Jean Wicki)	4:43.07
1976	E. Germany (Meinhard Nehmer)	3:40.43
1980	E. Germany (Meinhard Nehmer)	3:59.92
1984	E. Germany (Wolfgang Hoppe)	3:20.22

2-MAN BOB

		TIME
1932	United States (Hubert Stevens)	8:14.74
1936	United States (Ivan Brown)	5:29.29
1948	Switzerland (F. Endrich)	5:29.20
1952	Germany (Andreas Ostter)	5:24.54
1958	Italy (Dalia Costa)	5:30.14

1964	Great Britain (Antony Nash)	4:21.90
1968	Italy (Eugenio Monti)	4:41.54
1972	W. Germany (Wolfgang Zimmerer)	4:47.07
1978	E. Germany (Meinhard Nehmer)	3:40.43
1980	Switzerland (Erich Schaerer)	4:09.36
1984	E. Germany (Wolfgang Hoppe)	3:25.56

Figure Skating

MEN'S SINGLES

1908	Ulrich Sachow, Sweden
1920	Gillis Grafstrom, Sweden
1924	Gillis Grafstrom, Sweden
1928	Gillis Grafstrom, Sweden
1932	Karl Schaefer, Austria
1936	Karl Schaefer, Austria
1948	Richard Button, U.S.
1952	Richard Button, U.S.
1956	Hayes Alan Jenkins, U.S.
1960	David W. Jenkins, U.S.
1964	Manfred Schnelldorfer, Germany
1968	Wolfgang Schwartz, Austria
1972	Ondrej Nepela, Czechoslovakia
1976	John Curry, Great Britain
1980	Robin Cousins, Great Britain
1984	Scott Hamilton, U.S.

WOMEN'S SINGLES

1908	Madge Syers, Great Britain
1920	Magda Julin-Mauroy, Sweden
1924	Heima von Szabo-Pianck, Austria
1928	Sonja Henie, Norway
1932	Sonja Henie, Norway
1936	Sonja Henie, Norway
1948	Barbara Ann Scott, Canada
1952	Jeanette Altwegg, Great Britain
1956	Tenley Albright, U.S.
1960	Carol Heiss, U.S.
1964	Sjoukje Dijkstra, Netherlands
1968	Peggy Fleming, U.S.
1972	Beatrix Schuba, Austria
1976	Dorothy Hamill, U.S.
1980	Anett Poetzsch, E. Germany
1984	Katarina Witt, E. Germany

PAIRS

1908	Anna Hubler & Helnich Burger, Germany
1920	Ludovika & Walter Jakobsson, Finland
1924	Helene Engelman & Alfred Berger, Austria
1928	Andree Joly & Pierre Brunet, France
1932	Andree Joly & Pierre Brunet, France
1936	Maxie Herber & Emest Baier, Germany
1948	Micheline Lannoy & Pierre Baugniet, Belguim
1952	Ria and Paul Falk, Germany
1956	Elisabeth Schwartz & Kurt Oppelt, Austria
1960	Barbara Wagner & Robert Paul, Canada
1964	Ludmila Beloussova & Oleg Protopopov, USSR
1968	Ludmila Beloussova & Oleg Protopopov, USSR
1972	Irina Rodnina & Alexei Ulanov, USSR
1976	Irina Rodnina & Aleksandr Zaitsev, USSR
1980	Irina Rodnina & Aleksandr Zaitsev, USSR
1984	Elena Valova & Oleg Vassiliev, USSR

ICE DANCING

1976	Ludmila Pakhomova & Aleksandr Gorschkov, USSR

1980 Natalya Linichuk & Gennadi Karponosov, USSR
1984 Jayne Torvill & Christopher Dean, Great Britain

Alpine Skiing

MEN'S DOWNHILL	TIME
1948 Henri Oreiller, France	2:55.0
1952 Zeno Colo, Italy	2:30.8
1956 Anton Saller, Austria	2:52.2
1960 Jean Vuamet, France	2:06.0
1964 Egon Zimmermann, Austria	2:18.16
1968 Jean Claude Killy, France	1:59.85
1972 Bernhard Russi, Switzerland	1:51.43
1976 Franz Klammer, Austria	1:45.73
1980 Leonhard Stock, Austria	1:45.50
1984 Bill Johnson, U.S.	1:45.59

MEN'S GIANT SLALOM	TIME
1952 Stein Eriksen, Norway	2:25.0
1956 Anton Saller, Austria	3:00.1
1960 Roger Staub, Switzerland	1:48.3
1964 Francois Bonlieu, France	1:46.71
1968 Jean Claude Killy, France	3:29.28
1972 Gustavo Thoeni, Italy	3:09.62
1976 Heini Hemmi, Switzerland	3:26.97
1980 Ingemar Stenmark, Sweden	:40.74
1984 Max Julen, Switzerland	2:41.68

MEN'S SLALOM	TIME
1948 Ed Reinalter, Switzerland	2:10.3
1952 Othmar Schneider, Austria	2:00.0
1956 Anton Saller, Austria	194.7 pts.
1960 Emest Hinterseer, Austria	2:08.9
1964 Josef Stiegler, Austria	21:11.13
1968 Jean Claude Killy, France	1:39.73
1972 Francesco Fernandez Ochoa, Spain	1:49.27
1976 Piero Gros, Italy	2:03.29
1980 Ingemar Stenmark, Sweden	1:44.26
1984 Phil Mahre, U.S.	1:39.41

WOMEN'S DOWNHILL	TIME
1948 Heidl Schlunegger, Switzerland	2:26.3
1952 Trude Jochurn-Beiser, Austria	1:47.1
1956 Madeline Berthod, Switzerland	1:40.7
1960 Heidl Biebl, Germany	1:37.6
1964 Christi Haas, Austria	1:55.39
1968 Olga Pall, Austria	1:40.87
1972 Marie Therese Nadig, Switzerland	1:36.68
1976 Rosi Mittermaler, W. Germany	1:46.16
1980 Annemarie Proell Moser, Austria	1:37.52
1984 Michela Figini, Switzerland	1:13.36

WOMEN'S GIANT SLALOM	TIME
1952 Andrea Mead Lawrence, U.S.	2:06.8
1956 Ossi Reichert, Germany	1:56.5
1960 Yvonne Ruegg, Switzerland	1:39.9
1964 Marielle Goitschel, France	1:52.24
1968 Nancy Greene, Canada	1:51.97
1972 Marie Therese Nadig, Switzerland	1:29.90
1976 Kathy Kreiner, Canada	1:29.13
1980 Hanni Wenzel, Liechtenstein (2 runs)	2:41.66
1984 Debbie Armstrong (2 runs)	2:20.98

WOMEN'S SLALOM	TIME
1948 Gretchen Fraser, U.S.	1:57.2
1952 Andrea Mead Lawrence, U.S.	2:10.6
1956 Renee Colliard, Switzerland	112.3 pts.
1960 Anne Heggtveigt, Canada	1:49.6
1964 Christine Goitschel, France	1:29.86
1968 Marielle Goitschel, France	1:25.86
1972 Barbara Cochran, U.S.	1:31.24
1976 Rosi Mittlemaler, W. Germany	1:30.54
1980 Hanni Wenzel, Liechtenstein	1:25.09
1984 Paoletta Magoni, Italy	1:36.47

Nordic Skiing

MEN'S CROSS-COUNTRY EVENTS 15 KILOMETERS (9.3 MILES)	TIME
1924 Thorleif Haug, Norway	1:14:31
1928 Johan Grottumsbraaten, Norway	1:37:01
1932 Sven Utterstrom, Sweden	1:23:07
1936 Erik-August Larsson, Sweden	1:14:38
1948 Martin Lundstrom, Sweden	1;13:50
1952 Hallgeir Brenden, Norway	1:01:34
1956 Hallgeir Brenden, Norway	49:39.0
1964 Eero Maenlyranta, Finland	50:54.1
1968 Harald Groenningen, Norway	47:54.2
1972 Sven-Ake Lundbeck, Sweden	45:28.24
1976 Nikolai Bajukov, USSR	43:58.47
1980 Thomas Wassberg, Sweden	41:57.63
(Note approx. 18-km. course 1924–1952)	
1984 Gunde Svan, Sweden	41:25.6

30 KILOMETERS (18.6 MILES)	TIME
1956 Veikko Hakulinen, Finland	1:44:06.0
1960 Sixten, Jemberg, Sweden	1:51:03.9
1964 Eero Maentyranta, Finland	1:30:50.7
1968 Franco Nones, Italy	1:35:39.2
1972 Vyacheslav Vedenin, USSR	1:36:31.15
1976 Sergei Savaliev, USSR	1:30:29.38
1980 Nikolai Zimyatov, USSR	1:27:02.80
1984 Nikolai Zimyatov, USSR	1:28:56.3

50 KILOMETERS (31 MILES)	TIME
1924 Thorleif Haug, Norway	3:44:32.0
1928 Per Erik Hedlund, Sweden	4:52:03.0
1932 Veli Saarinen, Finland	4:28:00.0
1936 Elis Viklund, Sweden	3:30:11.0
1948 Nils Karlsson, Sweden	3:47:48.0
1952 Veikko Hakulinen, Finland	3:33:33.0
1956 Sixtan Jemberg, Sweden	2:50:27.0
1960 Kalevi Hamalainen, Finland	2:59:06.3
1964 Sixten Jemberg, Sweden	2:43:52.6
1968 Ole Ellefsaeter, Norway	2:28:45.8
1972 Paal Tyldum, Norway	2:43:14.75
1976 Ivar Formo, Norway	2:37:30.05
1980 Nikotai Zimyatov, USSR	2:27:24.60
1984 Thomas Wassberg, Sweden	2:15:55.8

40-KM. CROSS-COUNTRY RELAY	TIME
1936 Finland, Norway, Sweden	2:41:33.0
1948 Sweden, Finland, Norway	2:32:08.0
1952 Finland, Norway, Sweden	2:20:16.0
1956 USSR, Finland, Sweden	2:15:30.0
1960 Finland, Norway, USSR	2:18:45.6
1964 Sweden, Finland, USSR	2:18:34.6
1968 Norway, Sweden, Finland	2:08:33.5
1972 USSR, Norway, Switzerland	2:04:47:94

1976	Finland, Norway, USSR	2:07:59.72
1980	USSR, Norway, Finland	1:57:03.46
1984	Sweden, USSR, Finland	1:55:06.30

COMBINED CROSS-COUNTRY & JUMPING

		POINTS
1924	Thorleif Haug, Norway	453.800
1928	Johan Grottumsbraaten, Norway	427.800
1932	Johan Grottumsbraaten, Norway	446.200
1936	Oddbjorn Hagen, Norway	430.300
1948	Helkki Hasu, Finland	448.800
1952	Simon Slattvik, Norway	451.621
1956	Sverre Stenersen, Norway	455.000
1960	Georg Thorna, Germany	457,952
1964	Tormod Knutsen, Norway	469.280
1968	Franz Keller, W. Germany	449.040
1972	Ulrich Wehling, E. Germany	413.340
1978	Ulrich Wehling, E. Germany	423.390
1980	Ulrich Wehling, E. Germany	432.200
1984	Tom Sandberg, Norway	422.595

SKI JUMPING (90 METERS)

		POINTS
1924	Jacob Tharns, Norway	227.5
1928	Alfred Andersen, Norway	230.5
1932	Birger Ruud, Norway	228.0
1936	Birger Ruud, Norway	232.0
1948	Petter Hugsted, Norway	228.1
1952	Anders Bergmann, Norway	226.0
1956	Antti Hyvarinen, Finland	227.0
1960	Helmut Recknagel, Germany	227.2
1964	Toralf Engan, Norway	230.7
1968	Vladimir Beloussov, USSR	231.3
1972	Wojiech Fortuna, Poland	219.9
1976	Karl Schnabl, Austria	234.8
1980	Juoko Tormanen, Finland	231.5
1984	Matti Nykaenen, Finland	231.2

SKI JUMPING (70 METERS)

		POINTS
1964	Veikko Kankkonen, Finland	229.9
1968	Jiri Raska, Czechoslovakia	216.5
1972	Yukio Kasaya, Japan	244.2
1976	Hans Aschenbach, E. Germany	252.0
1980	Anton Innauer, Austria	266.3
1984	Jens Weissflog, E. Germany	212.5

WOMEN'S EVENTS

5 KILOMETERS (APPROX. 3.1 MILES)

		TIME
1964	Claudia Boyarskikh, USSR	17:50.5
1968	Toini Gustafsson, Sweden	16:45.2
1972	Galina Koulacova, USSR	17:00.50
1976	Helena Takato, Finland	15:48.69
1980	Raisa Smetanina, USSR	15:06.92
1984	Marja-Liisa Haemaelainen, Finland	17:04.0

10 KILOMETERS

		TIME
1952	Lydia Wideman, Finland	41:40.0
1956	Lyubov Kosyreva, USSR	38:11.0
1960	Maria Gusakova, USSR	39:46.6
1964	Claudia Boyarskikh, USSR	40:24.3
1968	Toini Gustafsson, Sweden	36:46.5
1972	Galina Koulacova, USSR	34:17.82
1976	Raisa Smetanina, USSR	30:13.41
1980	Barbara Petzold, E. Germany	30:31.54
1984	Marja-Liisa Haemaelainen, Finland	31:44.2

20 KILOMETERS

		TIME
1984	Marja-Liisa Haemalainen, Finland	1:01:45.0

15-KM. CROSS-COUNTRY RELAY

		TIME
1956	Finland, USSR, Sweden	1:09:01.0
1960	Sweden, USSR, Finland	1:04:21.4
1964	USSR, Sweden, Finland	59:20.2
1968	Norway, Sweden, USSR	57:30.0
1972	USSR, Finland, Norway	48:46.1
1976	USSR, Finland, E. Germany (20 km.)	1:07:49.75
1980	E. Germany, USSR, Norway (20 km.)	1:06:49.70
1984	Norway, Czechoslovakia, Finland (20 km.)	1:06:49.70

Ice Hockey

1920	Canada, U.S., Czechoslovakia
1924	Canada, U.S., Great Britain
1928	Canada, Sweden, Switzerland
1932	Canada, U.S., Germany
1936	Great Britain, Canada, U.S.
1948	Canada, Czechoslovakia, Switzerland
1952	Canada, U.S., Sweden
1956	USSR, U.S., Canada
1960	U.S., Canada, USSR
1964	USSR, Sweden, Czechoslovakia
1968	USSR, Czechoslovakia, Canada
1972	USSR, U.S., Czechoslovakia
1976	USSR, Czechoslovakia, W. Germany
1980	U.S., USSR, Sweden
1984	USSR, Czechoslovakia, Sweden

Luge

MEN'S SINGLES

		TIME
1964	Thomas Keohler, Germany	3:26.77
1968	Manfred Schmid, Austria	2:52.48
1972	Wolfgang Scheidel, E. Germany	3:27.58
1976	Detief Guenther, E. Germany	3:27.6888
1980	Bernhard Glass, E. Germany	2:54.796
1984	Paul Hildgartner, Italy	3:04.258

MEN'S DOUBLES

		TIME
1964	Austria	1:41.62
1968	E. Germany	1:35.85
1972	Italy, E. Germany (tie)	1:28.35
1976	E. Germany	1:25.604
1980	E. Germany	1:19.331
1984	W. Germany	1:23.620

WOMEN'S SINGLES

		TIME
1964	Ortun Enderien, Germany	3:24.67
1968	Erica Lechner, Italy	2:28.66
1972	Anna M. Muller, E. Germany	2:59.18
1976	Margit Schumann, E. Germany	2:50.621
1980	Vera Zozulya, USSR	2:36.537
1984	Steffi Martin, E. Germany	2:46.570

Speed Skating

MEN'S EVENTS

500 METERS (APPROX. 547 YDS.)

		TIME
1924	Charles Jewtraw, U.S.	0:44.0
1928	Clas Thunberg, Finland & Bernt Evensen, Norway (tie)	0:43.4
1932	John A. Sea, U.S.	0:43.4
1936	Ivar Ballangrud, Norway	0:43.4
1948	Finn Helgesen, Norway	0:43.1
1952	Kenneth Henry, U.S.	0:43.2
1956	Evgenly Grishin, USSR	0:40.2

1960	Evgenly Grishin, USSR	0:40.2
1964	Terry McDermott, U.S.	0:40.1
1968	Erhard Keller, W. Germany	0:40.3
1972	Erhard Keller, W. Germany	0:39.44
1976	Egeny Kulikov, USSR	0:39.17
1980	Eric Heiden, U.S.	0:38.03
1984	Sergei Fokichev, USSR	0:38.19

1,000 METERS

		TIME
1976	Peter Mueller, U.S.	1:19.32
1980	Eric Heiden, U.S.	1:15.18
1984	Gaetan Boucher, Canada	1:15.80

1,500 METERS

		TIME
1924	Clas Thunberg, Finland	2:20.8
1928	Clas Thunberg, Finland	2:21.1
1932	John A. Shea, U.S.	2:57.2
1936	Charles Mathlesen, Norway	2:19.2
1948	Sverre Farstad, Norway	2:17.6
1952	Hjalmar Andersen, Norway	2:20.4
1956	Evgenly Grishin, & Yurl Mikhailov, both USSR (tie)	2:08.6
1960	Roald Edgar Aas, Norway & Evgenly Grishin, USSR (tie)	2:10.4
1964	Anis Anston, USSR	2:10.3
1968	Cornelis Verkerk, Netherlands	2:03.4
1972	Ard Schenk, Netherlands	2:02.96
1976	Jan Egil Storhoil, Norway	1:59.38
1980	Eric Heiden, U.S.	1:55.44
1984	Gaetan Boucher, Canada	1:58.36

5,000 METERS

		TIME
1924	Clas Thunberg, Finland	8:39.0
1928	Ivar Ballangrud, Norway	8:50.5
1932	Irving Jaffee, U.S.	8:40.8
1936	Ivar Ballangrud, Norway	8:19.6
1940	Raider Llaldev, Norway	8.29.4
1952	Hjalmar Andersen, Norway	8:10.6
1958	Boris Shikov, USSR	7:48.7
1960	Victor Kosichkin, USSR	7:51.3
1964	Knut Johannesen, Norway	7:38.4
1968	F. Anton Maier, Norway	7:22.4
1972	Ard Schenk, Netherlands	7:23.61
1976	Sten Stensen, Norway	7:24.48
1980	Eric Heiden, U.S.	7:02.29
1984	Sven Tomas Gustafson, Sweden	7:12.28

10,000 METERS

1924	Julius Skutnabb, Finland	18:04.8
1928	Event not held, thawing of ice	
1832	Irving Jaffee, U.S.	17:24.3
1936	Ivar Ballangrud, Norway	17:24.3
1948	Ake Seyffarth, Norway	17:26.3
1952	Hjalmar Andersen, Norway	16:45.8
1956	Sigvard Ericsson, Sweden	16:35.9
1960	Krut Johannesen, Norway	15:46.6
1964	Jonny Nilsson, Sweden	15:50.1
1968	Jonny Hoeglin, Sweden	15:23.6
1972	Ard Schenk, Netherlands	15:01.3
1978	Piet Kleine, Netherlands	14:50.59
1980	Eric Heiden, U.S.	14:28.13
1984	Igor Malkov, USSR	14:39.90

WOMEN'S EVENTS
500 METERS

		TIME
1960	Helga Haase, Germany	0:45.9
1964	Lydia Skobakova, USSR	0:45.0
1968	Ludmila Titova, USSR	0:461
1972	Anne Henning, U.S.	0:43.44
1976	Sheila Young, U.S.	0:42.76
1980	Karin Enke, E. Germany	0:41.78
1984	Christa Rothenburger, E. Germany	0:41.02

1,000 METERS

		TIME
1960	Klara Guseva, USSR	1:34.1
1964	Lydia Skobikova, USSR	1:33.2
1968	Caroline Geijssen, Netherlands	1:32.6
1972	Monika Pflug, W. Germany	1:31.40
1976	Tatiana Averina, USSR	1:28.43
1980	Natalya Petruseva, USSR	1:24.10
1984	Karin Enke, E. Germany	1:21.61

1,500 METERS

		TIME
1960	Lydia Skoblikova, USSR	2:52.2
1964	Lydia Skoblikova, USSR	2:22.6
1968	Kaija Mustonan, Finland	2:22.4
1972	Dianne Holum, U.S.	2:20.85
1976	Galina Steperskaya, USSR	21:16.58
1980	Anna Borckink, Netherlands	2:10.95
1984	Karin Enke, E. Germany	2:03.42

3,000 METERS

		TIME
1960	Lydia Skoblikova, USSR	5:14.3
1964	Lydia Skoblikova, USSR	5:14.9
1968	Johanna Schut, Netherlands	4:56.2
1972	Stjan Baas-Kaiser, Netherlands	4:52.14
1976	Tatiana Averina, USSR	4:45.19
1980	Bjoerg Eva Jensen, Norway	4:32.13
1984	Andrea Schoene, E. Germany	4:24.79

5
The Heavyweight Championship Belt

"The Boston Strong Boy." "The Manassa Mauler." "The Brown Bomber." "The Brockton Blockbuster." "The Greatest."

One might well expect to see such nicknames taped to the back of a leather jacket strewn across a Harley-Davidson; or on the backup card of wrestling night at the sports arena; or even maybe on a post office wall. In fact they stand for people who would fit in all three contexts. They have the toughness of a street-fighting motorcyclist, the crowd-pleasing theatrics of a Monday night grappler, and the ability to attract the public's attention and fascination in the way that the FBI's Ten Most Wanted often has.

Who are these people and what do they do? The answer: they are all involved in the sport of professional boxing, and they all were, at one time or another, heavyweight champions of the world. It would be easier to identify them by their real names—John L. Sullivan, Jack Dempsey, Joe Louis, Rocky Marciano, and Muhammad Ali, respectively.

These men have all attained something about which most fighters only dream—the heavyweight championship belt. Of all the weight divisions in the world of boxing, the heavyweights receive the most notoriety and publicity. Their names are recognized throughout the globe, and when two of them get together to duke it out, they become international news.

More than any other sport, boxing has become internationally successful. Muhammad Ali is a prime example. On 1 October 1975 he fought Joe Frazier in a championship bout. By that time in his career Ali had become an international celebrity, receiving more publicity and attention than any king or president alive. The fight between Frazier and Ali, known as "the Thrilla in Manila," virtually brought nations to a standstill and commanded a worldwide television audience. Millions of dollars changed hands, and the two participants received their fair share. It was an extravaganza not to be matched in the entire world of sports.

But the sport was not always that way. Use of the fist undoubtedly dates back almost to the origins of prehistoric man. It was probably used by the caveman as a form of self-defense, before he discovered the use of clubs, knives, and other weapons. As civilizations developed, the use of the fist began to evolve into a type of sport. Boxing murals show evidence of it six thousand years ago in Egypt. Archeological excavations have revealed that around 1800 B.C. Crete built great palaces and theaters to house boxing competitions as well as bullfighting, rodeo, and dancing. Greek mythology is full of references to boxing. Odysseus, Theseus, and Pollux were all mythological characters renowned for their ability in the sport. It is not surprising, then, that boxing was included in the ancient Olympic games. From that point on, its popularity grew swiftly.

More than any other sport, boxing has taken on an international scope. And the division most watched is that of the heavyweights. (UPI photo)

The rules used during those times were quite different from those employed today. In ancient Greek boxing, for example, there were no rounds or weight divisions, and the bouts often turned into battles to the death. Fights were stopped when one man literally could not go on. Sometimes, if the boxers were too exhausted to continue, lots were drawn, and the winner would get a free punch at his opponent.

During its golden age in Greece, boxing was considered not just a sport, but an art and a science. It was a test of power, speed, cunning, agility, and endurance. Olympic heroes such as Theogenes (undefeated world champion from 464–468 B.C.) and Cleitomachus (world heavyweight champion from 225–215 B.C.) became legends throughout the land.

Despite this early interest boxing all but disappeared from A.D. 500 to A.D. 1700, due mainly perhaps to a severe restriction on individual liberty. Around the thirteenth century an Italian monk re-

portedly tried to keep the sport alive by promoting matches in his congregation.

The next time it reappeared with any real enthusiastic support was in England in the eighteenth century. Like its boxing predecessors, England at the time was a nation that freely and openly promoted athletics. One man in particular was responsible for the great strides that the sport took. His name was Jack Broughton. He was an expert fencer, broadsword and singlestick fighter, as well as a boxer. A well-educated, cultured man, Broughton constructed in 1742 an amphitheater devoted mainly to the instruction of self-defense and the promotion of prize fighting. He later published the first set of boxing rules. He also made a major contribution when he developed the boxing glove by studying some of the early equipment of the Greeks.

The popularity of boxing soon spread to Ireland, the United States, and other countries. In 1810 a former American slave, Tom Molyneux, traveled to England to take on the national champion, Tom

Cribb, in a series of fights, which the challenger eventually lost.

The first international heavyweight championship occurred some fifty years later. It was between the English champion at the time, a small, cunning man named Tom Sayers, and the current American champion, a six-foot, two-inch strong man from California named John Heenan. On 17 April 1860 the two battled it out at Farnborough, England. The bout lasted almost two and a half hours. Heenan knocked Sayers down twenty-five times, but the crafty Englishman retaliated by puffing up both the American's eyes so that he was practically blind. The police eventually broke up the fight, and it was declared a draw. Sayers was awarded the championship belt, on the rationale that he defended his title. He subsequently offered half of it to Heenan, who gratefully turned it down.

Fighting was definitely a game for John L. Sullivan. Born in Boston in 1858, the hefty Irish-American received much of his early recognition as bare-knuckle champion and later as the first champion of the padded-glove era. His exploits both in and out of the ring helped him win the hearts of Americans. "His championship was the most important thing in the world to him," comments his biographer, "with hard liquor and women combined running a close second."[1]

Though good-natured and likeable outside the ring, the Boston Strong Boy had a will and temperament that terrified opponents. On 7 February 1882, he won the title when he defeated Paddy Ryan in nine rounds at Mississippi City. He maintained his stature at the top until 7 September 1892, when an American named James Corbett defeated him and took the championship away.

One of Sullivan's most famous fights was in Mississippi on 8 July 1899, against Jake Kilrain. Sullivan had just returned from a fight in England. Little did he know what he was in for. In an epic battle the two exchanged blows for over three hours. Soon, the 108-degree temperature began to take effect, and after the seventy-fifth round a doctor from the New York Athletic Club told one of Kilrain's assistants that if Jake continued, he would likely die. The fight was then stopped, both men near exhaustion, and Sullivan was declared the winner.

His next and last big fight was against Jim Corbett, the brash, young challenger with a unique style. Corbett used quickness, agility, and the art of dodging. Sullivan, on the other hand, used the brute-strength, punch-it-out style of the past. Their fight represented the new against the old, and after the twenty-first round of their bout, the new was declared the champion. Sullivan bowed out gracefully, still the hero of the people, but a defeated champion. He left his mark on the American people and the sport itself. Almost single-handedly, he had introduced the big time world of boxing to the United States and prepared the ground for its universal popularity.

When he defeated Sullivan, Corbett proved that he was more than able to carry on the new tradition. Going on to England, he defeated English and European champion Charley Mitchell (whom Sullivan had never been able to beat) and made the first legitimate and undisputed claim to the heavyweight championship of the world.

Corbett then took on a tall middleweight named Bob Fitzsimmons. The fight, held in Carson City, Nevada, for a purse of fifteen thousand dollars, saw a local sheriff collect over four hundred guns from the fans entering the area. There was apprehension that spectators would get too involved and that violence would break out. The fight went on without any major incidents, however, and after six rounds Corbett was in control, having knocked his opponent out to the count of nine in one round. Fitzsimmons, however, battled back, and in the fourteenth round, after hitting Corbett with his famed solar-plexis punch, took the championship.

The new champ didn't fight again for two years. Instead, taking advantage of his position in the boxing world, he made money traveling with a theatrical troupe. He later popularized the saying "The bigger they are, the harder they fall."[2]

Along came a big, slow hulk named James Jeffries. Over 220 pounds, Jeffries took advantage of his size and developed a crouch that made him hard to hit. He utilized it successfully, and when he came up against Fitzsimmons, it resulted in an eleventh-round knockout.

Jeffries then piled up an impressive record. His string of victories included a twenty-third round KO of the talented Corbett. He never ducked a fight, and in 1902 he had a rematch with Fitzsimmons. The forty-year-old challenger put up a good battle, but Jeffries's crouch and punishing left proved too much once again. Fitzsimmons was knocked out in the eighth round.

In 1905 Jeffries, retiring to California, named Marvin Hart the new champion. The public had difficulty accepting this, for they felt that Hart hadn't earned the honor. In 1906 he fought a 175-pound Canadian named Tommy Burns and was defeated. Over the next two years Burns won thirteen straight matches against boxers from all over the world. Finally, on 26 December 1908 he met his match. He was a towering American named Jack Johnson. Their fight took place in Australia, and after fourteen rounds the police were forced to stop the fight because Burns was so badly beaten up. It was a milestone, for Johnson was the first black in history to be recognized as the heavyweight champion of the world. Because of his lifestyle and beliefs, he was also a very controversial man. Johnson was scorned by both blacks and whites for living with white women. When indicted on a federal morals charge, he chose to leave the country.

The nation was intent on finding a man to beat Johnson. Jeffries was summoned but, in the ensuing bout, was knocked out in the fifteenth round. He seemed unbeatable. Johnson was then forced into exile, and it took a six-foot, seven-inch, two hundred fifty-pound giant named Jess Willard to lure him out. The two met on 15 April 1915. In the early rounds of the bout Johnson had control. But as the fight wore on, Willard's strength began to show, and in the twenty-sixth round he knocked Johnson out. Controversy later surrounded the fight, as it did so often Johnson's life. When Johnson was lying on the canvas taking the count in the last round, photographs showed him shading his eyes from the sun with his arms. Questions were raised as to how a semiconscious fighter could casually do something like that. Johnson later claimed that he took a dive and could have gotten up. The question remained unanswered, but one thing was sure: Willard was the new heavyweight champion.

American fight fans rejoiced at Johnson's demise and Willard's success. As a champion, however, Willard was less than exciting. His fights were often described as dull and, when he took three years off to tour with a Wild West show, nobody complained.

Along came a new heavyweight from the West. Often referred to as "the Manassa Mauler," Jack Dempsey scored an incredible eighteen knockouts in 1918. Willard was finally coaxed into the ring for a fight with Dempsey the following year. It was the fourth of July, and most of the fireworks came from Dempsey's corner. Dempsey put on an awesome first-round display, battering the stunned Willard all over the ring. In the seventh knockdown the referees's count reached ten just after the bell sounded to end the round. One of the reasons for Dempsey's tremendous effort was that his manager, Jack Kearns, had reportedly bet ten thousand dollars on ten to one odds that Dempsey would knock out Willard in the first round. He was one second away from winning a hundred thousand dollars.

The fight went on, but for all intents and purposes it was over. At the end of the third round Willard's corner threw in the towel. It was a merciful gesture, for their fighter had already suffered a broken jaw, a split cheekbone, a flattened nose, a cut ear, and large red welts all over the body.

Dempsey soon proved to be one of the greatest fighters ever to enter the ring. But he too had to overcome early public scorn. Under Kearns's guidance the young Dempsey decided to continue to work rather than fight in the war. He was heavily criticized for being a "draft dodger", and fans found it difficult to support him. However, his unpopularity soon waned, and his achievements in the ring made him a folk hero.

Dempsey introduced the million-dollar gate to boxing with his historic fight with Frenchman Georges Carpentier in 1920. It was billed as an international extravaganza—the brutal, unshaven, tanned American against the flamboyant, fair-skinned Frenchman. Dempsey was in control of the fight from the first round, and in the fourth he knocked Carpentier down for the count. The count reportedly lasted over four four minutes, as the Frenchman took some time to recover from Dempsey's devastating blow. The fight ended, and Dempsey left no doubt as to who was world champion.

The town of Shelby, Montana, then put itself on the map by sponsoring a fight between Dempsey and a thirty-four-year-old light heavyweight named Tommy Gibbons. Hoping the promotion would initiate investments and a real estate boom, a group of local businessmen sponsored the fight and guaranteed Dempsey and his manager three hundred thousand dollars. The result was disastrous, not for Dempsey, but for Shelby. The champion won a rather uninteresting bout, and the city took a heavy loss as many of the banks were forced to close.

Dempsey then took on Argentina's Luis Angel Firpo, known as "the Wild Bull of the Pampas." Firpo had gained a reputation for his unorthodox style, his wild charges in the ring, and his devastating, club-like right hand. The stage was set for another classic international bout. The two met on 14 September 1923 at the Polo Grounds in New York. The following is an account of the first round:

At ringside Dempsey weighed 193; Firpo, 221. At the very outset, Dempsey went down for no count, caught by Firpo's right in the usual Dempsey rush at the first bell. Immediately afterward, Firpo went down for a count of three from Dempsey's left to the head. As Firpo got up, Dempsey dropped him again for a count of two, and again Firpo got up, [only] to be floored by Dempsey's left to the body for three. When Firpo jumped up again, Dempsey's right to the jaw stretched him out for the full count of nine. But Firpo arose again, and this time went down from a left to the body for two, followed by another knockdown for a count of six. When Firpo got up from this one, he rushed Dempsey, clubbed away at him, and knocked Dempsey out of the ring with a right."[3]

It was a brutal display of courage by both fighters. With the help of some ringside reporters Dempsey climbed back into the ring and continued the fight. In the second round Firpo, unable to absorb any more of those punishing blows, was knocked out. Though it didn't even last two full rounds, the championship fight was one of the most memorable in history.

Following the fight, Dempsey's interest turned away from boxing. He sailed to Europe and became involved in the stage and screen. He did not fight again for three years. Dempsey was truly a champion and hero of the American people.

A rising young heavyweight named Gene Tunney then decided that the time was ripe for an assault on the champion. Having studied Dempsey's style, Tunney felt that he had the key that would unlock the champ. The fight took place in Philadelphia on 14 September 1926, and Dempsey was the heavy favorite. Tunney surprised everyone as he boxed a superb match, administering devastating punishment throughout. When it was all over, a legend had been dethroned, and Tunney was king.

A rematch was later set up in Chicago. Dempsey was attempting something never before achieved—a former champion's regaining his crown. Tunney took control in the early rounds, but in the seventh, Dempsey hit the new champ with a barrage of punches that sent him reeling to the canvas. A new boxing rule stated that a fighter must move to a neutral corner after knocking down his opponent. After Dempsey floored Tunney, he lingered near the scene, as was his habit. The referee stopped right in the middle of the count and was forced to move Dempsey away. He walked back to the fallen boxer, started his count over, and by the time he got to nine, Tunney was up. It was a very controversial occurrence, for Tunney went on to win the bout and retain his crown. The so-called Battle of the Long Count was not soon forgotten. Tunney defended his title for the last time in a fight against Tom Heeney. About a month later he retired, a winner of sixty-seven fights and a loser of only one (to Harry Greb).

Tunney's retirement brought about problems in finding a successor. The spotlight became occupied by what many felt was a lackluster group of champions. On 12 June 1930 Germany's Max Schmeling and Boston's Jack Sharkey met to decide the issue. The fight ended in confusion in the fourth round.

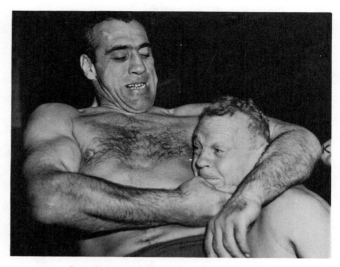

Massive Italian heavyweight Primo Carnera clowns for the camera. (Wide World photo)

The judges ruled that Sharkey fouled Schmeling, who was then declared the winner. The following year, when Schmeling refused to sign for a return bout, the New York State Athletic Commission stripped him of his crown. Finally, the two met in June 1932, and Sharkey won in a rather uneventful match.

A six-foot, six-inch, 270-pound Italian circus giant and wrestler then appeared on the scene. His name was Primo Carnera. When he fought Sharkey in June 1933, he easily defeated him with a powerful right hand uppercut. Carnera then took on a young Californian named Max Baer. Known for his punishing right hand and for his ability to take a punch, Baer was the logical challenger for the title. In the Baer-Carnera bout, after eleven rounds and twelve knockdowns, Carnera's corner signalled that their champ could take no more. The fight was over; Baer had ousted the incumbent. Though he sometimes acted like a killer in the ring, Baer was well-liked by the press and boxing fans alike. A good-looking, easy-going extrovert, he won fans wherever he ventured. And he went to venture to many places—except the ring. He appeared in vaudeville, movies, and on radio. Baer also occasionally fought in exhibitions, but avoided anything very strenuous.

Baer's next fight was against James Braddock in June 1935 at the same ring in Long Island where he defeated Carnera. Braddock was an intelligent boxer. He continued to circle to the champion's left, to avoid his devastating right. It was a defensive strategy, but it proved very offensive to Baer, who was never able to unleash. Braddock used the ploy wisely and successfully in dethroning the champion.

A bright new prospect then appeared on the horizon, and he had people talking. As an amateur, he won the national light heavyweight championship, and as a professional, he sported an impressive 24–0 record, seventy-five percent of which was by knockout. He was Joe Louis Barrow, known to most as Joe Louis, "the Brown Bomber." His outings included wins over Primo Carnera and Max Baer, and people thought he was ready. But along came Max Schmeling, who thought otherwise. The German studied Louis's style and believed he could beat him. And that's exactly what Schmeling did as he knocked out the young star in the twelfth round.

It turned out to be a minor setback for Louis. he bounced back a few months later to KO Sharkey in the third round. Then, on 22 June 1937 Louis met Braddock for the championship belt and defeated him soundly. Unlike many of his predecessors, Louis defended his title as often as physically possible. He beat Tommy Farr of England and, in a million-dollar gate at Yankee Stadium, disposed of the only man who had defeated him, Max Schmeling. It was an incredible fight. When the bell sounded in the first round, Louis rushed over to Schmeling, and just two minutes later, after an intense battering, the German was down and out.

From 1949–51 Ezzard Charles reigned supreme. (UPI photo)

Some twelve years after he had won the title, the great Joe Louis decided to retire. His list of victories included some respected fighters, like Billy Conn, Jersey Joe Walcott, and others. The Brown Bomber and his masterful ability to counterpunch had dominated the boxing world for over a decade. He had become another hero of the people. When he announced his retirement in 1949, the sport of boxing lost one of its greatest champions.

Louis dominated the ring from 1937 to 1949. When he left, a man named Ezzard Charles took a shot at the championship belt. A two-time National Amateur Middleweight champion, Charles gained the crown by defeating Walcott in a match set up by Louis and a group of promoters. After a second unsuccessful attempt, Jersey Joe finally took the title away from Charles in 1952. A year later he gave Charles a chance to win the title back, but decisioned him in fifteen rounds.

Looming in the wings was a fighter known to his followers as "the Brockton Blockbuster." Born in Brockton, Massachusetts, Rocky Marciano started his climb to fame as a member of the United States Army's boxing team. His aggressive offensive style and his powerful punching ability helped him spread many an opponent all over the canvas and his reputation all over the country.

On 23 September 1952 Marciano challenged

Joe Louis (the "Brown Bomber") strikes a fighting pose reminiscent of his 194–5 championship career. (UPI photo)

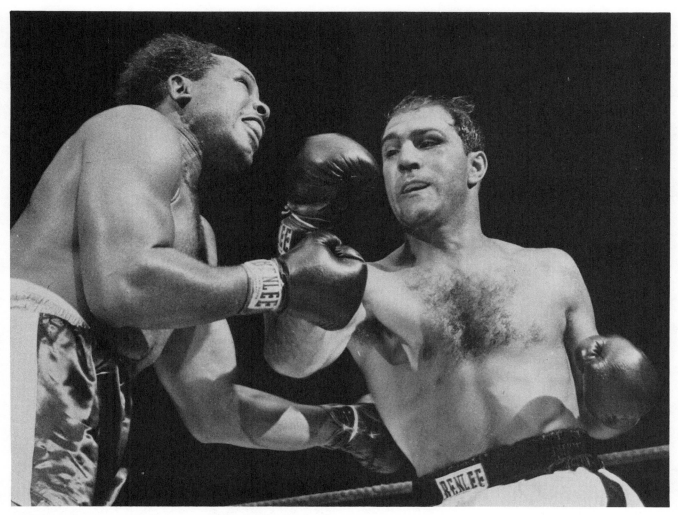

Rocky Marciano stuns challenger Archie Moore with a hard right to the head. (UPI photo)

Walcott for the championship. The fight went back and forth until Marciano's punishing punches took over in the thirteenth round. Marciano then knocked his opponent out and was declared to be the new champ. He remained on top until he retired on 27 April 1956. Having achieved a record unequalled in boxing—forty-nine fights without a loss or draw, including forty-three knockouts, the Brockton Blockbuster had proved that he was truly champion of the world. His untimely death in a private airplane crash in 1969 was one of the biggest tragedies ever to have occurred in the world of sports.

Floyd Patterson, an Olympic gold medalist in the middleweight division, was crowned the next heavyweight champion by virtue of his victories in a series of elimination bouts. His opponents were Archie Moore, Hurricane Jackson, and Joey Maxim. Patterson's quick, dodging style helped him defend the title on many occasions. But,

finally, in a title fight in New York a big Swede named Ingemar Johansson knocked out Patterson in only the third round. Then, on 20 June 1960 Patterson bounced back against the champion and knocked him out in the fifth round. It was the first time in history that a heavyweight actually regained his title.

In a third bout between the two, Patterson, maintaining his position as the champ, once again proved to be superior. It wasn't for long, however, as a young fighter named Sonny Liston entered the picture. Liston, a big man, had done much of his training behind the walls of a penitentiary. During his earlier years he associated with criminals and spent a lot of time with them—in prison. He got out long enough to knock out Patterson in the first round of their title fight. Liston then dispelled all doubts by repeating the feat when the two met again. From 1953 to 1956 he piled up an impressive seven knockouts and from 1958 to 1962 ran off another sixteen.

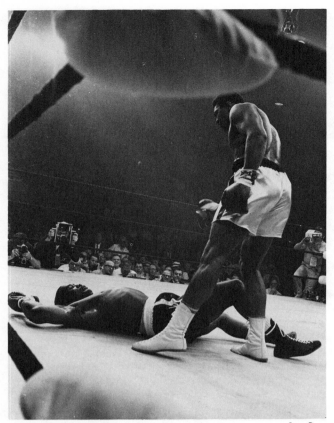

Cassius Clay stands over a fallen Sonny Liston in the first round of their title fight of May 1965. (UPI photo)

Like all other heavyweight champions before him, Liston eventually encountered an opponent who was younger, quicker, and more aggressive than he. This time, it was a youngster named Cassius Clay, who took seven rounds to dispose of the champ in 1964. In his first three years of professional boxing the hard-working Clay won nineteen fights. He was a talented boxer, and he knew it, and his tongue soon became as lightning quick as his jab. His constant boasting turned many fight fans against him, and when he became a Black Muslim and changed his name to Muhammad Ali, he lost even more support. But it was difficult not to admire his enormous talent. He dubbed himself "the Greatest," and many fight experts found that point hard to argue.

In 1963 Ali failed to pass a military preinduction test, but three years later he was reclassified 1-A. He refused to report for duty. As a Muslim minister, he claimed that war was against his religion. On 9 May 1967 a federal grand jury indicted him for refusing to serve, and he was soon stripped of his heavyweight title by the New York State Commission and the World Boxing Association.

In 1971 the Supreme Court overruled the con-

viction, and Ali began to stalk the championship again. He defeated Jerry Quarry and Oscar Bonavena and signed to fight the new champ, Joe Frazier. Frazier, the 1964 Olympic heavyweight champ, won the world title by beating Jimmy Ellis in a bout in New York in 1970. When Ali was stripped of his crown, Ellis was declared champion by the World Boxing Association, while Frazier, who declined to participate in their tourney, was declared champ in six other states. Frazier soon ended the debate by knocking out Ellis in the fifth round of their bout. Joe Frazier, was then recognized as the new champ.

A powerful puncher and relentless fighter, the former slaughterhouse worker Frazier has often been compared to the great Rocky Marciano. On 8 March 1971 in the middle of the comeback trail, Muhammad Ali met Frazier in a fight for the title. In the eleventh round Frazier began to take control of what had been a close fight. He almost knocked Ali out and continued the pressure in the twelfth and thirteenth rounds. In the fifteenth Frazier knocked Ali down for a count of eight, and the fight was decided. In his fortieth professional fight, Muhammad Ali was finally defeated. For the moment, at least, he was no longer "the Greatest."

On 22 January 1973 in Kingston, Jamaica, Frazier was knocked out in the second round of his fight with another Olympic champion, George Foreman. A huge man, Foreman packed a devastating punch. In June 1974 Foreman went on to dispose of Ken Norton, the highly ranked contender who broke Ali's jaw in 1973. Norton was knocked out in only the second round of the match.

Ali was still in hot pursuit of the crown which he felt was rightfully his. Finally, he managed to get the new champ, Foreman, to fight him in Zaire. Respecting his opponent's awesome punching power, Ali came out with a new strategy. Instead of standing toe-to-toe and punching it out with Foreman, he decided to stand back in the corner, protecting with his arms his upper body and face. Ali called it "rope-a-dope"—he hoped the champion, who had not been forced to go many rounds in the past, would punch himself out and tire. And that's exactly what happened. Instead of forcing Ali to come out of the ropes and box, Foreman attacked him relentlessly but did minimal damage. Finally, in the eighth round, fatigue set in on Foreman, and Ali knocked him out. His superior strategy having paid off, he laid claim once again to the championship belt. He was only the second heavyweight in history to regain the title.

About a year later, on 1 October 1975, Ali took on his long-time nemesis, the hard-punching

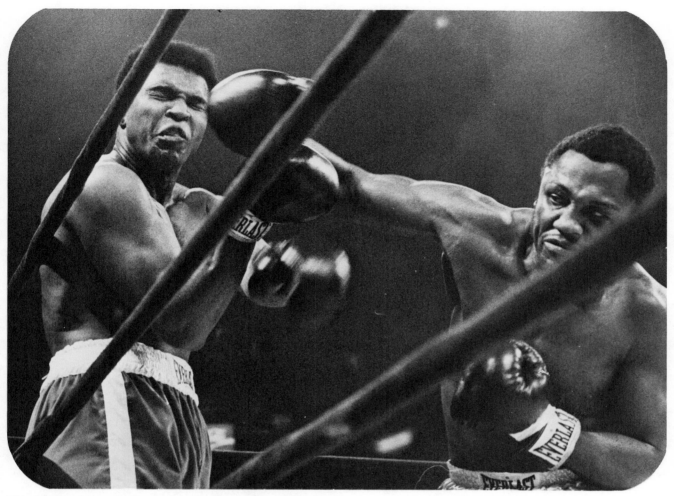

This hard right to the head of Muhammad Ali helped Joe Frazier win a unanimous 15-round decision and become undisputed heavyweight champion. (UPI photo)

Frazier. Taking place in Manila the fight lived up to all the prebout publicity. It was nothing short of a war. "It was like death," Ali later said. Frazier battered Ali so much that, by the eleventh round, the defending champ almost quit. What was even more incredible was the pounding Ali was giving Frazier. No matter how often or how hard he was hit, Frazier just kept going. Although totally drained, both fighters clubbed each other as if it were their last fight. From the first round on, it was pure action. But then, when the bell sounded for the final round, Frazier was unable to make it to the center of the ring. He threw in the towel, and Ali had shown once again why he was champion.

During the next two-and-a-half years Muhammad Ali put away six heavyweight challengers, including Jimmy Young, Ken Norton, and Earnie Shavers. Then, on 15 February 1978, he took on an up-and-coming young fighter named Leon Spinks.

Very unpolished, Spinks appeared to be an easy opponent. But what this Olympic hero lacked in experience, he made up for in unrelenting determination. Constantly chasing Ali around the ring and bulling him into the corners, Spinks defeated the champ and shocked the boxing world.

Following this unbelievable upset, the World Boxing Council recognized Ken Norton as its champion. The World Boxing Association, on the other hand, stayed with its newly crowned king, Spinks. Suddenly, there were two championship belts, and no one was quite sure who truly was the champ.

Both fighters took their own courses, which, unfortunately, were both short ones. It didn't take Norton long to lose his new crown, as he was defeated by a hard-hitting fighter named Larry Holmes. Showing that his victory was no fluke, Holmes mowed down the next eight fighters to step into the ring against him. The last in that string took place late in 1980 against an aging-but-game fighter named Muhammad Ali. Larry Holmes had defeated more than many peoples' doubts about his ability; he had defeated a legend.

Spinks's tenure on the throne was just as short as Norton's. Seven months after he defeated Ali, Spinks gave the former champion a rematch. Afterward, Ali was no longer a former champion. He defeated Spinks and won the championship for a record third time in his career. At that point Ali decided to call it quits and retire.

Ali's departure left the World Boxing Association with a chore. They had to fill his shoes and find another champion. It proved to be a very difficult task, but after a series of elimination bouts, John Tate became its man. Another Olympic boxer, Tate defeated Gerry Coetzee of South Africa in the final elimination to win the title. But, like Spinks, he soon learned that life outside the Olympic ring was not easy. On 31 May 1980 Tate took on a powerfully built ex-Marine from Los Angeles named Mike Weaver. It was Tate's first title defense. And it proved to be his last. The champ had the challenger well in hand for almost the entire fight. Then, in the twelfth and final round Weaver came alive and decked Tate with a hard right and two powerful left hooks. Though Tate had fought very well, the hard-hitting, courageous Weaver was awarded the heavyweight championship belt.

From 1978 to 1980 the heavyweight championship switched hands more often than a bad hand at a poker game. But unpredictability is part of the excitement that makes boxing an international sport. During his reign Muhammad Ali traveled the world as if he were a king, and he was treated as one. But, then, he was "the Greatest."

Heavyweight Champions

1882	John L. Sullivan
1892	James J. Corbett
1897	Robert Fitzsimmons
1899	James Jeffries
1905	Marvin Hart
1906	Tommy Burns
1908	Jack Johnson
1915	Jess Willard
1919	Jack Dempsey
1926	Gene Tunney
1930	Max Schmeling
1932	Jack Sharkey
1933	Primo Carnera
1934	Max Baer
1935	James Braddock
1937	Joe Louis
1949	Ezzard Charles
1951	Joe Walcott
1952	Rocky Marciano
1956	Floyd Patterson
1959	Ingemar Johansson
1960	Floyd Patterson
1962	Sonny Liston
1964	Cassius Clay (Muhammad Ali)
1970	Joe Frazier
1973	George Foreman
1974	Muhammad Ali
1978	Leon Spinks
1978	Ken Norton (WBC)
1978	Muhammad Ali (WBA)
1978	Larry Holmes (WBC)
1979	John Tate (WBA)
1980	Mike Weaver (WBA)
1983	Michael Dokes (WBA)
1983	Gerrie Coetzee (WBA)

6
The Davis Cup

The young American star, John McEnroe, had just beaten his Italian opponent Antonio Zugarelli to take a 1–0 lead. He walked back to the service line ready to start the second game.

Suddenly, some angry Italian fans began to heckle him from the stands. The emotional McEnroe responded with a barb of his own, and then, as the hecklers continued, lay down on the court in protest. Moments later, he collected himself, stood up, and prepared to serve. The crowd of over five thousand at San Francisco's Civic Auditorium applauded him wildly.

As McEnroe waited for the crowd to quiet down, Italy's self-proclaimed human mascot, Serafino, got out of the stands and quietly approached him from behind. When he was just a few feet away from McEnroe, the crowd roared with laughter, and McEnroe turned around and discovered him.

With a look of mock horror, the young American sprinted over to the sidelines and hid behind the bench. Serafino then dropped onto his back, mimicking McEnroe's earlier display. The crowd erupted once again as he just lay there. Serafino was no ordinary mascot. At five feet, five inches in height and a whopping 440 pounds, he looked, in the words of one writer, "like a human oil spill washed ashore."[1]

Then the problems really began. Serafino was

Known throughout the tennis world for his encounters with umpires and fans, as well as opposing players, America's John McEnroe has spearheaded their resurgent Davis Cup squad. (UPI photo)

stuck. He couldn't get up by himself. Later, with the help of three ushers and the prayers of the tournament officials, the enormous Italian cheerleader was helped up to his feet and led back to his seat.

"Vaudeville?" McEnroe said later, "I hope I can go straight onto the movie screen from here."[2]

It may not have been exactly what Dwight Davis had in mind, but when the sixty-ninth Davis Cup Final was completed in 1979, the United States had a convincing 5–0 victory over Italy.

Like most sports, tennis is a game of the young and energetic, the athletic, and well-conditioned. How is it, then, that the game's biggest attraction is an eighty-year-old trophy that reputedly can hold thirty-seven bottles of champagne? Maybe it's because, in the words of one authority, it has "crossed the Pacific a dozen times and made almost as many trips across the Atlantic. It has been locked up in bank vaults and guarded by armed policemen as if it were the crown jewels. Cracked three times and modified over the decades, it has nevertheless grown in value as ever more nations sought it as they would the Holy Grail."[3]

The Davis Cup began as a dream, the dream of a young Harvard tennis enthusiast, Dwight Filley Davis. It developed into the sport's most cherished trophy. Teams from all over the world vie in regional competition to determine who truly is king of the tennis racquet.

Born into a prominent St. Louis family, Davis decided, at the ripe age of twenty, that it was time to bring all the nations of the world together to partake in a single tournament void of politics, ideologies, and cultural differences. He also wanted to prove that American tennis could compete with the best.

Davis attended an exclusive Eastern prep school before going on to Harvard, of whose renowned tennis team he became a member. In 1899 he and teammate Holcombe Ward won the national doubles championship. It was the first of three straight for Davis.

Still, Davis was not content. The Harvard varsity, comprised of Davis, Ward, Malcolm Whitman, and Beals Wright, traveled to the West Coast to display their talents and stimulate interest in the game. Winning all but two of their matches against their Western opponents, their confidence skyrocketed. They began to think the unthinkable—that they could beat the superpower of tennis, Great Britain.

The young Americans played a very aggressive, wide-open game. They served hard, rushed the net, volleyed wildly, and employed a number of beguiling spins, the most notorious of which was known as "the American twist." The British, considered the world's best players at the time, employed a more conservative style, preferring to stay back at the baseline and rally from there.

The more they thought about it, the more confident and determined the young men from Harvard became. After returning to the East Coast, they presented their idea to the United States Lawn Tennis Association (USLTA). The president of the USLTA, Dr. James Dwight, confided to the boys that he had been trying unsuccessfully for years to set up such a match. The proposal was once again sent to the British Lawn Tennis Association, but this time the answer was yes!

To Davis, the contest was an extension of good will, and to show this, he donated a sterling silver bowl, which appropriately became known as "the Davis Cup." Thirteen inches high and eighteen inches in diameter, it weighed 217 ounces and had a value of seven hundred dollars.

In 1900 the British traveled to Boston to battle the Americans at the Longwood Cricket Club. They were a confident group, amused that the fledgling Americans challenged them to a match. The simple format consisted of two singles matches on the first day, a doubles match on the second, and two more singles matches on the final day.

The inaugural Davis Cup match was one to remember. On the opening day the United States jumped out to an amazing 2–0 lead on the strength of Whitman's 6–1, 6–3, 6–2 thrashing of Arthur Gore, and of Davis's victory over E. D. Black. This surprising result meant a doubles win the next day would give the Americans the cup in an unbelievable upset. Davis and Ward achieved just that, as they went out and aced their British opponents, Black and Roger Barrett, 6–4, 6–4, 6–4. The final day's singles competition was eventually suspended, and the United States had a 3–0 victory.

The British were not at all pleased with the results. They directed their frustration at what they felt were the unacceptable conditions under which the tournament was held. Complained Barrett:

The ground was abominable. The grass was long. Picture to yourself a court in England where the grass has been the longest you ever encountered; double the length of that grass and you have the courts as they were at Longwood at that time. The net was a disgrace to civilized Lawn Tennis, held up by guy ropes which were continually sagging, giving way as much as two or three inches every few games and frequently requiring adjustment. As for the balls, I hardly like to mention them. They were awful—soft and "mothery looking"—and when served with the American twist came at you like an animated egg plum . . .

They not only swerved in the air, but in hitting the ground broke surely from four to five feet . . . We had never experienced this service before and it quite nonplussed us. The spectators were most impartial and the female portion thereof not at all unpleasant to gaze upon.[4]

Well, not everything displeased them.

The next Davis Cup competition was in 1902 at the Crescent Athletic Club in Brooklyn, New York. The British arrived with a much stronger team, consisting of three Wimbledon champions—Reginald and Hugh Doherty, and Dr. Joshua Pim. After two days the favored British held a commanding 2–1 lead. On the final day, however, some outstanding singles play by Whitman and Bill Larned rallied the Americans to an impressive 3–2 win. The following year Britain and the Dohertys returned to America and finally captured the trophy.

In 1904 the competition expanded to include Belgium, Austria, and France. The following year Australasia (Australia and New Zealand) joined. Participation continued to grow, and the rules were eventually refined. The final round of play for the cup became known as "the challenge round." In the early years the defending champion had a bye to the final round, it was thus spared of the months of qualifying matches through which the other teams had to go. Teams were composed of four players, and a match between two nations was known as a "tie." The matches, played over three consecutive days, consisted of two singles, one doubles, and two more singles.

By 1921 teams from Japan, Spain, Denmark, Czechoslovakia, the Philippines, Argentine, Holland, India, Germany, Canada, and South Africa were participating. To accommodate the expansion, a system of zoning was set up. The qualifying matches were to be played in three zones—American, European, and Eastern. The winner from each zone was then to compete in interzonal matches. The winner of the latter was to go on to the challenge round against the defending champ.

The initial years of competition were dominated by the Americans and British. Soon, the teams from France and Australia began to flex their muscles. Led by Sir Norman Brookes, the Australasians took the cup away from the British in 1907. Four years later the English rebounded to capture it, only to lose the trophy to the Americans in 1913.

The outbreak of World War I in 1914 threatened the continuation of the tournament. During one of the preliminary rounds that year, a touchy situation developed. On the opposite side in the war, the Australians came up against the German team, consisting mainly of officers from the Kaiser's imperial staff. The match was played in Pittsburgh, and led by Brookes and Anthony Wilding, the Australians came out on top. They then went on to defeat the U.S., 3–2, in the challenge round.

After a four-year suspension due to war, Davis Cup competition resumed. In 1919 the Australians won it again by drubbing Great Britain, 4–1.

Then came Tilden. Known as "Big Bill," partly because of his immense stature and partly because of his enormous ability on the court, Tilden is regarded by many as the greatest player of all time. He and his lifetime associate, Bill Johnston, "Little Bill," teamed up to form one of the most unbeatable Davis Cup squads in American history. They were like "twin engines of destruction who ruled the courts as absolute potentates—monarchs of all they surveyed across the net."[5]

In 1920 the Tilden-Johnston team whipped their Australian opponents, 5–0, in the final round. They brought the trophy back to the United States, where it stayed until 1927.

But the legacy of Bill Tilden lived on. He was often called a showman because "he would allow his opponent to gain so big a lead as to make his own defeat appear inevitable. Then, from this precarious position he would launch a spectacular comeback that had the crowd cheering him and that invariably ended with an ovation from the stands

The legendary Bill Tilden led the United States to early domination of Cup play. (UPI photo)

when he won."[6] Critics pointed to his 1921 match against Zenzo Shimizu of Japan. Shimizu won the first two sets, 7–5, 6–4, but then Tilden came rushing back for an incredible 7–5, 6–2, 6–1 decision. It was later learned that after the third set Tilden went into the locker room and lanced open an enormous boil on his foot.

Big Bill was the center of attention no matter where he went or what he did. Once, while playing a match at the Orange Lawn Tennis club in New Jersey, the indignant star threatened to walk off the court because he was not used to playing in a "cow pasture." Another time, he invested a thirty-thousand-dollar inheritance in a production of *Dracula*, and, a frustrated Shakespearean actor, put himself in the title role. Both he and the play bit the big one. But on the tennis court Tilden reigned supreme. For seven years he kept the trophy on American soil.

The Davis Cup eventually became too big for its britches: no more space was available in which to list new winners. Its founder then added a four-hundred-dollar tray below the cup, which would fit addition names for the next thirty-five years.

Appropriately, the first two names inscribed on the new tray were those of Tilden and Johnston. In fact, their carvings were on the cup every year until 1927, when a group of upstart Frenchmen, known as "the Four Musketeers," appeared on the courts of the Germantown Cricket Club in Philadelphia. Led by Rene LaCoste and Henri Cochet, the Frenchmen pulled off an amazimg 3–2 upset. Teaming with LaCoste and Cochet were Jean Borotra and Jacques Brugnon.

When they returned to France, the victors were embraced by the people with open arms. They were considered national heroes. It was the first time that the trophy came to French soil, and that was where the natives felt it belonged. After all, France is the place where many historians believe the game of tennis originated. The sport was often mentioned in French ecclesiastical writings of the twelvth century. It was played at religious festivals, and bishops and archbishops were known to retire to the cloister for an exhilirating game of the racquet sport. Lawn tennis, on the other hand, was said to have been invented around 1874 by an English cavalry officer, Major Walter Clopton.

For the next five years the Four Musketeers were the center of attention in the tennis world. And they were a colorful group, indeed. Borotra, known as "the Bounding Basque," was the showman of the team. He wore a black beret, often fooled around on the courts, and had a reputation for wining and dining the ladies. "The Crocodile"—

that's what the young, volatile LaCoste was called—was a talented, determined player. Unfortunately, ill health ended his career when he was in his early twenties. Cochet, "the Magician," was very cool and nonchalant. He often claimed that he didn't even know how he made some of his incredible shots. Brugnon, a consistent, steady player, was known more for his brilliant doubles play than for his antics on the court.

In 1928, when the United States was to challenge the champion French, a controversy ensued. A USLTA rule stated that a player cannot write a report on a tournament in which he was about to play. Tilden had written some stories for one of the wire services on the agreement that they be published twenty-four hours after the event. That was the legal USLTA limit. However, three weeks before the challenge round match with the French, the article appeared, and Tilden's enemies demanded that he be barred from further Davis Cup competition. But the French, enraged, asked the American ambassador, Myron Herrick, to have him reinstated. In the name of international good will, Tilden was allowed to play. He went on to defeat LaCoste in one of his greatest matches ever, but the American Team failed to recapture the trophy.

The French continued to dominate the courts over the next four years, for a total of six straight Davis Cup championships. After their last victory, in 1932, not everyone was in agreement that they truly deserved it. The opponent was the American team once again. Borotra was facing Wilmer Allison in the fifth set, and the score was tied 2–2. As Allison was going for match point, the wily Borotra suddenly stopped play to change his shoes. The home crowd roared its approval. Allison waited impatiently. Finally, Borotra was ready, and resumed play. In the interim the momentum had changed, and the match went his way.

That was not the only controversy of the match. On the final day of the challenge round Borotra, "Putting on one of the finest acts of his career, using the volatile crowd as an instrument on which to play and as a weapon against his opponent, was said to have 'stolen the cup' after serving what clearly appeared to be a double fault at match point to Wilmer Allison."[7]

In 1933 Fred Perry and Henry Austin of Great Britain teamed up to take the trophy away from the French. They successfully defended it for the next three years. Then, a Californian named Don Budge entered the scene. Armed with an explosive backhand, he helped capture the trophy for the next two years for the United States. Like many top-notch players before him, Budge was subsequently lured into the ranks of professional tennis by a very lucrative contract.

In 1939 the Australians, led by Adrian Quist and John Bromwich, won the cup with a 3–2 triumph over the Americans. The outcome proved to be a bad omen once again. For the second time an Australian victory in the Davis Cup was followed by the outbreak of a world war. Competition was again postponed.

When the event resumed in 1946, the Americans were ready. Led by Jack Kramer and Ted Schroeder (well-known for his statement "I could play more wood shots than Sammy Snead"), they traveled down under to challenge the Aussies at Melbourne. They successfully overthrew their hosts, 5–0, and brought the cup back to the United States, where it remained for four years.

In 1950 Harry Hopman returned to captain the Australians and began what is known as "the Australian Era." Hopman was a tough man who imposed extremely high standards upon his players. Conditioning and discipline were essential. He soon became known as "the Miracle Man" for his

Once the number one player in the world, Rod "the Rocket" Laver helped bring Australia into the tennis spotlight. (photo by Dave Hasemyer)

uncanny ability to extract the maximum from his players. "He put his players through rigorous training grinds, both in the gymnasium and outdoors. He levied fines against players who broke curfew or picked up the wrong fork at the table. No one was better at raising a team to peak mental pitch before a big match."[8]

Hopman was so good that during the next nineteen years his Australian teams won the cup an amazing fifteen times! The Americans were the only ones to wrestle it away from them during their dynasty. They did so in 1954, 1958, 1963, and 1968. Time after time, Hopman came up with a top-notch performer to help maintain Australian dominance. His stars included Lew Hoad, Ken Rosewall, Ken McGregor, Frank Sedgman, Ashley Cooper, Malcolm Anderson, Roy Emerson, Rod Laver, Fred Stolle, John Newcombe, and Tony Roche. Most of these players were eventually lured into the pro ranks, but some, like Cooper, who married Miss Australia, lost interest for other reasons.

In 1958 a young man hit the scene who put the tennis world into a backspin. His name was Alex Olmedo, a member of the American team. He became known as "the Darling of Australia" and "the Tennis Hero of the World" by beating the first-ranked amateur, Cooper, by a 6–3, 4–6, 6–4, 8–6 score. Olmedo was a fiery twenty-two year old Peruvian, who would let nothing come between him and victory. Writes one authority:

"At one stage the referee, Cliff Sproule, and Olmedo had a gentle tug of war (one newsman reported it as a "wrestle") for possession of a towel. This was when, having fallen on the slippery court, Alex walked to the courtside and picked up a towel to wipe the mud off his hands and racquet. Alex continued to towel himself as well, thus breaching the rules, a violation Sproule tried to prevent the next time it happened. The result was a tugging match for the towel, with Olmedo winning. When he fell another time and lost his racket, [the Australian coach] Hopman rose from his chair and retrieved it for him. Olmedo took the racket from him but otherwise ignored Hopman as he continued to the stand and made with the towel again."[9]

Olmedo won the hearts of both the Australian fans and tennis enthusiasts all over the world. He received a standing ovation from the Australian crowd of over eighteen thousand upon his victory over Cooper. In Peru thousands cheered in the streets. The Chamber of Deputies gave him a standing ovation when they heard the news. He was decorated with the Order of Sport by the minister of education.

Though the Aussies continued to dominate cup play, the United States, led by Arthur Ashe, did manage a victory every few years. Ashe, a gifted young athlete from UCLA, was known to have a difficult time channeling his ability. "I'll start thinking about anything but the match, he once remarked, "girls, a horse race. I don't know. At Sydney this past year, I was playing John Newcombe in the finals. I won the first set. Then all of a sudden I started thinking about the stewardess, Bella, I had met. Oh-h-h-h. She was Miss Trinidad of 1962. I just kept seeing her—this gorgeous face, this beautiful creature—and the next thing I know, the match is over and Newcombe's won."[10]

Finally, in 1968, the Australian dominance waned. Depleted by the exodus to the pros, they fielded a young, inexperienced team. Bill Bowrey, Ray Ruffels, and youngsters Phil Dent and John Alexander were sent into battle against the more powerful, experienced American team of Ashe, Clark Graebner, and the Unviersity of Southern California's championship doubles combination of Bot Lutz and Stan Smith. (Smith, was denied a job as a ballboy at the cup match against Mexico eight years earlier because officials judged him to be too clumsy to run across the court.)

The Australian fans sensed doom, as the Americans, 10–1 favorites, came to town. With attendance at the matches down about eighty percent, the wild enthusiasm present during the previous two decades was nowhere to be found. Hopman was unable to come up with another miracle, and the Americans walked off with an impressive 4–1 win—and the cup.

The 1969 final was between the United States and Romania; Australia was conspicuously absent. Though the Australian Laver and his cohorts were considered to be the best tennis players in the world at the time, they were denied eligibility because they were contract professionals. In their place the jocose Aussies fielded two koala bears and a wallaby.

The Romanians were a talented group, led by their brash stars Ion Tiriac and Ilie Nastase. They smashed their way into the final round in both 1969 and 1971, but both times they were stopped by the more experienced Americans.

1971 marked the end of the challenge round.

Romania's brash Ilie Nastase led his squad into the Davis Cup finals in both 1969 and 1971. (photo by Dave Hasemyer)

One of the new stars to brighten the American Davis Cup effort is Vitas Gerulaitus. (photo by Dave Hasemyer)

Since then, the defending champ, has had to play through the long series of interzonal matches to the final, instead of taking the traditional bye.

The 1970s will probably be best known in tennis history as the decade that the "Big Four" (The United States, Australia, France, and Great Britain) were finally dethroned. In 1974 South Africa captured the trophy by beating India by default, and in 1975 Sweden knocked off Czechoslavakia, 3–2. Toward the end of the decade the United States reasserted its superiority. Its 5–0 trouncing of Italy in 1979 served as a challenge to others for the future. Comments a national sport magazine: "The fact is that it may be very difficult to stage a competitive Davis Cup over the next few years, what with the number of American players crowding the top of the international rankings."[11] With McEnroe, Jimmy Connors, Vitas Gerulaitis, Roscoe Tanner, Eddie Dibbs, and youngsters Peter Fleming, Brian Teacher, Hank Pfister, and Eliot Teltscher, the deck is certainly stacked. But then, in Davis Cup play anything can happen, and anyone can reach the pinnacle. "The Davis Cup, more than any other lawn tennis event, separates the men from the boys. To win for youself is one thing; to win for your country is another."[12]

The Australian squad proudly surrounds the Davis Cup. (UPI photo)

Davis Cup Results

1900	United States 3, British Isles 0	1946	United States 5, Australia 0
1901	United States (by default)	1947	United States 4, Australia 1
1902	United States 3, British Isles 2	1948	United States 5, Australia 0
1903	British Isles 4, United States 1	1949	United States 4, Australia 1
1904	British Isles 5, Belgium 0	1950	Australia 4, United States 1
1905	British Isles 5, United States 0	1951	Australia 3, United States 2
1906	British Isles 5, United States 0	1952	Australia 4, United States 1
1907	Australasia 3, British Isles 2	1953	Australia 3, United States 2
1908	Australasia 3, United States 2	1954	United States 3, Australia 2
1909	Australasia 5, United States 0	1955	Australia 5, United States 0
1910	Australasia (by default)	1956	Australia 5, United States 0
1911	Australasia 5, United States 0	1957	Australia 3, United States 2
1912	British Isles 3, Australasia 2	1958	United States 3, Australia 2
1913	United States 3, British Isles 2	1959	Australia 3, United States 2
1914,	Australasia 3, United States 2	1960	Australia 4, Italy 1
1919	Australasia 4, British Isles 1	1961	Australia 5, Italy 0
1920	United States 5, Australasia 0	1962	Australia 5, Mexico 0
1921	United States 5, Japan 0	1963	United States 3, Australia 2
1922	United States 4, Australasia 1	1964	Australia 3, United States 2
1923	United States 4, Australasia 1	1965	Australia 4, Spain 1
1924	United States 5, Australasia 0	1966	Australia 4, India 1
1925	United States 5, France 0	1967	Australia
1926	United States 4, France 1	1968	United States 4, Australia 1
1927	France 3, United States 2	1969	United States 5, Rumania 0
1928	France 4, United States 1	1970	United States 5, West Germany 0
1929	France 3, United States 2	1971	United States 3, Rumania 2
1930	France 4, United States 1	1972	United States 3, Rumania 2
1931	France 3, Great Britain 2	1973	Australia 5, United States 0
1932	France 3, United States 2	1974	South Africa defeated India by default
1933	Great Britain 3, France 1	1975	Sweden 3, Czechoslovakia 2
1934	Great Britain 4, United States 1	1976	Italy 4, Chile 1
1935	Great Britain 5, United States 0	1977	Australia 3, Italy 1
1936	Great Britain 3, Australia 2	1978	United States 4, Great Britain 1
1937	United States, 4, Great Britain 1	1979	United States 5, Italy 0
1938	United States 3, Australia 2	1980	Czechoslovakia 4, Italy 1
1939	Australia 3, United States 2	1981	United States 3, Argentina 1
		1982	United States 3, France 0
		1983	Australia 3, Sweden 2

7
The Lombardi Trophy

Winning is not everything. It is the only thing.
Mental toughness is essential to success.
Success demands singleness of purpose.
Fatigue makes cowards of us all.
The harder you work, the harder it is to surrender.
I demand a commitment to excellence and to victory, and that is what life is all about.[1]
—Vince Lombardi

The Lombardi Trophy: the most coveted award in the sport of professional football. In 1980 a hundred thousand people crammed into the Rose Bowl in Pasadena to watch the Los Angeles Rams take on the Pittsburgh Steelers. Over 102 million viewers tuned in to their television sets all over America to watch the best in the National Football League battle it out.

Named after the late Vince Lombardi, the great coach of the Green Bay Packers, the Lombardi Trophy is awarded every year to the winner of the National Football League (NFL) championship game—the Super Bowl.

The Lombardi Trophy symbolized the standard of excellence that is so often associated with the legendary Lombardi. From 1959 to 1967 Lombardi coached the Packers with the unrelenting determination of an army drill sergeant. In his ten seasons he won five NFL championships and was the winning coach in the first two Super Bowls. This period

became known as "the Lombardi Era," and the city of Green Bay was soon called "Titletown, U.S.A." To Lombardi, football was more than just a game; it was a yardstick of life itself. "Some of us will do our jobs well and some will not," he said, "but we all will be judged by only one thing—the result."[2]

Professional football in America has a long, illustrious history, dating back to before 1900. Probably the biggest development in the sport was the merger of the two rival leagues, in 1966. The union between the established National Football League and the young, untested American Football League produced one of the great spectacles of sport, the Super Bowl. Initially dubbed the AFL-NFL World Championship Game, it was inaugurated in 1967 at the Los Angeles Coliseum.

The first two participants were the Green Bay Packers of the NFL and the Kansas City Chiefs of the AFL. Officials of both leagues looked on anxiously to see what the result would be. Green Bay was a heavy favorite, and the odds makers proved to be correct. Behind two third-quarter touchdowns and their famous "Packer Power Sweep," Green Bay brushed by the Chiefs by a 35–10 score.

Quarterback Bart Starr had a field day. His main targets were wily veteran wide receivers Carroll Dale and thirty-four-year-old Max McGee, who was placed in the lineup because the other starter, Boyd Dowler, was sidelined with a shoulder injury.

The Lombardi Trophy. (National Football League photo)

McGee turned in an outstanding performance, catching seven passes for 138 yards and two touchdowns. On the ground the Packers were just as impressive as Jim Taylor and Elijah Pitts rolled through holes opened up by guards Jerry Kramer and Fuzzy Thurston.

After the game Packers coach Lombardi tried to put the game in perspective. "In my opinion the Chiefs don't rate with the top names in the NFL. They are a good football team with fine speed, but I'd have to say NFL football is better. Dallas is a better team, and so are several others. That's what you wanted me to say wasn't it? Now I've said it."[3] The issue had been settled; the NFL was still boss.

The Packers reasserted their league dominance the following year at the Orange Bowl in Miami, in Super Bowl II. This time the opponent was the Oakland Raiders. The result was much the same. Wrote a national sportswriter: "Watching films of the Raiders a few nights before the game, the Packers all broke up when their coaches replayed a scene in which one Oakland safety bowled over the other Oakland safety in the open field, thus allowing the opposition to score the easiest of touchdowns. Said Lee Roy Caffey, the Packers' right-corner linebacker, 'It's pretty tough to get up again when you've already been on the stick for the two big games in the NFL playoffs.'"[4]

Green Bay jumped out to a 16–7 halftime lead and followed it up with ten unanswered points in the third quarter. Defensive back Herb Adderley intercepted a pass and ran it back sixty yards for a touchdown to settle the score. The mighty Packers had once again proven too much for their AFL opponent, as they snuffed the Raiders, 33–14. "It wasn't our best effort," Lombardi said after the game. "All year it seemed like as soon as we got a couple touchdowns ahead, we let up. Maybe that's the sign of a veteran team, such as ours. I don't know."[5] Following the contest Lombardi retired from his head coaching position to take on the job of full-time general manager of the Packers.

The Super Bowl returned to Miami in 1969 for contest number three. The NFL's representative, The Baltimore Colts, were favored by up to three touchdowns. They were led by the golden arm of quarterback Johnny Unitas, and the consistent play of his backup, Earl Morrall. Their opponent was the New York Jets and its brash young signal called Joe Namath. The contest was billed as "the long hair versus the crew cut;" youth versus experience.

Everyone expected the Colts to win, and win big. Everyone, that is, except Namath. Before the game he went to an awards dinner at the Miami Touchdown Club. "The Jets are going to win Sunday. I'll guarantee you,"[5] he cockily predicted. He even went a step further by saying "Earl Morrall would be a third string quarterback on the Jets. There are maybe five or six better quarterbacks than Morrall in the AFL."[7] His remarks made national headlines, and they did not set well with the Colts.

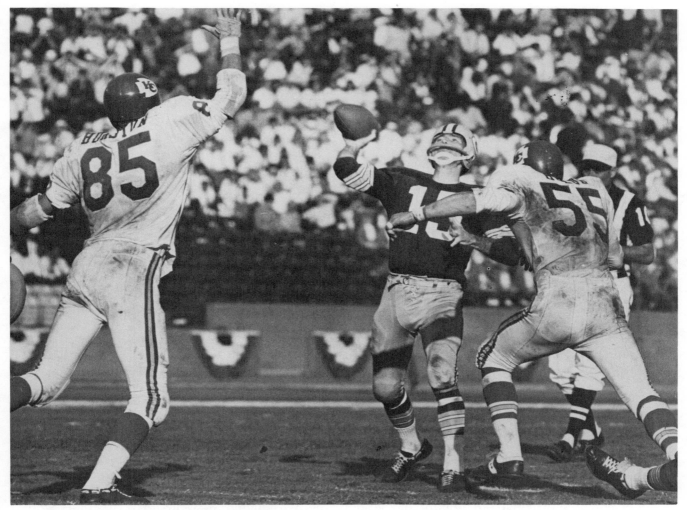

Bart Starr of the Green Bay Packers goes back to pass as Chuck Hurston (85) and E. J. Holub (55) of the Kansas City Chiefs close in, in the first Super Bowl in 1967. Green Bay won, 35–10. (photo by Vernon Biever)

National Football League Commissioner Pete Rozelle presents the Super Bowl Trophy to Packer Coach Vince Lombardi after their victory over Kansas City. (photo by Vernon Biever)

When the game began and the hitting started, the Colts soon realized that it was not just idle talk. On the second play of the game Jet fullback Matt Snell bulled up the middle and knocked out Colt safety Rick Volk. Namath, who completed seventeen of twenty-eight passes for 206 yards, engineered the Jets to a 16–0 lead. Late in the game the Colts turned to their star, Unitas, who was sidelined with an injury. He came off the bench to lead the Colts to a quick touchdown, but it was a matter of too little, too late. Behind Namath and Snell, who rushed for 121 yards, the Jets pulled out a 16–7 victory. The NFL's reign was over. "Hello, world." Jet placekicker Jim Turner said afterwards. "Welcome to the American Football League."[8]

The fourth Super Bowl was played in New Orleans, and once again the AFL sent in the Kansas City Chiefs. Under Coach Hank Stram, a self-proclaimed offensive revolutionary, the Chiefs brought with them a totally redesigned offense. Before the game quarterback Len Dawson had been linked to a federal gambling investigation in Detroit. The Chiefs were two-touchdown underdogs, but that didn't bother them.

Minnesota was not impressed with Stram's talk of "the offense of the future," nor with their "three hundred or so plays." The "Purple-People Eater" defense was known for its ability to crush opposing quarterbacks, and this time they had their sights set on Dawson. "The offense of the 70's will die the first time we get Lenny Dawson on the pass rush. He's not going to survive under a heavy rush."[9]

Dawson, undaunted by the threats or the investigation, went out and completed twelve of seventeen passes for 142 yards and a touchdown. The "Purple-People Eaters" were put on a starvation diet as Stram's multiple formation offense totally confused the Vikes. With men in motion to the left and to the right, Minnesota didn't know which end was up. Wide receiver Otis Taylor had a field day running under Dawson's passes, and the Chiefs breezed to a 23–7 triumph. A Minnesota coach later replied, "That offense of the future stuff is nothing to laugh at. We were cautious all game because their offense was so complicated. We just could never figure out what they were going to do next."[10]

Dawson was eventually cleared of any impropriety off the field, and his performance on the field silenced the critics. "The best thing about this game is that we don't have to answer for it the next three years, like we did last time," Dawson said.[11] He then heard the phone ring. It was President Nixon calling to congratulate him.

Super Bowl V returned to the friendly confines of the Orange Bowl in 1971. The Baltimore Colts, now a member of the other league, were up against the NFL's perennial powerhouse, the Dallas Cowboys. The game had officially become known as "the Super Bowl." Indeed, it was a super game.

There were eleven interceptions and fumbles in the game, and neither team was able to gain a sizable lead. It was a seesaw battle. With five seconds left, the score was tied 13–13. The Colts had the ball on the Dallas twenty-five-yard line. The Cowboys called a time-out. The fifty thousand fans at the stadium inched up closer to the edge of their seats. Baltimore's twenty-three-year-old rookie placekicker nervously paced around the huddle as the team prepared for the potential game-winning field goal. Dallas had already caused one of his extra points to go astray.

The Colts lined up for the field goal. Dallas called another time-out, but referee Norm Shachter disallowed it because the ball had not been put in play since the last one. O'Brien readied himself for the kick, and then suddenly yelled to his holder, Earl Morrall, "The wind, Earl; where's the wind?"

Morrall calmly replied, "There is no wind; just kick the ball straight!"[12] O'Brien approached the ball and gave it his best boot. The ball sailed toward the right goalpost, veered back to the left, and dropped through the uprights. It was good. O'Brien jumped in the air triumphantly. He had just kicked the Colts to a 16–13 victory.

"I've had luck decide against us so many times I'm sick of it," said Colt guard Bob Vogel. "I quit being proud years ago when we lost games we should have won. The way I look at it, we're going to get the Super Bowl ring because we won the games that counted this year. We deserve it."[13]

In Super Bowl VI at New Orleans, the Cowboys got revenge. Their victim was the Miami Dolphins, and the score was 24–3. The Cowboys set a team rushing record with 252 yards, as they ran up sixty-nine plays to the opponent's forty-four.

"My biggest disappointment was that we never challenged," said Miami Coach Don Shula. "They completely dominated."[14] After Miami had defeated Baltimore for the right to go to the Super Bowl, President Nixon gave Shula a telephone call to suggest a play. "The Cowboys are a good team," Shula said, quoting Nixon, "'but I think you can hit Paul Warfield on the down-and-in pattern.'"[15] The Dolphins tried it and the Cowboys stopped it. "We made sure they didn't complete that pass on us,"[16] Dallas Coach Tom Landry said.

Los Angeles was the scene for Super Bowl VII. Don Shula, already a two-time loser in the game, brought in his undefeated Miami Dolphins to face the Washington Redskins. The Redskins were a two-point favorite, but the Miami defense, led by Manny Fernandez, Nick Buoniconti, and safety Jake Scott, totally shut them off.

The Dolphins were ahead 14–0 late in the fourth period when a strange thing happened. Miami placekicker Garo Yepremian lined up for a forty-two-yard field goal. The snap from center Howard Kindig was low, and holder Earl Morrall tried to place it quickly. The kick was blocked by Bill Brundige of Washington. Yepremian picked up the deflected ball, ran to his right, and tried to pass it. The ball slipped out of his hands, however, and was intercepted by Mike Bass, who ran it forty-seven yards for a touchdown. Suddenly, the score was 14–7, and there were still two minutes, seven seconds remaining in the contest. Washington was unable to mount another threat in the waning minutes, and the Dolphins came away with a 14–7 win and a perfect 17–0 season. "This is the first time the goat of the game is in the winner's locker room," Yepremian said. "I should have fallen on the ball, but my mind went blank."[17]

Continuing its winning ways the following year,

Miami climaxed its season with another appearance in the Super Bowl. Minnesota was the opponent, but it didn't make much difference. Running back Larry Csonka had a field day as he rushed for 145 yards on thirty-three carries. Miami dominated from beginning to end. Not even a totally blown play in the third quarter, could keep them from the end zone. With the ball on the Viking two-yard line, quarterback Bob Griese called a play in the huddle, and the Dolphins lined up at the line of scrimmage. Suddenly, Griese realized he had forgotten what count the ball was to be snapped on. He turned to his fullback, Csonka, and asked him, "What's the count?" Csonka thought for a moment. "It's on two, isn't it?" he replied. "No, no, it's on one," the other running back, Jim Kiick said.[18] Griese finally agreed with Csonka. He walked up to the center, Jim Langer, and got ready. Langer snapped it on one, and the startled Griese juggled the ball, turned, and fumbled it into the arms of Csonka, who gathered it in and stumbled into the end zone for a touchdown. "Bob had that wide-eyed look when he gave me the ball," Csonka said afterward. "I'm just happy I didn't cause him to drop the ball."[19]

Despite the momentary lapse the Dolphins went on to crush Minnesota 24–7. It was their third Super Bowl appearance and their second triumph. It was Minnesota's second time around and their second failure.

Super Bowl IX began what will probably become known as "the Pittsburgh Dynasty." Making their first championship appearance, the Steelers faced those perennial bridesmaids, the Vikings. Viking quarterback Fran Tarkenton was determined to be a winner this time around. There were four things he forgot to take into account. The were L. C. Greenwood, Mean Joe Greene, Dwight White, and Ernie Holmes—the Pittsburgh defensive front four. They were awesome. They totally dominated the Viking offensive line and shut down the Minnesota offense.

Franco Harris rushed for 158 yards, breaking Csonka's record, and the Steelers outrushd the Vikings 249 yards to 17. (That's right—17.) The Vikings managed only 17 yards rushing during the entire game. Pittsburgh led by a slim 2–0 margin at the end of the first half, but the lead expanded after the intermission, and the Steelers went on for a 16–6 win. It was the team's first championship in its forty-two year history. For owner Art Rooney it really was a super Bowl.

Pittsburgh's Victory in Super Bowl IX served notice to the rest of the NFL. And when the Steelers showed up again the next year in Miami, no one was really surprised. Least of all, the Dallas Cowboys, their opponent.

This time, however, it was not the Pittsburgh defense that was dominant. The Cowboys proved to be more than a worthy opponent for the championship Steelers. Two big plays turned out to be decisive in the contest. One of them could simply be called "Lynn Swann." The talented Steeler wide receiver almost single-handedly broke the backbone of the Cowboy defense. He caught four passes for 161 yards, but it was his reception late in the fourth quarter that helped determine the outcome.

The Steelers were leading 14–10 and there was only a little over three minutes left in the game. Steeler quarterback Terry Bradshaw went back to pass on third down. The Cowboys blitzed him, and just as he was releasing the ball downfield, he was hit by a Dallas linebacker and knocked unconscious. The ball sailed through the air in the direction of Swann, who was covered by Mark Washington. The acrobatic wide receiver pulled in the pass and glided into the end zone for a touchdown. Meanwhile, the woozy Bradshaw was being helped to the sideline and eventually the locker room. Later, when his head cleared, Bradshaw was told that his pass had gone for a touchdown.

The other crucial play in the contest came minutes later. The Steelers led 21–17, but Dallas was driving for the possible game-winning score with only minutes remaining. Quarterback Roger Staubach launched a pass into the end zone, where it was intercepted by Pittsburgh defensive back Glen Edwards. The threat, drive—and game— were over.

Super Bowl XI pitted two teams that had been in

Pittsburgh Steeler wide receiver John Stallworth gathers in a pass over two Los Angeles Ram defenders in Super Bowl XIV. Stallworth went all the way for a touchdown on the play, in a game the Steelers won 31–19. (Pittsburgh Steeler photo)

the game before but had never won. It was the Oakland Raiders, losers of Super Bowl II, against the Minnesota Vikings, losers of Super Bowls IV, VIII and IX. The frustrations of one of these teams was, unfortunately, to be continued.

Early in the game the Raiders drove down the field only to have their placekicker, Errol Mann, miss a twenty-nine-yard field goal. Oakland Coach John Madden was irate. "Don't worry," quarterback Kenny Stabler told his coach. "There's more where that came from."[20] And he was right. The Oakland line, consisting of Art Shell, Gene Upshaw, Dave Dalby, George Buehler, and John Vella totally dominated the Viking defensive front four. "When you've got the horses, you ride them," Stabler said after the Raiders's impressive 32–14 win. "We're not a fancy team. We just line up and try to knock you out of there."[21]

The twelfth Super Bowl in the Superdome in New Orleans brought with it a Cinderella story. Nobody's preseason pick to be there, the Denver Broncos somehow knocked off both the Raiders and the Steelers and earned its way into their first championship game. Although fairy tales sometimes come true, the Dallas Cowboys did their best to make sure this one didn't.

The game was billed as the battle of the defenses. It was Denver's "Orange Crush" defense against Dallas's "Doomsday Defense." It turned out to be doomsday, however, as both the Bronco offense and defense were crushed by the potent Dallas ball club. The final score was 27–10, and at times it wasn't even that close. Dallas controlled the ball for thirty-nine minutes and gained 325 yards. The inspired Cowboy defense caused four Denver fumbles and intercepted four passes in the first half alone. After the game Dallas defensive lineman Harvey Martin, commented, "Orange Crush is soda water, baby. You drink it. It don't win football games."[22]

As they prepared for a rematch with the Dallas Cowboys in Super Bowl XIII, the Pittsburgh Steelers weren't too happy. Cowboy lineback Hollywood Henderson said that Dallas was going to win, 31–0. He also said that Terry Bradshaw was dumb and that Jack Lambert looked like Dracula. Henderson made a big mistake. The last thing anyone would want to do is give a team like Pittsburgh added incentive. It was considered by most experts to be the best team in pro football, if not in the history of the game.

Bradshaw came out and played one of the best games of his career. By halftime the Steeler quarterback had passed for an incredible 253 yards, a Super Bowl record. On the day he ended up with 318 yards in passing and a record four touchdowns.

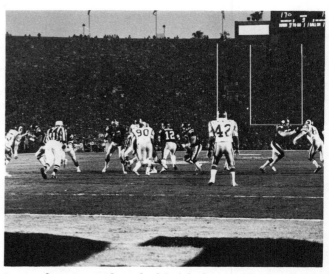

Ram safety Dave Elmendorf (42) looks over the Pittsburgh offense in the third quarter, as the Steelers drive toward their goalline. (Pittsburgh Steeler photo)

He was voted the game's Most Valuable Player as Pittsburgh rolled to a 35–31 victory and their third Super Bowl win.

Super Bowl XIV, in 1980, brought together "the City of Champions" and "the Team without a City." Fielding a team that had won three of the last five Super Bowls in football and that was winning the World Series in baseball, Pittsburgh was appropriately dubbed "the city of champions" by the American media. Pittsburgh's opponent this time was the Los Angeles Rams, "the Team without a City." The Rams had just completed their final season in the historic Los Angeles Coliseum. They finished with a 9–7 record, and they were more often booed than cheered by the hometown fans. Because of differences with Coliseum management, the Rams decided to move to Anaheim Stadium in Orange County for the 1980 season. Then they found themselves in the Super Bowl in Pasadena in January. But who would they be playing for, the Los Angeles fans or the Anaheim fans? Tackle Doug France quickly settled the issue: "They [LA fans] know it's not theirs. In Orange County, when the [baseball] Angels lost their last game, the fans made them come back on the field. Our fans couldn't wait for us to get off the field."[23]

And by the time Super Bowl XIV was over, neither could the Steelers. Underdogs, by ten to twelve points the fired-up Rams disregarded the odds makers and went out and pushed the champion Steelers to the brink. Reported a national sports magazine:

It was an emotional Super Bowl and easily the best of the fourteen played so far. It was the way

Super Bowls are supposed to be played, but haven't been. The score changed hands six times before it ended Pittsburgh 31, Los Angeles 19, but only the guys who laid the 11 points with the bookies read it as a 12-point Steeler win. The Rams made it that close. They stayed in it because of a sustained intensity that brought them great honor, because of an unexpectedly brilliant performance by young quarterback Vince Ferragamo, and because of a tackle-to-tackle ferocity that had the Steeler[s] defense on its heels much of the afternoon.[24]

With the victory, their fourth Super Bowl championship, Pittsburgh assured itself of a spot in pro football history. But it was not just a triumph for the team, it was a victory for the conference. When the Super Bowl began, football hierarchy worried whether the young American Football Conference would be able to compete with the more talented national conference. Eighteen years later the question has been answered. The American Conference has won twelve of the eighteen Super Bowls, and the only NFC teams to win have been the Green Bay Packers, the Dallas Cowboys, the Washington Redskins, and the San Francisco 49'ers. As defensive tackle Henry Jordan of the Packers said after

Super Bowl II: "The other league is getting better. If they improve as much each year, they'll be on a par with us soon."[25]

Super Bowl Results

1967	Green Bay Packers 35, Kansas City Chiefs, 10
1968	Green Bay Packers 33, Oakland Raiders 14
1969	New York Jets 16, Baltimore Colts 7
1970	Kansas City Chiefs 23, Minnesota Vikings 7
1971	Baltimore Colts 16, Dallas Cowboys 13
1972	Dallas Cowboys 24, Miami Dolphins 3
1973	Miami Dolphins 14, Washington Redskins 7
1974	Miami Dolphins 24, Minnesota Vikings 7
1975	Pittsburgh Steelers 16, Minnesota Vikings 6
1976	Pittsburgh Steelers 21, Dallas Cowboys 17
1977	Oakland Raiders 32, Minnesota Vikings 14
1978	Dallas Cowboys 27, Denver Broncos 10
1979	Pittsburgh Steelers 35, Dallas Cowboys 31
1980	Pittsburgh Steelers 31, Los Angeles Rams 19
1981	Oakland Raiders 27, Philadelphia Eagles 10
1982	San Francisco 49'ers 26, Cincinnatti Bengals 21
1983	Washington Redskins 27, Miami Dolphins 17
1984	Oakland Raiders 38, Washington Redskins 9

8
The Podoloff Cup

What were they going to do? Football season was over, and it would be months before baseball would begin. Some form of recreation, some sport, was needed to fill the interim, but nobody was quite sure what it would be. The year was 1891, and young James Naismith, a physical education instructor at the International Young Men's Christian Association (YMCA) Training School in Springfield, Massachusetts, decided that he would try to solve the dilemma.

Driven indoors because of the bad weather, Naismith and his physical education class experimented with many activities. He tried rugby, but it was too rough to be played in a gymnasium, and there were too many injuries. Lacrosse and soccer were also given a shot, but they too proved unsuccessful. As none of the available sports seemed adequate, Naismith's frustation grew.

So did his sense of adventure. He decided to try something new. A ball was needed, and it had to be big enough so that other equipment was not necessary. He outlawed running with the ball to avoid the roughness of the other sports, and he decided to use an elevated goal to bring in the idea of skill and aim. Then Naismith devised thirteen rules for the game, and decided to use peach baskets as the goals. The baskets were hung on the gym's balcony, about ten feet above the floor.

In the event that the new sport didn't work, Naismith promised that he wouldn't experiment further. It was a great success, however, and the class loved it. Except for the soccer ball that was used, the equipment was primitive, compared to the modern game. When the school recessed for Christmas, many of the students introduced the game to their friends in their hometowns. "Basketball" quickly became popular. It was soon played in high schools, colleges, and in the public in general.

On 6 June 1946 a group of businessmen met in New York City to organize a professional basketball league. They established the Basketball Association of America (BAA). The businessmen, who were arena owners, chose Maurice Podoloff, a New Haven lawyer, as commissioner of the league. At the time he was also commissioner of the American Hockey League. The original BAA had eleven teams—Boston, New York, Philadelphia, Providence, Toronto, Washington, Chicago, St. Louis, Cleveland, Detroit, and Pittsburgh. Despite some tough early years Podoloff held the league together.

In 1947 the National Basketball League (NBL) came into operation, and the two leagues became immediate rivals. In the 1949–50 season the leagues merged to form the National Basketball Association (NBA). With Podoloff as its first president, the NBA grew and prospered, and basketball soon challenged the two other professional sports, football and baseball.

In 1956 an award was instituted to recognize the "most valuable player" in the league. Becoming known as the Podoloff Cup, it was recognized as a symbol of excellence. Players throughout the league were judged not only on their talent and performance but also on their contribution to the team as a whole.

The first recipient of the trophy was a young forward named Bob Pettit of the St. Louis Hawks. A graduate of Louisiana State University, Pettit was originally drafted by the Milwaukee Hawks in 1954. In his first season the six-foot, nine-inch forward was selected as Rookie of the Year. He was on the road to greatness, but for Bob Pettit it had not always been that way. When he first tried out for his high school basketball team, he was cut. He finally made the squad in his senior year, but throughout his career he was considered too skinny and too light for the sport. A determined athlete, he proved himself time and time again.

In just his second year in the pros Pettit won the Podoloff Cup. That season he led the league in scoring with a 25·7 average and in rebounding with a 16·2 average, and was selected Most Valuable Player (MVP) of the all-star game. Known as a smooth shooter and an intelligent ball player, Pettit gave his all to the game throughout his career. In the 1956–57 NBA championship game against the Boston Celtics he played with his wrist in a cast. The Hawks eventually lost, though four of the games were decided by only two points. "When I fall below what I know I can do, my belly growls and growls. Anytime I'm not playing up to my very best, I can count on a jolt of indigestion,"[1] Pettit said.

Pettit continued to assault the league and those who doubted his ability, and in 1959 he won his second Podoloff Cup. But injuries soon took their toll on the superstar, and in 1965 he shocked the sports world by announcing his retirement. Many thought he was at the peak of his game at the time.

In 1957 a flashy, unpredictable guard hit the scene. Bob Cousy was his name, and the magic he could perform with a basketball often left opponents reeling in disbelief. An all-American at Holy Cross College in Massachusetts, he went virtually unnoticed by the pros. Cousy was drafted by the Tri-Cities Hawks and then was traded to the Chicago Stags, which later folded. Eventually, his name was drawn from a hat by Walter Brown, owner of the Boston Celtics. It was one of the luck-

The second player ever to win the Podoloff Cup, Bob Cousy was one of the few guards in the history of the game ever to take the award. Following his amazing career with the Boston Celtics, Cousy went on to coach the NBA's Cincinnati Royals. (UPI photo)

iest moves that the Celts ever made. Cousy was one of the best small playmaking guards ever to play the sport. He tried to make the game fun and interesting, and his clever ball handling and passing attracted fans. Nicknames such as "the Houdini of Hardcourt" and "the Mobile Magician" were soon thrown his way.

Known primarily for his playmaking, Cousy was also an excellent scorer. He led the team in scoring for four straight seasons and once scored fifty points in a game. On another occasion he collected twenty-eight assists in a contest. Cousy helped develop the fast break and the behind-the-back pass. During his career the Celtics ran away with six NBA championships. In 1957 he won the Podoloff Cup after one of his best seasons ever. "Cousy was one of the greatest all-around basketball players in the game," said former coach Red Auerbach. "Undoubtedly, he was the best backcourt player."[2] He retired at the end of the 1962–63 season and went on to coach Boston College and the NBA's Cincinnati Royals.

The next man to win the MVP was one of Cousy's

teammates, Bill Russell. In fact he won it again, and again, and again, and again. The six-foot, nine-inch center for the Celtics was without a doubt the most successful pro in the history of the sport. Though he didn't dominate the league as a scorer, in his thirteen seasons playing in the Boston Garden, he brought home eleven NBA Championship banners. He also won the coveted Podoloff Cup five times (1958, 1961, 1962, 1963, and 1965).

A winner—that's the only way to describe Russell. All through his career, wherever he went, success followed. At the University of San Francisco he led the Dons to fifty-five consecutive victories and national championships in 1954–55 and 1955–56. He then led the U.S. team to the gold medal in the 1956 Olympics. The St. Louis Hawks had the original draft rights to Russell, but they traded them to the Celtics for forwards Cliff Hagan and Ed Macauley. Another shrewd move by the Celts. Instantly, Boston became a winner, and Russell was largely responsible.

A defense specialist, Russell virtually revolutionized the game. As a rebounder, shot-blocker, and intimidator Russell was unsurpassed. There were better offensive players in the league, such as his long-time rival, Wilt Chamberlain of the Philadelphia '76ers. They were the two behemoths of basketball, each with his own specialty, and when the two met, sparks flew. "I've been in seven playoffs with Boston," Wilt said. "When it all came down to the final game . . . Boston won six."[3] Known for his clutch play, Russell was eventually appointed player-coach by Celtic management in 1966. Through it all he always maintained his sense of perspective and his sense of humor—although not always in that order. "The best player I've got is me," he said. "I'm the one I have to bear down on most."[4] After his retirement from the Celtics, Russell went on to become coach and general manager of the Seattle Supersonics. During his four-year tenure with the expanding Supersonics, the team went to the play-offs twice.

The two giants dominated the game from 1960 to 1968. During that period the Podoloff Cup was won by either Russell or Chamberlain eight out of the nine times. While Russell was busy blocking shots and winning championships, Wilt the Stilt was setting every scoring record in the book.

Born in Philadelphia, Wilt was a track star as a youth. He played college ball at Kansas University before dropping out to join the Harlem Globetrotters. The following year he entered the NBA, playing for the Philadelphia Warriors. During his rookie year he averaged 37·6 points per game, and the trend was set. It didn't take long for Chamberlain to become the most awesome offensive weapon in the game. During the 1961–62 season Wilt averaged an incredible 50·4 points and collected 100 points in a contest against the New York Knickerbockers. He led the league in scoring for seven straight years and won the Podoloff Cup four times—in 1960, 1966, 1967, and 1968.

Despite Walton's well-balanced attitude, injuries continued to dominate his professional career. In 1979 he signed with the expansion San Diego Cliphad a difficult time relating to his coaches. Despite these difficulties, Chamberlain attained the ultimate goal in 1966. It had often been said that he couldn't win the big one, but that year he proved his critics wrong by taking the '76ers to the NBA Championship. The seven-foot giant was later traded to the Los Angeles Lakers, whom he proceeded to lead to thirty-three straight wins in 1971 and their first NBA crown in twelve years.

By 1973 Wilt held or shared forty-three NBA records. He then jumped to the rival American Basketball Association (ABA) to become player-coach of the San Diego Conquistadors. In response the Lakers obtained a restraining order that prevented him from playing. As the athlete that he was, he soon became involved in another sport—professional volleyball. He bought a franchise in the International Volleyball Association, became league president, and spent his spare time playing with his own Big Dipper volleyball squad. Throughout his career in sports, whether it was in track or basketball or volleyball, Wilt Chamberlain stood tall.

In 1964 a young man from the University of Cincinnati stole the show from the two big men. Averaging 31·4 points and eleven assists per game, the "Big O," Oscar Robertson, won the Podoloff Cup in what was considered his greatest year as a pro. Of this tremendous ball handler and playmaker, the Celtics coach Auerbach once said, "There is nothing Oscar can't do. He's so great he scares me."[5]

As for Pettit, success did not always lay on Robertson's doorstep. He had to go out and earn it. He was the first black ball player in the history of the University of Cincinnati. "For a fellow his size, Oscar has to be the greatest player of his time," said Phog Allen, University of Kansas coach.[6] Robertson graduated with a degree in business administration and went on to become co-captain of the 1960 Olympic team, which won the gold medal.

Robertson was drafted by the pros in the first round by the Cincinnati Royals, and despite his efforts and heroics he was unable to capture that elusive NBA Championship. An outstanding playmaker and shooter, he was also blessed with great body agility. "We were playing Cincinnati, and

OSCAR ROBERTSON
GUARD   6'5"

MILWAUKEE
BUCKS

With the help of "Mr. Inside," (Kareem-Abdul Jabbar) "Mr. Outside" (Oscar Robertson) dribbles toward the basket and a world championship for the Milwaukee Bucks. (Milwaukee Buck photo)

Earl Strom was one of the officials," said NBA forward Tom Meschery. "Somehow, I wound up guarding Oscar after a switch. Well, Oscar throws the ball behind his back, heads for the basket, and leaves me behind. It was a fantastic move, split-second like always with him. Just as the ball goes in, Strom calls walking. Oscar gets real excited and starts screaming at him, "How can you call that walking, you never saw that move before!"[7]

In the latter part of his career the versatile Robertson was traded to the Milwaukee Bucks. He was soon nicknamed "Mr. Outside" and along with "Mr. Inside," Lew Alcindor, led the Bucks to the championship. Having finally achieved his long-time goal, Robertson retired in 1974.

In 1969 Wes Unseld, a bull of a man from the University of Louisville, joined the Baltimore Bullet franchise as a rookie. Before acquiring Unseld, Baltimore finished last in the division. In his first season with the Bullets he was selected Rookie of the Year, an all-star, and league MVP, and led the Bullets to the play-offs. Originally a forward, the six-foot, eight-inch Unseld was eventually moved to center, where he found a home. Although small in height for the position, he more than made up for it with his overwhelming strength and speed. "I'm referred to as the guy who does the dirty work that each team has to have somebody to do," Unseld said. "I rebound, take the ball out of bounds, set picks—that's it. I'm not too involved in the offense. . . . As for me, I don't care what I'm outstanding as. They tell me what they want to do, and I try to do it."[8]

Big men continued to score well in the selection of the Podoloff Cup, as the following year, in 1970, another center won the award. His name was Willis Reed, and he played for the New York Knickerbockers. A second-round draft pick out of Grambling College, Reed had been a forward before he was moved to center. A quick, intelligent, and aggressive player, Reed led the Knicks to championships in 1969–70 and 1972–73. In 1970, when he

When the New York Knicks were on top of the basketball world it was their big center, Willis Reed, who kept coming up with the big plays and the emotional lifts. (NY Knick photo)

was chosen as the league MVP, the Knicks were matched up against the Los Angeles Lakers in the finals. Reed was suffering from a hip injury at the time, and it was doubtful that he would be able to play in the final game. That contest, played in Madison Square Garden in New York, will go down in history as a classic. Reed limped out onto the court for warm-ups, and the chances of his playing didn't look good. As the fans could tell, he was not at full strength, and without their big center the Knicks would be in trouble. When the game began, Reed was not in the starting lineup, and the tension grew. Suddenly, he got up from the bench and hobbled over to the scorers' table. He was about to go into the game. The partisan crowd went wild. He was their hero; they loved him and knew that he was going to save their team. It was like a New Year's celebration. Limping up and down the court, he immediately made his presence felt. The Knicks started to control the contest and when

Reed sank a couple of jump shots, pandemonium reigned. It was still early in the game, but the outcome had already been decided: New York was champion of the NBA, and Willis Reed was champion of the world. "When I quit playing ball," he said. "I want people to look back and say, not that I was great, but that I gave 100 percent."[9]

"The greatest all-around player of all time": that's how many basketball experts refer to Kareem-Abdul Jabbar, the six-time winner of the Podoloff Cup. He won it in 1971, 1972, 1974, 1976, 1977, and 1980, and may add to the collection in the future. known as Lew Alcindor before he took the Muslim name in 1971, he dominated the sport from his beginnings at Power Memorial High School in New York, through his collegiate days at the University of California at Los Angeles (UCLA), and on into his professional career with the Milwaukee Bucks and the Los Angeles Lakers. "They can talk theory all they want, but if [he] comes to play, we

KAREEM ABDUL-JABBAR
Center   7'2"

MILWAUKEE BUCKS

Considered by many to be the greatest player in the history of the game, Kareem-Abdul Jabbar has won a record six Podoloff Cups. (Milwaukee Buck photo)

can just go home," said Bob Cousy, then coach of the Cincinnati Royals. "He just toyed with us. Let's face it: he scores against us whenever he feels like it. There's no way we can beat these guys when he's playing."[10]

Jabbar was drafted by the Bucks, whom he led to the NBA Championship in just his second year. Combining the offensive prowess of a Chamberlain and the defensive intimidation of a Russell, he was a force to be reckoned with. A quiet, introspective man off the court, Jabbar is often a fierce competitor. In a 1977 play-off series against the Golden State Warriors he scored forty or more points in four of the seven games. In 1980 he suffered a severely injured ankle in the fifth game of the championship series against the Philadelphia '76ers. He continued to play despite the injury, and the Lakers won the contest and the NBA crown. Defenses have often resorted to anything to try to stop him.

As a result, he has resorted to wearing protective glasses to save his eyes. Maurice Lucas of the Portland Trailblazers summed it up best after the Blazers beat the Lakers in the Western Conference Finals in 1977: "Jabbar would never give up. He's the most respected player in the league because he never bows his head. Such great inner strength! You may beat his team, but you never beat him."[11]

In 1973 the Celtics came up with another outstanding center to lead the team. This time, it was Dave Cowens of Florida State University. Cowens was a scrappy, aggressive player, whom the Celts knew they wanted right from the start. "He was so good in one game against Dayton, I kept hoping he'd make a mistake because there were scouts all over the place that night, and I figured if they saw the same potential in Cowens that I did, I was dead,"[12] Red Auerbach said. Like so many before him, Cowens was originally drafted to play forward but was eventually moved to center because of his skill at the position.

Known to have practiced long hours, Cowens of-

95

DAVE COWENS

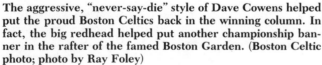

The aggressive, "never-say-die" style of Dave Cowens helped put the proud Boston Celtics back in the winning column. In fact, the big redhead helped put another championship banner in the rafter of the famed Boston Garden. (Boston Celtic photo; photo by Ray Foley)

ten shot until his arms ached. He was largely responsible for putting the Celtics back on top after the departure of Russell. A small man for his position, he made up for it with his intensely aggressive play. For his great performance during the 1973 season he was awarded the Podoloff Cup. He followed that up by leading the Celtics to the NBA Championship in 1974 and 1976. When a broken foot sidelined Cowens during the 1975 campaign, the Celtics record reflected it.

In a shocking move in 1976 Cowens announced that he was tired of basketball and that he was leaving the Celtics. He said that he needed a leave of absence, and that's exactly what he took. The following season Boston was back in the play-offs, mainly because Cowens was back in uniform. His

enthusiasm, talent, and all-around hustle returned to Boston Garden. "Every player should really be able to play all parts of the game," Cowens said. "I think that some players limit themselves. You can't be effective if you do."[13]

Most of the time defensive players are the ones who complain about not being noticed and not receiving enough publicity. But in 1975 the cup was won by a man who for years had been claiming that his achievements were going unrecognized. This was Bob McAdoo of the Buffalo Braves. He led the league in scoring three straight years and was voted Rookie of the Year in 1972. "I do not think anyone pays much attention to what I'm doing. About the only way I'll get people to notice me is for us to win the NBA Championship."[14] An outspoken player, he felt that his biggest disadvantage was playing for a team that wasn't a contender. At six-feet ten-inches, he was lanky, but he had a great shooting touch, even if his style was considered unorthodox. "You've got one of the ugliest shots I've ever seen," all-pro guard Jerry West once told him at a basketball camp. "I don't know how the ball goes in. But don't change it because the ball goes in."[15]

In 1974 he could hold it no longer. "I'm not going to lie about it. I think I should win the Most Valuable Player Award this season. I think I'm giving the best players as much trouble as they're giving me. I think I can go to the hoop as well as anyone."[16] Although he was probably right, he still didn't get his wish. It wasn't until the following year that he finally received the recognition that he felt was due. Having averaged over thirty-four points and fourteen rebounds a game that season, McAdoo finally won the Podoloff Cup.

In 1978 another big center arrived from the campus of UCLA. Like Jabbar before him he could run, pass, shoot, rebound, and dominate the league. "This is a basketball player, the essence of what the game is all about,"[17] said former Celtic great John Havlicek. His name was Bill Walton, and the talent of this six-foot eleven-inch redhead was abundant.

Born in La Mesa, California, Walton went to UCLA and became another product of Coach John Wooden's school of basketball superstars. "He's as fine a team player as you'll ever see,"[18] said Wooden. Known for his hustle and unselfish play, Walton was often sidelined with nagging injuries. He underwent a knee operation after his senior year in college, had bone spurs that caused him to miss a few games with the team that drafted him— the Portland Trailblazers—and in the 1975–76 season suffered a broken toe and a fractured wrist, which caused him to miss thirty-one games.

A controversial man both on and off the court,

Walton tried to keep the sport of basketball in its proper perspective. "My responsibility to myself and to my teammates is to win every game I possibly can. And I do whatever is required of me to accomplish that goal. Playing ball is a full-time job. You have to work around the clock and learn to become a physical fitness person because it's your body and your mind that are earning money for you. They're getting the job done. I have a responsibility to myself to be as healthy as possible, mentally, spiritually, and physically. I play a lot of basketball, lift weights, ride a bicycle, eat the proper foods, get the proper rest, and meditate."[19]

Despite Walton's well-balanced attitude injuries continued to dominate his professional career. In 1979 he signed with the expansion San Diego Clippers a multi-million dollar contract, and the town welcomed back their boyhood hero. The jubilation, however, was short-lived as Walton was struck down again with an ankle injury. As Walton made only a few appearances on the court, his team finished near the bottom of the division. When Walton is healthy, he can be awesome. Against Philadelphia in the 1977 finals, he averaged over twenty points and twenty rebounds per game, as Portland came back from a two-game deficit to win the series, 4–2. That year Walton was selected as league MVP.

Often referred to as "the Chairman of the Boards," the 1979 winner of the Podoloff Cup was exactly that. When six-foot, eleven-inch Moses Malone was in the area, nobody got a rebound. And that means *nobody*. Drafted directly into the pros out of Petersburg High in Virginia, Malone virtually dominated the backboards. They were his territory, his homestead, and strangers weren't welcome. Especially strangers with a differently colored uniform. Wrote one sports authority: "Malone is . . . the undisputed offensive rebound leader. No single player has ever meant so much to his team as a rebounder. No player has ever pulled down a higher rate of rebounds. It would seem that this year [1979] he has been the single most effective rebounder ever to play the game."[20] Malone was also a potent scorer, averaging over twenty-three points a game for the Houston Rockets. Like many before him, he was a giant among giants. In its twenty-seven year history the trophy has been awarded to a center twenty-two times. Moses kept the streak alive in 1982 when he won the trophy again.

Professional basketball has seen many spectacular players in its long history. But it is difficult to find one quite like Julius Erving, who has stunned crowds with unbelievable physical acrobatics on the hard court. Known as "Dr. J." to basketball enthusiasts, the sharpshooting forward for the Philadelphia '76'ers has helped make his team one of the most successful playoff contenders in years. Averaging 24.6 points per game, Erving led the Sixers into the playoffs as favorites to take it all. In 1980 they made it to the finals only to be stopped by the Los Angeles Lakers and their sensational rookie Magic Johnson. Their frustration continued the next year as the rejuvenated Boston Celtics knocked out Dr. J. and Philadelphia in the Eastern Conference finals. Erving's efforts, however, earned him the respect and admiration of players and fans alike—and the 1981 Podoloff Cup.

The Podoloff Cup is a very symbolic award. It is given every year to the player deemed most valuable to his team. But it is much more than that. It is a symbol of the sport itself. The athletes who have won the cup have shaped and reshaped the game. Whether it's on an around-the-back-pass by Bob Cousy, a blocked shot by Bill Russell, a slam-dunk by Wilt Chamberlain, a flashy drive by Oscar Robertson, or a crashing rebound by Moses Malone, the result is the same—two points for the sport of basketball. From its humble beginnings with a peach basket and a soccer ball, basketball has grown into one of the three major sports in a sports-crazy nation. And the winners of the Podoloff Cup have been largely responsible.

Podoloff Cup Winners

1956	Bob Pettit, St. Louis
1957	Bob Cousy, Boston
1958	Bill Russell, Boston
1959	Bob Pettit, St. Louis
1960	Wilt Chamberlain, Philadelphia
1961	Bill Russell, Boston
1962	Bill Russell, Boston
1963	Bill Russell, Boston
1964	Oscar Robertson, Cincinnati
1965	Bill Russell, Boston
1966	Wilt Chamberlain, Philadelphia
1967	Wilt Chamberlain, Philadelphia
1968	Wilt Chamberlain, Philadelphia
1969	Wes Unseld, Baltimore
1970	Willis Reed, New York
1971	Lew Alcindor, Milwaukee
1972	Kareem-Abdul Jabbar, Milwaukee
1973	Dave Cowens, Boston
1974	Kareem-Abdul Jabbar, Milwaukee
1975	Bob McAddo, Buffalo
1976	Kareem-Abdul Jabbar, Los Angeles
1977	Kareem-Abdul Jabbar, Los Angeles
1978	Bill Walton, Portland
1979	Moses Malone, Houston
1980	Kareem-Abdul Jabbar, Los Angeles
1981	Julius Erving, Philadelphia
1982	Moses Malone, Houston
1983	Moses Malone, Philadelphia

9
The World Cup

Probably the only sport that can truly claim a world championship is soccer. Every four years over a hundred countries participate in what has become a legend in the world of sports—the World Cup.

For some, the World Cup has become a tradition. The team from Brazil, for example, has shown its athletic prowess by winning three championships. For others, it has been a forum for political exhibitionism. In the 1934 games Italy's Benito Mussolini used the competition as a means of flaunting to the world his fascist policies. For still others, the cup has been a road to international recognition. Superstars such as Pélé of Brazil, Franz Beckenbauer of West Germany, and Johann Cruyff of the Netherlands have used their team success to further their individual careers.

But to no one, is it merely a game. To the followers of soccer it is more than a pastime; it is a lifestyle. According to estimates, over twenty million people play organized soccer. The governing body of the game, the Federation Internationale de Football Association (FIFA), has 142 nations on its membership roles.

Even more amazing than the number of athletes who play soccer, is the even greater number of people who are fans of the sport. The 1974 World Cup was televised to over 750 million viewers throughout the globe. And at the 1950 cup final, held in Rio de Janeiro, a world record attendance mark was set when 199,850 fans showed up for the championship game between Brazil and Uruguay.

To the followers of the sport of "football" (as it is known everywhere except in the United States), what is important is not how the game is played but whether it is won or lost. In the 1978 finals in Argentina, muggings, beatings, and riots reportedly followed the outcome of some of the games. In England the violence reached such great proportions that severe security measures had to be taken at many of the Saturday contests.

Soccer is a game of the masses. It is the sport of the common people. It requires no special equipment and no elite club memberships. All that is required is a ball and some open space. In fact most of the early balls were nothing more than inflated animal bladders.

Soccer had its origin in China two hundred years before Christ. Called *isu chu* ("kick ball"), this ancient Chinese game was part of military training, and the severed head of an enemy warrior was used as the ball. The Japanese and Romans also developed early versions of the sport.

It wasn't until the sixteenth century that soccer really began to catch on. In Renaissance Florence each team had twenty-seven participants who, oddly enough, all donned formal attire when they played. In England the game was known as "mob football," and it was frequently banned by law.

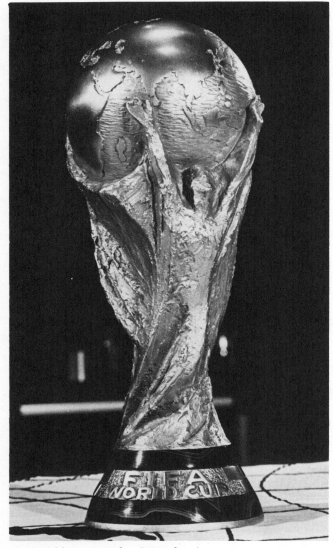

The World Cup Trophy. (UPI photo)

Each Shrove Tuesday the townspeople of Derbyshire competed in what became a brutally violent game. The teams often numbered in the hundreds, and the game ended when one side forced the ball through the other's goal. Through the Act of 1314, King Edward II decided that anyone caught playing football in London would go to prison. This attitude toward the sport continued into modern times, as the English Puritans considered football "a bloodie and murthering practice rather than a felowly sport or pastime."[1]

In 1823 William Webb Ellis inadvertently picked up the ball and began to run with it. The result—rugby was born. The Irish caught onto the spirit of the game, and in the sixteenth century they developed their own version. It was even rougher than mob football. The teams, representing towns, numbered in the hundreds. The fields were miles long, and the squads battled and battered each other until the ball reached the gates of the opposing team's town.

The game eventually was refined, and in 1863 it took a giant step forward. On 26 October eleven representatives of London clubs met at Freemasons' Tavern and founded the Football Association. Formal rules were set up. Numerous other leagues and associations were soon formed. In 1904 the idea of a world championship took shape. On 21 May four Frenchmen got together in Paris and decided to formulate a worldwide organization for soccer. They were Robert Guerin, a lawyer, C. A. W. Hurschman, a banker, Henri Delaunay, a printer, and Jules Rimet, a publisher. This was the beginning of FIFA. It wasn't until twenty-six years later, in 1930, however, that the first World Cup competition was actually held.

Uruguay, a nation with a proud soccer tradition, was chosen as the site of the first world championship game. To show its dedication to the new tournament, the host country built the 100,000-seat Centenary Stadium in Montevideo in just eight short months. It also offered to pay all expenses of the visiting teams.

Four European teams—Belgium, France, Romania, and Yugoslavia—decided to compete. They were joined by Argentina, Chile, Mexico, Brazil, Bolivia, Peru, Paraguay, and the United States. For their efforts in coming the long distance, the European squads received a grand reception when they arrived in Uruguay. The hospitality was not extended, however, when the teams ventured onto the playing field.

In the tourney's opening game, France met Mexico. A precedent was set for the brutal style of play as the French goalie was kicked in the jaw and knocked unconscious. Despite this mishap the French won, 4–1.

In the next round France came up against Argentina, a finalist against Uruguay in the 1928 Olympic Games. After the two squads battled to a scoreless tie, an unfortunate thing happened. With nine minutes left in the game, Argentina was given a free kick. The referee raised his hand to start play. The French, expecting a whistle, waited and watched as their opponents kicked the ball, untouched, into their net. The score: Argentina 1, France 0. France bounced back and minutes later forward Marcel Langiller found himself in a one-on-one situation with the Argentine goalie. Just as he was about to give it his best shot, the referee blew his whistle ending the game. Argentina joy-

Franz Beckenbauer is considered one of West Germany's greatest soccer players ever. In 1974 the Germans beat a tough squad from the Netherlands, 2–1, to win the World Cup. (UPI photo)

fully raced off the field while the French angrily raced after the referee, claiming that there were still six minutes left in the contest. Embarassed, the official checked his watch, realized his error, and resumed the game. But the damage had been done: the French had lost that elusive ally, momentum. Argentina held on for the last few minutes and came away with a most unusual victory.

Identical 3–0 wins over Belgium and Paraguay put the United States in the semifinal game against Argentina. In that game Argentina used physical tactics and sidelined numerous American players with injuries. The violence continued until the U.S. trainer could take it no longer. He raced onto the field in pursuit of the official. When he caught up to him, he threw his medical bag onto the ground in disgust. A bottle of chloroform in the case broke, and the fumes engulfed the two. Weak-kneed, the trainer was assisted to the sidelines.

Overmatched, the Americans went down to defeat, 6–1, and Argentina advanced to the championship against host Uruguay. Uruguay made it to the

finals through an equally impressive 6–1 victory over Yugoslavia.

Uruguay and Argentina were bitter rivals, and the stage was set for their championship encounter. Thousands of fans poured into the city for the final. Soldiers with bayonets encircled the stadium. At halftime Argentina led, 2–1. In the second half, however, the home team staged a remarkable comeback with three goals to secure the game and the first World Cup.

The 1934 competition was held in Italy during the reign of Benito Mussolini. According to an Italian press release, "The ultimate purpose of the tournament was to show that Fascist sport partakes of great quality all stemming from one unique inspiration, the Duce."[2] With thirty-two competing nations the tourney was much larger and longer than the previous one. The Italian team, bent on making a good display, lured four of Argentina's best players onto their squad. Born during Fascist rule, they claimed that anyone of Italian ancestry was an Italian. Enraged, Argentina sent only a token squad to the games. The tourney began, and the field was slowly but surely whittled down. In the semifinals, Italy overcame a stubborn Austrian squad, 1–0, and Czechoslovakia defeated Germany, 3–1. In the championship game the Czechs scored first. But Italy, sparked by a tremendous crowd, countered with a goal of its own. The game ended in a tie and was sent into overtime. The contest continued to go back and forth, but finally, the inspired Italians managed to push through a score and win the championship.

The threat of world war in 1938 also proved to be a threat to the World Cup. Of the thirty-six nations that agreed to participate, only fifteen actually entered. Despite the political tensions the games were held in France, and the tradition of brutal play continued. In a second-round contest between Czechoslovakia and Brazil, the violence became so dominant that only seventeen of the twenty-two starting players finished. The game ended in a 1–1 tie and was replayed the next day. In that rematch the Czechs fielded only six players, and the Brazilians, nine. The game was much less violent, and Brazil went on to win, 2–1.

Italy was Brazil's semifinal foe. Still recovering, the Brazilians benched two stars, Tim and Leonidas, and went on to lose, 2–1. Reportedly, they did not use their two stars in this match because they were saving them for the finals!

In the finals, Italy, with its wide-open offensive style, faced the more conservative team from Hungary. For the second straight time Italy rose to the occasion and outplayed their opponent, 2–1.

Many World Cup soccer stars, such as Johann Cruyff of the Netherlands, have gone on to great professional careers. (UPI photo)

World War II caused the World Cup championship to be discontinued. When they invaded Rome, the Nazis launched an all-out search for the trophy. Fortunately, the Italians had wisely hidden the prize in a bank vault in Switzerland.

The games finally resumed in 1950 in Brazil. Only thirteen nations competed, mainly because of political problems with iron curtain countries. The biggest upset in the history of Cup competition occurred when the upstart team from the United States defeated one of soccer's powerhouses, England, by a 2–1 score. Back in England soccer fans went into a state of shock. But the U.S. team eventually lost its momentum and was knocked off by Chile, 5–2.

For the third time in four World Cup championships the host nation made it to the finals. This time it was Brazil, and its opponent was the always formidable squad from Uruguay. Over two hundred thousand people packed the stadium for the final, and the police were called in to control the mobs. Brazil scored first, early in the second half, and the crowd went crazy. But Uruguay, refusing to fold, came back to win, 2–1, and destroy Brazil's dream. Back in Uruguay the celebration was enormous. Three people died of heart attacks while listening

to the match on the radio, and five more died during wild postgame parties in the streets.

The 1954 cup competition in Switzerland at times more closely resembled a boxing match than soccer. In a quarter final game between Hungary and Brazil, points could have been awarded for blows rather than goals. When Hungary's Nandor Hidegkuti scored, his pants were literally ripped off by angry Brazilian defenders. Two players were ejected for exchanging blows on the field. But the game continued, and so did the brawling. The whistle finally blew, ending the contest. Undaunted, both teams headed to their locker rooms, where they proceeded to finish the fight that they started on the field. Police intervened and broke it up. Hungary had won the match, 4–2, and advanced to the next round.

Considered to have the best team in the world at the time, the Hungarians boxed their way into the finals against a scrappy team from West Germany. Jumping out to a 2–0 lead, they seemed to be heading for an easy victory. Then the weather changed, and so did the fortunes of the West Germans. As the rain began to come down, so did the Hungarian defense, and the Germans poured through them for three goals and their first World Cup. Thousands rioted in the streets of Budapest in disbelief. Hungary was supposedly the best team in the world, but they had been knocked out in the final round.

The 1958 cup championship in Sweden turned out to be a show of dominance by the young Brazilian team. The trademark of the World Cup, violent play, continued, but the Brazilians were able to transcend it with some fancy footwork. Let by Garrincha and seventeen-year-old superstar Pélé, they went on to defeat Sweden, 5–2. They did a repeat performance in the 1962 games in Chile, beating Czechoslovakia, 3–1. They were a strong young team with a bright future.

The soccer world was in awe as the national teams prepared for the 1966 competition in England. With two straight championships behind it, Brazil would be tough to beat. Because of a defensive-minded strategy and an injury to Pélé, however, the Brazilians were eliminated early. Consecutive 3–1 defeats to Hungary and Portugal, along with some brutal play, knocked Pélé and his teammates out of the tourney.

England played flawless defense throughout the competition. Allowing only one goal in five contests, they found themselves matched up against the tough West Germans in the finals. Taking place in Wembley Stadium before one hundred thousand English enthusiasts, the confrontation proved to be one of the most exciting in cup history. With only minutes left in the contest the home team came from behind to take a 2–1 lead. Then, with just thirty seconds remaining, the West Germans broke through for a goal to send the match into overtime. But the English refused to fold, and behind Geoff Hurst's second and third goals of the afternoon, they broke the contest open, 4–2, and won their first World Cup.

The 1970 World Cup finals in Mexico pitted a couple of two-time winners, Italy and Brazil. Pregame favorites, the South Americans played like the champions that they were, winning, 4–1. It was truly a milestone—three World Cup titles.

In 1974 West Germany hosted the competition. As the financial rewards for winning had grown, so had the intensity of the competition. Teams were not there to compete; they were there to win. President Mobutu Sese Seko of Zaire gave his national team instructions as they prepared to depart—"Win—or die!"[3] He also gave them each a Volkswagen, a witch doctor, and a supply of mon-

key meat to last throughout the tournament. Unfortunately, they were shut out three straight times, and when they returned home, they were stripped of their automobiles.

At the end of the twenty-four-day tourney, only West Germany and the Netherlands remained in the competition. Playing "total football," the two teams put on a tremendous performance in the finals. But it was the defense of the host team that prevailed as it held on for a hard-fought 2–1 victory. Stopping the relentless Dutch attack time and time again, Goalie Sepp Maier turned in an outstanding performance for the winners.

In 1978, for the seventh time in eleven tournaments, the home team—in this case, Argentina—made it to the finals. It came away with an inspiring 3–1 victory over a talented squad from the Netherlands. Brazil, which won only four games and tied three, placed third in the competition.

After their team's victory the people of Argentina went into a state of ecstasy. The celebration con-

The greatest soccer player in the world—Pélé of Brazil. (UPI photo)

103

sisted of one party after another, one song after another, one toast after another. For the next four years, until the next World Cup games in Spain in 1982, the people of Argentina knew that they would sit on top of the world. Rightly so, for winning the World Cup is no small achievement. After years of playoffs and qualifying, traveling and practicing, a select few finally gets to compete for the cup.

To the South Americans, winning the World Cup is something like being given sainthood. To the English, it's like being granted knighthood. But to the people of America, it's like something out of Robin Hood. It's a fantasy they can't quite grasp. Soccer in the United States is still in its infancy, and Americans have trouble comprehending the fever that has engulfed the soccer world.

Brazil and Italy may not win many wars or political battles, but they have accomplished something that no other country can boast—three World Cups. Without a doubt, soccer is the world's most popular sport. There are numerous championships, such as the FA Cup and the European Cup, for which national teams compete. But there is only one World Cup. There is only room for one at the top. There is only one tournament that can make the world stop to watch it. Yes, there is only one World Cup.

World Cup Results

1930	(Uruguay) Uruguay 4, Argentina 2
1934	(Italy) Italy 2, Czechoslovakia 1
1938	(France) Italy 4, Hungary 2
1950	(Brazil) Uruguay 2, Brazil 1
1954	(Switzerland) West Germany 3, Hungary 2
1958	(Sweden) Brazil 5, Sweden 2
1962	(Chile) Brazil 3, Czechoslovakia 1
1966	(England) England 4, West Germany 2
1970	(Mexico) Brazil 4, Italy 1
1974	(West Germany) West Germany 2, Netherlands 1
1978	(Argentina) Argentina 3, Netherlands 1
1982	(Spain) Italy 3, West Germany 1

10
The America's Cup

If ever an award was appropriately named, it was the America's Cup. Since its inception in 1851, the United States has won the trophy every time, with one exception. With *Australia II*'s shocking 4–3 upset of *Liberty* in 1983, one of the longest winning streaks in sports history was broken. Despite the loss, it has been a very one-sided competition.

Every three years a challenger makes a new bid to take the cup away from the New York Yacht Club, and until 1983 every challenger had failed. It was a tradition of which American yachtsmen were proud and confident. Then along came Alan Bond of Australia with his skipper John Bertrand, and the Americans, under Dennis Conner, were defeated. A 132-year reign was over. "The story goes that on one occasion, when Emil ("Bus") Mosbacher, the great American helmsman, stood gazing at the America's Cup in its special place at the New York Yacht Club, he turned to the commodore and asked, 'What do you think we will put in its place if we lose?' The answer was short and to the point: 'The skull of the guy who lost it.' "[1]

How is it that a sport, such as yachting, could be so thoroughly dominated by a single nation? The answer, it appears, goes back to the history of the sport itself.

In the 1850s, American clipper ships reigned as the world's best commerce vessels, but it was England that produced superior yachts and was considered the leader in the sport. In 1851, however, an American yacht sailed over to England and challenged seventeen local boats to a race. The course was charted around the Isle of Wight, and the American ship won handily. The winning yacht, appropriately named *America*, was presented with a trophy that was eventually named after it.

The cup was brought back to the New York Yacht Club and placed on display. Yachtsmen throughout the nation were proud, for they had beaten the English at their own game. No plans had been made to set up an annual competition, but the thought was soon tossed about within the hierarchy of the sport. The idea of setting up an international competition to promote the sport, as well as good will among nations, soon became a reality. After hard work and many false starts it became an overwhelming success. Millions of dollars have been spent by yachtsmen in order to win the coveted trophy, originally known as the Hundred Guineas Cup (that's what it cost).

When the sport began, the English had many advantages over the Americans. In England there were many yachts—typically owned by the rich, the nobility, and the gentry. It was an established

In 1851 the *America* traveled to the Isle of Wight and defeated England's highly regarded sailing ships in what was the first running of the America's Cup competition. (UPI photo)

sport, and there were already many clubs in existence. The English were unquestionably the masters of the seas. On the other hand, in the United States there were relatively few yachts, and most of them were owned for pleasure, not for competition. Around 1840 it became more of a sport and clubs began to spring up. They appeared in New York, Boston, Charleston, New Orleans, and a few other cities along the East Coast. Many of these clubs eventually folded, but the big one, the New York Yacht Club, survived. Its first commodore, Colonel John Stevens, turned the one-room clubhouse on the Hudson into the sport's hotspot of the country. It had a fairly good-sized fleet of ships by 1850. The New York Yacht Club's rival, the famous Royal Yacht Squadron, had been sailing yachts as far back as 1815. But the 35-year difference in development was not enough to dampen the enthusiasm of the crew of *America* as they

headed out on their famous voyage.

Modeled after some pilot schooners, *America* was built by members of the New York Yacht Club. Constructed primarily to be sent abroad, the ship was originally contracted to be finished by 1 April 1851. Invitations were soon received from the commodore of the Royal Yacht Squadron, the earl of Wilton, to bring the yacht over for some races. The construction of *America* was supervised by George Steers, with considerable help from Commodore Stevens. The two soon became painfully aware that the yacht would not be ready on time. They accepted the invitation from the English, but it wasn't until 18 June that the craft was delivered.

After purchasing *America*, Commodore Stevens, and six business associates entered it in some local races. After chalking up a few impressive victories, *America* headed for England with thirteen men aboard and with the nation's hopes nestled firmly in its sails. The New York owners believed that such a venture would also be financially profitable, as betting on yacht races was common.

America docked in France for three weeks for repairs and refitting. On 31 July the yacht sailed for England and the Isle of Wight. It anchored about six miles off the island. The next morning, when the fog was blown away, an English cutter named *Laverock* stood proudly in the water, waiting anxiously to bait the foreigner into a race. Though tempted to refuse the challenge to avoid exposing his boat's true speed, Commodore Stevens decided to take on *Laverock*. The two boats headed off toward the Isle, and *America* won by a comfortable margin. The race revealed the yacht's superiority to the English. It also killed off any bets the Americans had been hoping to make.

Though impressed with *America*'s performance, the English were not as awed with its appearance. Vastly different from the English boats, she was often criticized for her heavy masts, for her lack of a fore-topmast, and for her long, sharp bow.

For many weeks Commodore Stevens went about trying to set up races with the English, but there were no takers. He tried anything and everything. The refusal of the English yachtsmen to take up the challenge resulted in heavy criticism from the local people and press. Finally, the Royal Yacht Squadron notified Stevens that *America* would be welcome to participate in a regatta around the Isle of Wight on 22 August. To the winner the club would present a trophy, costing 100 guineas.

As the course was in local waters, which only the English yachtsmen knew, the Americans were at a disadvantage. Nevertheless, Stevens accepted the invitation and entered *America* into the race. Matched against seventeen of the best schooners and cutters in existence, the new American yacht faced a true test.

The race began at 10 A.M.. Starting out in last place, *America* had a less than auspicious opening. The yacht, however, soon showed her speed, as she passed opponents left and right. She eventually moved into first place. When she crossed the finish line at 8:37 that evening, she was a full eighteen minutes ahead of her closest challenger, *Aurora*. The Americans had done it! They had proven their point to the English and to the rest of the world. The cup was then presented to Commodore Stevens by the Royal Yacht Squadron, and history's precedent was set. The name was then changed from the Hundred Guineas Cup to the America's Cup, and it became the permanent property of the winning yacht.

About a week after her victory *America* sailed a challenge race over twenty miles against *Titania*. She won again, this time by a whopping fifty-two minutes. After this victory the syndicate that owned *America* decided to sell her, rather than sail the ship all the way back to the United States. From this point on, the history of *America* is as diverse, and at times tragic, as the people who have owned her.

Lord John de Blaquiere bought the yacht for $25,000 and, as a true Englishman, began making modifications to fit England's sailing philosophy. Among these was a shortening of the masts. In 1852 he raced *America* and had only moderate success. Lord Blaquiere then sailed in the Mediterranean for awhile, and in 1853 he sold the boat to Lord Templeton. Lord Templeton used her for a year. The yacht was then found washed up in the mud at Cowes on the Isle of Wight, where she remained until 1859. *America* was bought again, and, in wretched shape, was rebuilt to her original form. Another English yachtsman then purchased her, changed her name to *Camilla*, and took her to the West Indies. He raced her on and off and then sold her to a Savannah man, who turned her into a gunboat for the South during the Civil War. Now known as *Memphis*, she was eventually chased up the St. John's River in Florida, where she was run aground and deserted. The United States government eventually confiscated the ship, repaired her, and put her to use in its own fleet under her original name. She served with the U.S. fleet until 1864, when she was sent to the U.S. Naval Academy as a training ship.

In 1870, nineteen years after the original race in England, a yacht called *Cambria* was sent to challenge for the cup. Despite her trials and tribulations, *America* was chosen as one of the representatives of the cup. She proved up to the task, as she finished ahead of her opponent, restored her dignity, and helped keep the cup in the States. The winner of the race was a yacht named *Magic*, but *America* made an important contribution. Following the race the United States government sold *America* to General Benjamin Butler of Massachusetts. Her glory days were over, but she had shown the world the efficiency of her design. General Butler used her often but in 1916, after she had spent many years docked in Boston Harbor, he sold her to C. H. W. Foster of the Eastern Yacht Club. Five years later, he, in turn, sold her to some local yachtsmen, who presented her back to the United States Naval Academy. The government had no money appropriated to maintain her, and sadly, in 1945, she was dismantled. Her parts were distributed as souvenirs.

Several years after winning the first America's Cup, the original owners of *America* presented the trophy to the New York Yacht Club. They wanted the cup to be used for an international yachting competition as an instrument of good will. In a letter to the yacht club, they wrote: "It is to be distinctly understood that the Cup is to be the property of the Club, and not of the members thereof, or the owners of the vessels winning it in a match, and that the condition of keeping it open to be sailed for by yacht clubs of all foreign countries . . . thus making it perpetually a Challenge Cup for friendly competition between foreign countries."[2]

Upon receiving the letter, the New York Yacht Club sent notice to clubs all over the world to inform them of the competition. It was eleven years before the first challenge was returned. The eventual result, however, has been some of the most outstanding yacht races the world has ever seen.

After a lull during the Civil War, interest in yachting revived. Recognizing American ships as the best on the seas, the English set out to improve their yachts. In 1868 James Ashbury, an Englishman who owned *Cambria*, challenged the New York Yacht Club to a race for the cup. The two parties took over a year to work out the exact details of the race. The parties came to terms after *Cambria* defeated one of America's best, *Dauntless*, in a transAtlantic race.

The race was run on 8 August 1870 on the club's home course on New York Bay. The English yacht was pitted against the whole club fleet. Among the entries was the old *America*, placed in the race by the naval academy because of strong public sentiment. It was a small schooner named *Magic*, however, that stole the show and went on to win the race. Ashbury's *Cambria* finished in tenth place, some twenty-seven minutes behind *Magic*. *America*, thought to be a dead ship, finished an impressive fourth. Following the cup competition, *Cambria* competed in several races and lost most of them. Ashbury eventually took her back to England and sold her. American superiority on the seas had been maintained.

Despite his failures in the United States, Ashbury, a true yachtsman, refused to give up. Building a new schooner, *Livonia*, he was ready to again challenge for the cup the following year. He tried to set up another match with the New York Yacht Club. Many details had to be worked out. Ashbury protested against the idea of competing against the club's whole fleet and also argued about the site of the race, the number of races to be run, and the type of boat the Americans could use. Finally, after many long hours of negotiation, the two parties agreed to sail a series of seven races, alternating between two of the yacht club's courses. The first yacht to win four races was to win the cup. *Livonia* was to represent the Royal Harwich Yacht club.

The four boats selected by the New York Yacht Club to defend the cup were *Palmer*, *Columbia*, *Sappho*, and *Dauntless*. Although there were four representatives, only one was allowed to sail in each race. The first three races pitted *Columbia* against her English counterpart. The opening duel was won by the *Columbia*. It was an impressive victory, as she crossed the finish line a full twenty-five minutes ahead of *Livonia*. The next two races were split. Though *Columbia* won the second, Ashbury protested the way the American ship rounded the outer mark. Stating that no specific directions were given on this score, the yacht club denied the protest. In the third race, *Livonia* won, and *Columbia* suffered extensive damage.

Leading 2–1, the Americans decided that *Sappho* would carry the burden of defending the trophy. And that she did well, as she swept the next two races and decided the competition. Decided it, that is, for everyone but Ashbury. Still irate over the *Columbia* turn in the second race, he filed another protest. This one, too, was eventually rejected. Ashbury then had a private match with *Dauntless* but lost. To demonstrate his protest he continued to show up at the starting line of the cup races. Announcing that the races had already been decided the New York Yacht Club refused to send out a competitor. Ashbury, on the other hand, claimed that the Americans had forfeited, and he demanded the cup. The New York Yacht Club refused his requests, and he returned to his homeland in an uproar. Bad feelings between American and English yachting circles followed. In England the New York Yacht Club underwent some severe criticism, and it was many years before an English yachtsman was even to make an attempt for the cup.

The next challenger came five years later, in 1876, from the Royal Canadian Yacht Club in Toronto. The yacht they put up as the challenger was *Countess of Dufferin*, owned by a syndicate run by the vice commodore of the club, Major Charles Gifford. The boat was built by Alexander Cuthbert, a Canadian designer with a reputation for fast vessels. Once again, the regulations for the race were questioned by the challengers, and certain compromises were made. The race was to consist of a series of three runs, and the first boat to win two was to be declared the winner. Also, the Americans agreed to select one vessel to defend the cup, rather than having the option of picking from many in the same race.

The New York Yacht Club selected a schooner named *Madeline*, a highly successful racer, to defend the cup. A polished craft, *Madeline* took advantage whenever possible and swept *Countess of*

Dufferin in two straight races, winning by almost eleven minutes in the first and by over twenty-seven in the second. In the second race, *America* ran alongside the two yachts, although she was not officially entered in the competition. Finishing about eight minutes behind *Madeline*, she turned in an admirable performance. What was even more incredible was that she finished over nineteen minutes ahead of the Canadian challenger.

Not discouraged by the result, Cuthbert and the Canadians returned home, bent on the idea of making a better showing the next time. He set about constructing a craft that he was sure would be able to defeat the Americans. In 1881 his plan finally came to fruition. His creation, *Atlanta,* was unveiled and prepared for the race. As in 1876, however, Cuthbert suffered a lack of financial support, which proved to be very costly.

This time, the New York Yacht Club sent out an iron sloop named *Mischief*, which had gained the right to defend the cup by winning a series of highly competitive trial races. *Mischief* proved troublesome enough to Cuthbert and his amateur crew (which was all he could afford) as it swept past the Canadian yacht for two consecutive victories. Once again, the races were not close. *Mischief* won by over twenty-seven and thirty-eight minutes, respectively. It was a one-sided match, which pit a finely turned instrument against a crude, undermanned, underfunded, and outclassed opponent.

Determined not to let this happen again, the hierarchy of the New York Yacht Club decided to make some changes. They approached the only living member of the syndicate that originally won it. He was George Schuyler. Schuyler was asked to revise and update the original deed of gift. The new document stipulated that (1) the challenged club was to face its opponent with one and only one boat; (2) the challenger was to sail to the port where the race was to take place; (3) once a yacht was defeated in a cup race, it was not to reappear in competition for two years; and (4) a challenging club must have for its annual regatta "an ocean water course on the sea or an arm of the sea." These new rules all but eliminated competition from the Canadian clubs on the Great Lakes.

Once the rules were settled, invitations to a match were sent out once again all over the world. In 1885 the club accepted two challenges—one from Sir Richard Sutton, owner of the cutter *Genesta,* and one from British navy lieutenant W. Henn, owner of the cutter *Galatea*. *Genesta* was to race first and *Galatea*, the following year. *Puritan,* a centerboard sloop built especially for the race, was to defend the cup. The first run was set for 7 September; however, as the boats waited at the starting line that morning, a problem arose—there was no wind. The next day they lined up again, but just before they were to begin, *Puritan,* trying to cross *Genesta's* bows, ripped her mainsail through her opponent's bowsprit and tore it off.

An executive committee pulled up alongside the English boat and informed them that the race was theirs. *Puritan* was totally in the wrong, and *Genesta* needed only to sail the course alone under the seven-hour limit in order to secure the victory. Sutton, however, in a move of true sportsmanship, declined the offer. He had come there to race, he said, and as soon as he could repair his boat, the race could start over. On September 11 the two boats met at the starting line once again. This time it was a fair start. Due to flat winds, however, it took the yachts about six hours to make their way around the halfway mark. The committee members recalled the boats and decided to try again on the fourteenth. With good winds, the race was off. Over six hours later *Puritan* crossed the finish line, winning by over sixteen minutes. The second race was much closer. *Genesta* led most of the way, but *Puritan* overtook her in a strong finish and won by only one minute, and thirty-eight seconds. It was the closest finish yet in cup competition. The *Genesta-Puritan* race greatly aided relations between English and American yachting circles, and the *Galatea* race the following year strengthened those ties.

In 1886 Lt. William Henn's *Galatea* representing the Royal Northern Yacht Club of Scotland, sailed over. As was the custom, the New York Yacht Club held trial races to determine who would be the American representative. Entrants included *Atlantic*, *Puritan*, *Mayflower,* and *Priscilla*. Winning the first two races easily, *Mayflower* was chosen to defend the cup. And that she did, as she whipped past the English challenger and won by large margins in two straight races.

Soon after the *Galatea-Mayflower* race, the Royal Clyde Yacht Club of Scotland proposed a race. The challenge was issued on behalf of Mr. James Bell, who, as head of a syndicate, had constructed a yacht called *Thistle*. Its design had been kept highly secret, and in America reports spread like wildfire of her great success in English races. Realizing the heavy responsibility in front of them, the Americans constructed *Volunteer* for the sole purpose of taking on *Thistle*.

The secrecy surrounding *Thistle* caused such speculation that it drove a New York newspaper manager to send a diver down to observe her bottom and outline it. The resulting report and picture were, however, considered highly inaccurate, and the controversy continued. Because of her success abroad, it appeared that *Thistle* would present the greatest challenge thus far. But once again American design proved superior as *Thistle* went down in defeat in two straight races.

American domination in the sport of yachting had by this time become widely recognized. The pattern had been set, and it would continue through the history of the cup races. What *America, Magic, Columbia, Sappho, Madeleine, Mischief, Puritan, Mayflower,* and *Volunteer* started, was to be continued by a host of equally illustrious successors. Throughout the entire history of the America's Cup, the United States has lost only one, and the coveted trophy remained in the hands of its original owner for many years.

In 1893 another deed of gift was drawn up by Schuyler. He added a clause stating that a challenger must announce himself ten months in advance of a race and give the exact dimensions of his boat. This revision caused many difficulties, for it meant that a challenger had to have his yacht constructed and in racing form a full year in advance. It also gave the cup defenders time to go over the challenging ship's dimensions and construct a superior yacht. Despite the many questions raised about the new deed, Schuyler and the New York Yacht Club defended it and planned to utilize it.

The next two challengers came from Lord Dunraven of England. Driven by his quest for the cup, he sailed across the Atlantic in 1893 in his cutter *Valkyrie II*. In a series of intense letters Dunraven persuaded the executives of the New York Yacht

'One of the more colorful skippers in the competition was Atlanta's Ted Turner. (UPI photo)

Club to waive many of the new clauses. Dunraven had constructed a very large yacht; and when the Americans learned of its size, they discovered that they were unprepared to meet such a vessel. They decided they would have to build a boat of their own of equal dimension—and *Vigilant* was born. After surviving some strenuous trial races, she proved she was ready for the big test.

The English earl brought a good boat with him, but as it turned out, it was not quite good enough. *Vigilant* outlasted *Valkyrie* in three straight races by margins of approximately five minutes, ten minutes, and forty seconds, respectively. It proved to be a very close competition, and Dunraven, not convinced that the Americans were superior, challenged again in 1895.

This time he brought with him *Valkyrie III*, a new boat that more closely resembled the American yachts. The New York Yacht Club countered with a ship appropriately named *Defender*, and the race was set. On 7 September the two yachts set out on the course. To the delight of the numerous spectator boats that lined the race, *Defender* took an early lead. As the two glided past the halfway mark, *Valkyrie III* began to fall behind. Taking full advantage, *Defender* pulled away to an eight-minute victory. A fierce competitor, Dunraven was not pleased. Following the race, he protested the number of excursion boats and the waterline of *Defender*. He claimed that his opponent's boat was lower in the water than it was when measured for the race. The executives of the yacht club, however, found that the American yacht was within the rules. Two days later, as the boats waited for the start of the race, *Valkyrie III* accidentally collided with *Defender,* snapping the latter's topmast. The boats sailed off despite the incident, and the visitor won by forty-seven seconds. The Americans filed a protest. The committee found Lord Dunraven's yacht to be guilty of a foul, and he forfeited the victory. Oliver Ieslin, head of the syndicate that owned *Defender,* offered to resail the race, but Dunraven, turned it down. Furious at the result of the two protests, he went to the extreme of pulling his yacht off the course just after the start of the third race. *Defender* sailed the course alone and captured the cup for the United States.

Lord Dunraven returned to England, still bitterly protesting what he felt was the unsportsmanlike treatment he received. A committee of highly regarded yachtsmen conducted an extensive investigation. Dunraven still insisted that his boat had been fouled by *Defender* and not vice versa. After much testimony and deliberation, the committee found the charges to be totally untrue, and Ieslin and *Defender* were judged to be innocent of any wrongdoing. The decision of the respected committee ended a bitter controversy that had rocked the yachting world.

During the next thirty-two years five attempts were made to capture the cup, all of them by the same man. He was Sir Thomas Lipton, who represented the Royal Ulster Yacht Club of Belfast. A wealthy man, he was knighted in England and was known as a good sportsman and a fair-minded gentleman. Unfortunately, he had to fall back on all those qualities as his yachts failed in all five attempts to win the trophy.

In 1899 Lipton's *Shamrock* broke a mast in the second race and was forced to drop out. He was defeated by *Columbia* in three straight races, all by wide margins. After the race the New York Yacht Club elected the Briton to honorary membership. Two years later Captain Charley Barr and *Columbia* proved again to be too much for him. His new boat *Shamrock II*, however, lost by a total margin of only five minutes. It was the best performance of a foreign boat in cup competition to date. Lipton's next challenger, *Shamrock III*, also lost in three straight races, this time to *Reliance*, Captain Barr's new yacht.

World War I interrupted Lipton's siege on the cup, but it didn't dampen his enthusiasm. In 1920 he reappeared on the scene with another challenge and another boat—*Shamrock IV*. His opponent was *Resolute*. It proved to be a fantastic battle. *Shamrock* opened the competition with two consecutive victories—something no challenger had ever done

In 1977 Turner's *Courageous* defeated *Australia* in four straight races. (UPI photo)

before. To take the cup all she had to do was win one of the next three races. The third race finished in a dead heat; however, because of the time allowance, *Resolute* was given the victory and remained alive. The narrow win seemed to spark the Americans, as they came back to pull out the next two races and successfully defend the trophy. Once again Sir Thomas's hopes were dashed.

Lipton made his final challenge for the cup in 1930. His *Shamrock V* battled *Enterprise*, the first class-J sloop ever entered. Though Lipton's newest boat had much potential, it was never realized. In the third race *Shamrock's* mainsail tumbled down, and she dropped from the race. It mattered little, for *Enterprise* sandwiched her opponent's bad luck with some good runs and an eventual 4–0 win. Lipton's fifth attempt ended like all the others, in failure, and the America's Cup remained in America. The following year, in 1931, Sir Thomas Lipton died, and the sport of yachting had lost one of its greatest competitors and gentlemen.

Rumors arose as to a challenge the next few years, but it wasn't until T. O. M. Sopwith, representing the Royal Yacht Squadron, came forward, that one was submitted. Sopwith skippered his own yacht, *Endeavor*. It was the first time in the history of the cup that a British yacht owner would command his own boat, and hopes were high for an English victory.

The Americans had great difficulty deciding whether to counter with *Yankee* or *Rainbow*. A series of trial races gave no clear indication as to who was faster. Finally, it came down to one race. *Rainbow* won by one second, and she was named the representative.

As the competition began, things looked grim for the home team. *Endeavor* took two straight wins. In the third race the British boat had a healthy lead, and victory seemed imminent. Suddenly, out of the blue a miracle occurred. *Rainbow* appeared, sped by her opponent, and won by three minutes. In the fourth race—which Sopwith protested, to no avail—*Rainbow* again won. The American craft then took the next two races to secure the series, 4–2. It was the closest cup match ever sailed. *Endeavor* was the faster boat, but *Rainbow*, under skipper Mike Vanderbilt, proved to have a quicker crew on the seas.

In 1937 Sopwith made another attempt for the trophy, this time with what he felt was an even faster boat, *Endeavor II*. Unfortunately for him, he came up against one of the fastest boats ever to compete, *Ranger*. The buildup for the race was tremendous, but for the Englishman, the results weren't. Vanderbilt's *Ranger* won the first two races by over seventeen and eighteen minutes, re-

San Diego's Dennis Conner sailed right through the trial races and into the 1980 finals. (San Diego Hall of Champions photo)

Conner's yacht, *Freedom*, helped keep the coveted Cup in the United States by winning in five races. (San Diego Hall of Champions photo)

spectively. The matter was settled, and she went on to win, 4–0.

The American domination continued. The next race was sailed in 1958, when *Columbia* beat England's *Sceptre,* four races to one. It was the first attempt at the cup by the Aussies, who were enthused by their showing. In 1964 the New York Yacht Club decided to give the next challenge to England and her representative, *Sovereign.* The result was the same. America's *Constellation* beat her four straight times.

Before another challenge was accepted, the club set forth a new policy that required a three-year interval between races. Accordingly, the next competition took place in 1967 against an optimistic group of Australians, representing the Royal Sydney Yacht Squadron. Their boat, *Dame Pattie,* had proven successful in home races. Her opponent, *Intrepid,* was considered a superboat. She proved to be just that, eliminating *Pattie* in four straight races. Three years later, in 1970, she defeated Australia's *Gretel II,* four races to one. Defending the cup in two straight competitions was quite an achievement.

In 1974 a flamboyant millionaire named Ted Turner entered the scene with his yacht *Courageous.* Turner, who also owned baseball's Atlanta Braves and basketball's Atlanta Hawks, skippered his yacht to consecutive 4–0 thrashings of Australia's *Southern Cross* and *Australia* (in 1977). In 1980 Turner sought his third consecutive victory but met a stumbling block in the form of Dennis Conner. The prerace trials boiled down to a duel between the crafty Southern skipper and the determined San Diegan sailor. Conner and his yacht, *Freedom,* won the showdown and received the right to face the once-defeated *Australia.* *Freedom* proved up to the task, and the Aussie challenger was subdued in five races.

Then, in 1983, Bond was finally successful. It was not an easy task for the Australians, for they had to overcome a 3–1 deficit before they went on to their historic win. It was a victory not only for an underdog, but for creative genius, too. Their revolutionary winged keel helped them become heroes to the world. To break a 132-year winning streak is quite an achievement, but as Conner so aptly put it, "You're talking about national pride."

America's Cup Winners

1851   *America* (United States) 1, England 0
1870   *Magic* (United States) 1, *Cambria* (England), 0
1871   *Columbia* (United States) 2, *Livonia* (England), 1
       Sappho (United States) 2, *Livonia* (England) 0
1876   *Madeleine* (United States) 2, *Countess of Dufferin* (Canada), 0
1881   *Mischief* (United States) 2, *Atlanta* (Canada) 0
1885   *Puritan* (United States) 2, *Genesta* (England) 0
1886   *Mayflower* (United States) 2, *Galatea* (England) 0
1887   *Volunteer* (United States) 2, *Thistle* (England) 0
1893   *Vigilant* (United States) 3, *Valkyrie II* (England) 0
1895   *Defender* (United States) 3, *Valkyrie III* (England) 0
1899   *Columbia* (United States) 3, *Shamrock I* (England) 0
1901   *Columbia* (United States) 3, *Shamrock II* (England) 0
1903   *Reliance* (United States) 3, *Shamrock III* (England) 0

1920   *Resolute* (United States) 3, *Shamrock IV* (England) 2
1930   *Enterprise* (United States) 4, *Shamrock V* (England) 0
1934   *Rainbow* (United States 4, *Endeavor* (England) 2
1937   *Ranger* (United States) 4, *Endeavor II* (England) 0
1958   *Columbia* (United States) 4, *Sceptre* (England) 0
1962   *Weatherly* (United States) 4, *Gretel* (Australia) 1
1964   *Constellation* (United States) 4, *Sovereign* (England) 0
1967   *Intrepid* (United States) 4, *Dame Pattie* (Australia) 0
1970   *Intrepid* (United States) 4, *Gretel II* (Australia) 1
1974   *Courageous* (United States) 4, *Southern Cross* (Australia) 0
1977   *Courageous* (United States) 4, *Australia* (Australia) 0
1980   *Freedom* (United States) 4, *Australia* (Australia) 1
1983   *Australia II* (Australia) 4, *Liberty* (United States) 3

11
The Cy Young Award

I ran regularly to keep my legs in shape. In the spring I'd run constantly for three weeks before I ever threw a ball. And I worked hard all winter on my farm, from sunup to sundown, doing chores that not only were good for my legs, but also for my arms and back. Swinging an axe hardens the hands and builds up the shoulders and back."[1]

—Denton True Young

Whether in the business world, politics, or sports there are uncounted "secrets of success." They are as varied and unusual as the people who utilize them. In athletics they often border on the bizarre. But for Denton True Young, known to his protégés as "Cy," the "secret" was nothing more than swinging an axe and running in the fields on his farm. Sounds logical for a football player or a marathon runner. Young, however, was a baseball pitcher, a species known more for its unusual antics than for its physical conditioning.

As pitchers go, Denton was no ordinary thrower. He was nicknamed "Cy" because, according to a local sportswriter, his warmup pitches battered the Canton ball park so badly that it looked like a cyclone hit it. "I had the benefit of a larger strike zone—from the top of the shoulders to the bottom of the knees—and, I admit, some of my cut-plug tobacco would get on the ball."[2]

It's not often that a sports star will downplay his own ability or try to diminish his achievements. But to Cy Young it really didn't matter; the records spoke for themselves. In fact his achievements in the sport of baseball were so great that many have tried to duplicate them (but probably not his training routine).

By the time Young retired from the game in 1912, numerous pitching records had been rewritten. Many of them still have his name inscribed on them today. His lifetime statistics included twenty or more victories in sixteen different seasons; thirty or more wins in five seasons; 818 games started (a major league record); 751 games completed (a major league record); 7,377 innings pitched (another record); 511 games won (a record); and 313 games lost (unfortunately, a record).

Naturally, it was not always easy for the former rail-splitting farmer-boy. In 1890 he signed as a pitcher for Canton for the Tri-State League. When he first reported to the team, he was laughed at by the other players. Through performance on the field, however, he soon earned their respect.

Young's career in pro baseball was characterized by his inconsistent pitching and his travels from one team to another. After playing with Canton, he was sold to the Cleveland Spiders of the National League. In 1901 he went to Boston of the American League. He then became the highest paid player of the time—the Red Sox paid him $3,000. In 1909 Young was sent back to Cleveland of the American

League, where he played until he closed out his career with Boston.

Cy played pro ball for an incredible twenty-two years. When he started, there was no mound, and the catchers played bare-handed. The changes in the game didn't really affect him, for he was easily adaptable. In 1904 he pitched a perfect game against Philadelphia. It was just one of three no-hitters he tossed in his career.

In 1912, at the age of 45, Cy Young decided to call it quits. He retired from the game and went back to the farm. In 1956, a year after he died, Baseball Commissioner Ford Frick initiated the Cy Young Award, given every year to the top pitcher in the league. In 1967 the honor was expanded to two awards—one for the top National League pitcher and one for the top American League pitcher.

The winner of the first Cy Young Award was Don Newcombe of the Brooklyn Dodgers. Newcombe had earlier been selected as the Most Valuable Player in the National League. Despite his outstanding season, which he finished with a 27–7 record, controversy surrounded his winning the award. Many people felt that "Newk's" teammate Sal Maglie was more deserving. Maglie finished

with a 13–5 record, but many of those wins came during Brooklyn's important pennant drive. He also came through with a clutch no-hitter during that stretch run. Newcombe, on the other hand, had trouble winning near the end, and many fans began to label him a "choke" pitcher. But Newcombe, without a doubt, was the best pitcher in either league that year. His performance statistics proved that.

Another important question was raised following this initial voting. Each of the sixteen cities having a big league franchise was given one vote for the trophy. The president of the National Baseball Writers Association appointed a writer in each town to take part in the selection. Since, however, there were two different leagues with schedules that did not mix, it would have been impossible for writers in one league to observe pitchers in the other. Consequently, many people wondered how American League writers could vote for Newcombe, a pitcher they had never seen. Newcombe received ten of the sixteen first-place votes so some of them had to have selected him. The question was raised for many years until the rule change in 1967.

In 1957 the second Cy Young Award was awarded to Warren Spahn of the Milwaukee

Don Newcombe of the Brooklyn Dodgers sported a 27–7 record in 1956 and was awarded the first Cy Young Award. (Los Angeles Dodger photo)

Considered the best left-handed pitcher in the league at the time, Warren Spahn led the Milwaukee Braves to their first pennant ever. (National Baseball Hall of Fame photo)

115

Braves, who led his club to their first pennant ever. During his career, Spahn was considered the best left-hander in the league. His statistics bore that out—thirteen times he won twenty or more games; he had two no-hitters, won 363 games, and played on three pennant winners. In 1940 Spahn signed with the Braves for eighty dollars a month, not much by modern standards. As a pitcher, he worked very hard, studying the batters' weaknesses and strong points inside and out. Spahn and Milwaukee's other star pitcher, Johnnie Sain, formed one of the best "one-two punches" in baseball. Sportswriters for the Braves had a saying—"Spahn and Sain and pray for rain."[3] In 1947 they each won twenty-one games, but the Braves finished in third place. To say the least, they didn't have much support. A durable player who found it difficult to quit, Spahn was still playing ball in 1963 at the age of forty-two. That year he won twenty-three games, lost only seven, posted a 2·60 earned run average, and generally amazed everyone in the baseball world. "Spahn is what I call a go-to-sleep pitcher," said Charlie Dressen, a professional manager for many years. "The manager says Spahn's gonna pitch tomorrow and then get a good night's sleep."[4]

The Cy Young Award is a trophy that represents the individual excellence put forth by professional pitchers. It soon became apparent that the position honored was a very important one to the success of the team as a whole. In baseball it is often said that nothing beats good pitching. From 1957 through 1969 the relationship between good pitching and success was very apparent. During that period eleven of the sixteen Cy Young winners led their squads into World Series competition. Warren Spahn got it started in taking the Braves to the series in 1957. The next year the New York Yankees had a banner season, and their ace on the mound was a man named Bob Turley. He led the Yanks to a World Series championship and also won the Cy Young Award. Vern Law did it for the Pirates in 1960; Whitey Ford for the Yankees in 1961; Sandy Koufax won two Cy Youngs and two world championships, in 1963 and 1965; and Jim Lonborg did it for the Boston Red Sox in 1967 (the first year two Cy Youngs were given). The list is a long one, and the relationship is more than coincidental. Success breeds success, and the Cy Young winners were pushing their teams to the top.

Winning the award also brought with it a fair amount of fame and glory. Two pitchers who got their share of headlines were Whitey Ford and Sandy Koufax. Known as the "thinking man's pitcher," Ford was a local boy-turned-hero. Born and raised in New York City, he was an instant crowd favorite with the local baseball enthusiasts.

Considered one of the best pitchers in the history of the game, Sandy Koufax of the Los Angeles Dodgers was widely known for his no-hitters, and his three Cy Young Awards. (Los Angeles Dodger photo)

The Yankees made the most of the situation and of Ford's talents. The clutch southpaw compiled ten World Series victories and a lifetime record of 236–106 for the Yanks during their glory years. In 1961 the Yankees won the series, and Ford won the Cy Young, the only one of his career. A competitive athlete, he retired at the age of thirty-eight and went right into another less taxing sport—harness racing.

While Ford was dazzling Eastern baseball fans, Sandy Koufax was out West dazzling visiting baseball teams. The hard-throwing leftie was often referred to as "the greatest pitcher in the history of the game," and his performances showed why. From 1962 to 1966 he won 111 games and lost only 34, pitched four no-hitters, a perfect game, won five Earned Run Average (ERA) titles, and led his Los Angeles Dodgers to three pennants and two world championships. He possessed an overpowering fastball and a devastating curveball that often left batters reeling is disbelief.

When Koufax first entered professional baseball, he didn't set the world afire with his performances. In fact he was so wild when he first reported to the Dodger training camp at Vero Beach, Florida, that his teammates refused to even take batting practice against him. He was known as "that wild lefty." His first six years were dismal at best, and he considered quitting. Fortunately for the Dodgers he

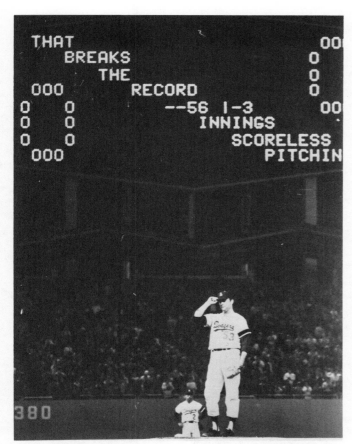

THAT
BREAKS
THE
RECORD
--56 1-3
INNINGS
SCORELESS
PITCHIN

380

With record-breaking Don Drysdale teaming up with Koufax, the Dodgers had one of the most unbeatable pitching staffs in the league. (Los Angeles Dodger photo)

gave it one more try. Right when Koufax and the Dodgers were flying along at peak performance, a problem developed. Koufax's left arm began to bother him, and it was soon diagnosed as arthritis. Koufax tried to continue to pitch, soaking his painful appendage in ice after every game. But it was just a matter of time before he was forced to retire. At the age of thirty-six he became the youngest player ever to be elected to the Baseball Hall of Fame.

Winning teams were not the only ones to produce successful pitchers during this period. One of the sternest tests in sports for an athlete is to maintain a high level of performance when his team is not. But that's exactly what Early Wynn, Dean Chance, and Mike McCormick did. Playing for an expansion team, the California Angels, Chance made his presence immediately felt. He helped keep the struggling Angels respectable and, for his efforts, was awarded the Cy Young in 1964. McCormick's performance three years later for the San Francisco Giants earned him similar accolades and his very own Cy Young Award.

Pitchers such as the great Early Wynn typified the determination and stamina that make great athletes. Ever since Wynn was a little boy, his father wanted him to become a pitcher. During his twenty-three years in the major leagues, he was known to be a battler whenever he stepped onto the mound. He played for three different clubs—the Washington Senators, the Cleveland Indians, and the Chicago White Sox. Although he was a very successful hurler in the professional ranks, the lower leagues weren't always as graceful to him. In the minors the very first batter he faced greeted him in a very unfriendly manner—by hitting a grand slam!

Many of the pitchers who won the Cy Young were also great athletes in other sports. Bob Gibson and Ferguson Jenkins are examples. Gibson won the award in 1970 while playing for the St. Louis Cardinals of the National League. Jenkins, of the Chicago Cubs, won it the next year. When Gibson was a young boy, he suffered various childhood illnesses, including pneumonia, which severely hampered his activity. The determined young boy bounced back and became an excellent athlete, playing basketball and baseball in both high school and college. Jenkins, born in Ontario, Canada, was strong in those sports, as well as in ice hockey. The two men had many other things in common. They were both clutch pitchers with a varied arsenal from which to choose. They were both big, strong, durable throwers. They both played in the National League. They both won the Cy Young Award during their careers. And, oh yes, they both, at one time or another, played basketball for the Harlem Globetrotters!

In any sport it is rare for two people in the same family to reach the top of the hill. But in this case, the old saying "Like father, like son" never had a truer meaning. When a father is a very successful semipro pitcher, what else can his sons do? That's the way brothers Gaylord and Jim Perry looked at it. Growing up with baseball all around them, they adapted very easily. When Jim was a senior in high school and his little brother Gaylord was just a sophomore, they led their team to the state championship. Jim went on to sign with the Cleveland Indians and embark on a very successful pro career. In 1970 he was awarded the Cy Young as he finished with a 24–12 record. He was the ace of the Minnesota Twins pitching staff at the time. Then, after seventeen years and 215 victories Jim decided to hang up the cleats.

Gaylord also made it into the major leagues, and for a pitcher he was quite a hit. He signed with the San Francisco Giants and was later traded to the Cleveland Indians. In 1972, while playing with the Indians, he won the Cy Young. Finding it nearly impossible to hit him, batters often accused him of putting "foreign substances" on the surface of the ball. Finally, in 1974, he admitted to the illegal pitch and promised never to use it again. Despite the controversies, Gaylord was a talented thrower. He invented a very successful pitch, which he called "the hard-slider." Late in his career he was playing with the hapless San Diego Padres of the National League. Destined to finish with a team near the bottom, Perry responded by winning his second Cy Young Award. What made it even more significant was that he was the first pitcher ever to win it in both the National and American leagues. Gaylord followed this achievement up by becoming the third pitcher in history to win 100 or more games in both leagues. Gaylord Perry was definitely a talented baseball player. But, then, he had good examples in front of him.

Up until 1974 the Cy Young Award was dominated by starting pitchers. Relievers, the men who are called when the game is on the line, were conspicuously overlooked. Performing during clutch, pressure-packed moments, a relief pitcher can make or break a season for a team. In 1974 a pitcher of remarkable durability emerged from the bullpen

of the Los Angeles Dodgers. His name is Mike Marshall. Appearing in no less than 106 of his Team's 162 games that year, Marshall set a league record for number of appearances in a single season. Behind the strength of his bionic arm Los Angeles made it to the World Series, and Marshall was rightfully awarded the Cy Young.

Three years later, in 1977, another reliever came out of the pen to take the bull by the horns. He was leftie Sparky Lyle of the Yankees and his ability to stop late inning rallies was uncanny. Known as "the Count," he was largely responsible for putting the proud New York organization back on top of the baseball world. As the top reliever in the game, he was rewarded with the Cy Young.

In 1979 the Chicago Cubs of the National League's Eastern Division finished in second-to-last place. By most accounts, it was a dismal year but there was one bright element. His name was Bruce Sutter, Chicago's top relief pitcher. The only way the Cubs could spell relief that season was S-U-T-T-E-R. Using his own variety of pitches, which were hard to classify, he struck out 110 batters and had a respectable 2·23 ERA. When it was

Gaylord Perry was the only pitcher in the history of baseball ever to win the Cy Young Award in both the American and National Leagues. (San Diego Padre photo; Natl. Baseball Hall of Fame photo)

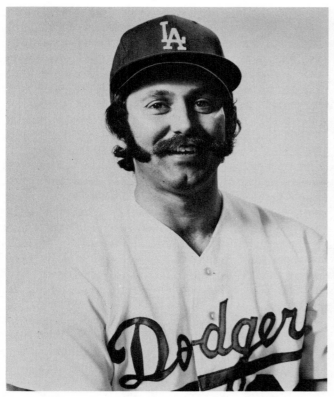

The Dodger's durable Mike Marshall set a record for pitching appearances during a season, and became one of the few relief pitchers to win the Cy Young Award. (Los Angeles Dodger photo)

Another great reliever was the Yankees' Sparky Lyle. (New York Yankee photo)

announced that Sutter won the Cy Young, people realized once and for all that he was no cub when it came to relief pitching.

"Maybe I was the best pitcher," said Mike Flanagan of the Baltimore Orioles after he won the award in 1979. "But I was also on the best team."[5] A simple thought, but it carried with it a very significant meaning. The best teams in the league were producing the best pitchers, and vice versa. Once again, there was an obvious connection between success on the mound and success in the standings. Great pitchers like Denny McLain of Detroit, Tom Seaver of the Mets, Steve Carlton of the Phillies, Mike Cuellar and Jim Palmer of the Orioles, and Ron Guidry of the Yankees came along, and their teams were suddenly in the play-offs.

The correlation between the World Series and the Cy Young once again appeared, but the road that it took to get there differed for each traveler. Take, for example, Tom Seaver, the three-time Cy Young winner from the New York Mets. The hard-throwing right-hander almost single-handedly turned a cellar-dwelling loser into a World Series contender. A confident and competitive ball player, Seaver couldn't understand or accept his

Hard-throwing Tom Seaver almost singlehandedly turned the cellar-dwelling New York Mets into a World Series contender. (Natl. Baseball Hall of Fame photo)

119

teammates' negative attitude and often told them so. He could understand hardship but found it hard to live with. When Seaver was in college, at the University of Southern California (USC), he was a very successful pitcher. He then experienced some problems that cut short his collegiate career and made him value the game even more. When Seaver was a senior in 1966, the Atlanta Braves signed him to a $40,000 bonus. There was only one problem—he hadn't graduated yet. Baseball Commissioner William Eckert voided the contract because the Braves violated a rule in signing a college player. USC then ruled the young pitcher ineligible to play any more collegiate ball because he signed a professional contract. Once Seaver graduated, Eckert held a drawing to determine negotiating rights to the star pitcher. The Mets won and signed him to a $50,000 bonus.

Seaver brought with him more than just a strong right arm. He brought with him a powerful attitude and a will to win. In 1969, the year he won his first Cy Young, the Mets found themselves wrapped up in a fight with the Chicago Cubs for the Eastern Division title. On 8 July the Cubs traveled to New York to do battle against the Mets, who were five games behind them at the time. Nobody really considered the lowly New Yorkers to be serious contenders. Before the first game of the series, Chicago's star third baseman, Ron Santo, pointed out rather emphatically that the Cubs were more experienced and talented than the Mets at just about every position on the field. The Mets opened the crucial series with a come-from-behind 4–3 victory, which left some of the Cubs a bit ruffled. The next night the visitors were bent on evening the score. But they came up against a brick wall in the name of Tom Seaver. Not only did he beat the division leaders, 4–0, but also allowed them only a single hit during the entire game! The shutout helped provide the spark that allowed the Mets to overtake the Cubs, win the division title, and go on to the World Series.

Another pitcher known for his clutch performances and his ability to get his team into the playoffs is Steve Carlton of the Philadelphia Phillies. In 1980 Carlton was an influential factor in his squad's very successful season. The Phillies staged one of the greatest comebacks in the history of the club that year, as they overtook the division-leading Montreal Expos in the last week of the schedule and went on to a World Series championship. It was a banner year for Philadelphia and for its big left-hander, who was awarded the Cy Young for his contributions.

As successful as he was, things were not always right for Steve Carlton. Early in his career, winning

seemed to be one pitch away from the aspiring young thrower. In 1970, while he was playing for the St. Louis Cardinals, he lost nineteen games. He was a very talented but frustrated man. One day, he received a letter from a night watchman in Tucson, Arizona. It was not an ordinary fan letter, for it was advising the young pitcher to espouse "the power of positive thinking." After reading the letter, Carlton decided that he had nothing to lose by taking the watchman's advice. Letters began to arrive every week from Arizona, and Carlton was slowly but surely won over to this new way of thinking. The next year, in 1971, Carlton made a great comeback and recorded twenty victories. "The night watchman's letters made me realize that man is the only animal who puts limitations on himself," Carlton said. "Defeat? I never consider it. Pressure? It doesn't exist. I take every game as it comes. When one ends, I start getting ready for the next one."[6]

Denny McLain of the Detroit Tigers was another interesting story. In 1968 he won the American League Cy Young Award and, not coincidentally,

With the help of an Arizona night watchman, Steve Carlton made one of the great comebacks in baseball and went on to lead the Philadelphia Phillies to the World Championship in 1980. (Natl. Baseball Hall of Fame photo)

the Tigers won the World Series, 4-3, over the St. Louis Cardinals. The next year, although Detroit didn't make it to the series, McLain was again voted the league's most outstanding pitcher, tying Mike Cuellar of the Baltimore Orioles. McLain was impressive on the mound, achieving something of which every pitcher dreams but few ever realize— thirty victories in one season.

Injuries have often cut short the career of many promising athletes. Sports can be a very demanding profession, both mentally and physically—as Jim Palmer of the Baltimore Orioles found out. Born in New York City, Palmer went to high school in Arizona, where he was all-state in football, basketball, and baseball. In 1963 he signed with the Orioles and two years later was playing in the major leagues. He immediately made his presence felt, as Baltimore made it to the series and Palmer, at the age of twenty-one, pitched a dazzling shutout against its opponent, the Los Angeles Dodgers. The man on the mound for Los Angeles that day was Sandy Koufax.

Later on in his career Palmer experienced some difficulties. Soreness developed in his right arm, and he was sent to the minor leagues. Palmer rigorously protested. Finally, he decided to go to a noted bone specialist, Dr. Robert Kerlan. The doctor injected cortisone into the pitcher's arm at a spot different from where other physicians had put it. The move proved successful as Palmer was cured, and worked his way back into the major leagues. In 1973 he posted a 22–9 record with a 2·40 ERA and won the Cy Young. The very next year, however, the Baltimore ace developed another arm injury. It was diagnosed as tendonitis, but the pain in the arm persisted. He decided to go back to Dr. Kerlan. Once again the previous diagnosis was found to be incorrect. Dr. Kerlan discovered a strained nerve and recommended that the pitcher sit out six weeks to rest it. Palmer took his advice and returned to the club in August, just in time to pitch thirteen games and help the Orioles make it to the playoffs. The next two years he continued his outstanding pitching as he won two more Cy Youngs. To many athletes, injuries such as these would have crippled a career in sports. But Jim Palmer used his head. He changed his style from a hard-throwing pitcher to a technician of control—and the rest is history.

In 1980 Steve Stone of the Baltimore club won the Cy Young for his amazing season. Joining him on the Oriole staff that year were Palmer and the previous year's winner, Mike Flanagan. The three Cy Young winners gave the Orioles one of the most formidable pitching rotations in the history of the game. In the past other teams had produced more

In 1971 left-hander Vida Blue hit the scene for the Oakland Athletics, and they subsequently dominated baseball for the next few years. (Natl. Baseball Hall of Fame photo)

Southpaw Randy Jones combined with Gaylord Perry to give the lowly San Diego Padres some top-notch pitching. (San Diego Padre photo)

than one Cy Young winner, but never had three graced the same team all at once. In the early 1970s the Oakland A's dominated the American League and were led by their great throwers. Among them were Vida Blue, the 1971 winner, and Jim ("Catfish") Hunter, who won it in 1974. The Los Angeles Dodgers, in their glory days, had the combination of Sandy Koufax and Don Drysdale on which to lean. Even the San Diego Padres have been graced with some outstanding pitchers. With 1976 winner Randy Jones and the unstoppable Gaylord Perry on their squad, opposing batters did not always have it easy at San Diego Stadium.

Whether it's for a World Series champion or a last-place finisher, the Cy Young Award is the highest individual recognition that a pitcher can attain. To be recognized as the best in baseball is quite an honor. It represents not only the success of the player who wins it but a standard of excellence that every athlete seeks. During his twenty-two years in the major leagues Cy Young became one of the most respected pitchers in the game. He was so revered that he became more than just a sports celebrity; he was a cultural hero. His memory, like the pitching records he set, will live on forever.

> Y is for Young,
> The Magnificent Cy;
> People batted against him,
> But I never knew why.[7]
>
> —Ogden Nash

Cy Young Award Winners

1956 Don Newcombe, Dodgers
1957 Warren Spahn, Braves
1958 Bob Turley, Yankees

1959 Early Wynn, White Sox
1960 Vernon Law, Pirates
1961 Whitey Ford, Yankees
1962 Don Drysdale, Dodgers
1963 Sandy Koufax, Dodgers
1964 Dean Chance, Angels
1965 Sandy Koufax, Dodgers
1966 Sandy Koufax, Dodgers
1967 (NL) Mike McCormick, Giants; (AL) Jim Lonborg, Red Sox
1968 (NL) Bob Gibson, Cardinals; (AL Denny McLain, Tigers
1969 (NL) Tom Seaver, Mets; (AL) tie; Denny McLain, Tigers, Mike Cuellar, Orioles
1970 (NL) Bob Gibson, Cardinals; (AL) Jim Perry, Twins
1971 (NL) Ferguson Jenkins, Cubs; (AL) Vida Blue, A's
1972 (NL) Steve Carlton, Phillies; (AL) Gaylord Perry, Indians
1973 (NL) Tom Seaver, Mets; (AL) Jim Palmer, Orioles
1974 (NL) Mike Marshall, Dodgers; (AL) Jim Hunter, A's
1975 (NL) Tom Seaver, Mets; (AL) Jim Palmer, Orioles
1976 (NL) Randy Jones, Padres; (AL) Jim Palmer, Orioles
1977 (NL) Steve Carlton, Phillies; (AL) Sparky Lyle, Yankees
1978 (NL) Gaylord Perry, Padres; (AL) Ron Guidry, Yankees
1979 (NL) Bruce Sutter, Cubs; (AL) Mike Flanagan, Orioles
1980 (NL) Steve Carlton, Phillies; (AL) Steve Stone, Orioles
1981 (NL) Fernando Valenzuela, Dodgers; (AL) Rollie Fingers, Brewers
1982 (NL) Steve Carlton, Phillies; (AL) Pete Vuckovich, Brewers
1983 (NL) John Denny, Phillies; (AL) LaMarr Hoyt, White Sox

12

The Sullivan Memorial Trophy

Wilma Rudolph was born in Tennessee in 1940. Her parents, who were very poor, were forced to work the fields in order to survive. As a baby, Wilma was often very sick. In fact there was doubt at one point that she would even live. She was stricken with double pneumonia, scarlet fever, and polio, which left her legs paralyzed.

For years Wilma received treatment to bring feeling back to the lower part of her body. She was a very determined young girl and finally, at the age of eight, she walked. With the aid of special leg braces her mobility began to return. Until she was eleven years old, she had to wear special shoes to help with her development.

Soon the eager young Wilma became involved in sports. There was one that she took a special liking to—running. Having been denied the ability for so long, she now treasured the gift of competition. She ran track in grade school and displayed great talent. Wilma then decided to go to Tennessee State University to pursue the sport that she had grown to love.

While at college, she trained very hard and set many goals for herself. One of them was to become the best runner in America. In the 1960 Olympic Games Wilma qualified for the United States squad. The dedicated twenty-two-year-old trackster showed the world what it's like to run. And run she did as she won the 100-meter dash and the 200-

meter race, and was a member of the winning 400-meter relay team. She became the first American woman to win three gold medals at the Olympic Games. She was truly America's greatest female runner.

When she returned home, her achievements were lauded, and she became a very popular figure. Then, in 1961, she was recognized once again. Wilma Rudolph was awarded the Sullivan Memorial Trophy. The Sullivan Memorial Trophy is given every year by the Amateur Athletic Union (AAU) to the athlete deemed the most outstanding in the nation. The selection of Wilma Rudolph in 1961 may not have seemed overly significant at the time of the announcement, but no one could have more appropriately represented the principles and values idealized in the trophy. The inscription on Wilma's trophy read: "To the athlete who by her performance, example, and influence as an amateur has done the most to advance the cause of sportsmanship."[1]

In sports the word *amateur* takes on many definitions. Amateur athletes are those who do not receive monetary compensation for their performances. They participate solely out of love for the sport itself. Who else could better exemplify the true meaning of *amateur* than Wilma Rudolph? Unable even to walk for much of her life, she turned into one of the most gifted athletes in

The courage of trackster Wilma Rudolph typifies the spirit of the amateur athlete. (UPI photo)

America. Her dedication, hard work, and love for life showed that the AAU knew what it was doing when it presented her with the Sullivan Memorial Trophy.

The trophy, in existence since 1930 (when immortal golfer Bobby Jones won it), has become one of the most prestigious awards presented each year. It symbolizes not only talent and performance but also determination, sportsmanship, and dedication to the ideal of amateur athletics.

James E. Sullivan, after whom the trophy was named, was the principal organizer of the AAU. In addition to serving twenty-five years on the AAU and on the American Olympic Committee, he was president of the American Sports Publishing Company and the athletic editor of various New York newspapers. The award was named after him to commemorate "the man to whose efforts, more than [those of] any other single individual, is due the credit for the marvelous growth of amateur athletics in America."[2]

The Sullivan Memorial Trophy is unique in the world of sports. Many awards are annually presented to athletes in a specific sport such as football, baseball, and basketball. The Sullivan, however, can be given to an athlete in any sport. The list of winners includes tracksters, swimmers, ice skaters, rowers, football players, gymnasts, golfers, basketball players, divers, and tennis players. Furthermore, it is given only to amateur athletes, a unique breed, for they compete solely out of love for the sport. But the most unusual aspect of the award is that it can be presented to either a male or a female. It can therefore be considered one of the forerunners of equal rights in athletics.

Since 1930, two sports have been predominant in the Sullivan winners' circle. They are track and swimming. From Glenn Cunningham in 1933 to the great Bruce Jenner in 1976, the trend has been maintained. The first swimmer to win the Sullivan was Ann Curtis in 1944, but it wasn't until the Olympian efforts of the 1960s and 1970s that swimmers became heavily noticed. Despite the overwhelming number of winners from these two sports, the winners are not predictable. In 1979 a young man named Kurt Thomas won the trophy. He was the first gymnast to capture it.

Many of the athletes who have won the Sullivan are bound together by one common trait—courage. Wilma Rudolph is a prime example. Three others that come to mind are Bob Mathias, Glenn Cunningham, and Jim Ryun.

Born on 17 November 1930 in Tulare, California, Bob Mathias was very sick as a boy. At various times during his childhood he suffered from anemia, chicken pox, severe nosebleeds, measles, and whooping cough. He had generally poor health until he was about twelve years old. When he entered high school, he became interested in athletics and went out for three sports—football, basketball, and baseball. At the urging of the track coach, he started training for the decathlon as a senior.

At the age of seventeen, Mathias won the United States Decathlon Championship and made the Olympic team for the 1948 games. He was the youngest athlete ever to compete on an American squad. This resulted in his often being referred to as the "baby" of the team.

When the games began, Mathias proved to be the surprise of the competition. He threw the discus so far that it went off the marked field. He pole vaulted in the dark, fog, and rain and ran the 1500-meter race on a soft, muddy track. Despite the obstacles, Mathias came away with the gold medal. For his remarkable performance he was also awarded the Sullivan trophy that year.

A similar success story is that of Glenn Cunningham. When he was a boy, Glenn ran three miles to and from school every day with his brother, Floyd. One day Floyd decided to start the stove at the schoolhouse. He picked up what he thought was a container of coal oil and threw it on the stove—but it was gasoline instead! The resulting fire killed Floyd and severely burned young Glenn's legs. Doctors predicted that he would never walk again. He was on crutches for a year and was almost always in pain.

A determined young man, Glenn set his sights high, and by the time he was in high school he was participating in basketball, football, and track. He soon developed a special feeling for running, and track became his favorite sport. In 1932 he made the Olympic team in the 1500-meter run. A courageous and tireless performer, he soon set world records, and in 1933 he won the coveted Sullivan. For Cunningham, running was more than just a sport or a game; it was a meter of life. Said he:

People can't understand why a man runs. They don't see any sport in it, argue that it lacks the sight-thrill of body contact, the color of rough conflict. Yet the conflict is there, more raw and challenging than any man-versus-man competition. In track it is man against himself, the cruelest of all opponents. The other runners are not the real enemies. His adversary lies deep within him, in his ability, with brain and heart, to control and master himself and his emotions.[3]

In 1966 a tall, skinny twenty-year-old from Kansas began to make big strides in the mile run. At a meet in Berkeley, California, he smashed the existing world record in the mile with a time of 3:51·3—over two seconds better than the previous mark. Jim Ryun had become one of the premiere runners of his time. As a boy, Ryun didn't have it so well. He almost died of peritonitis after an acute appendicitis attack. He also had a hernia and inner ear damage. But Ryun was not to be denied; no obstacle was too great. In 1966 the AAU recognized his efforts and presented him with the Sullivan.

Ryun's victory in 1966 gave further support to the fact that runners were highly esteemed by the Sullivan voters. Some of the greatest runners in track-and-field history have been awarded the prestigious trophy. The 1934 winner, Bill Bonthron, a middle-distance runner from Princeton, won three of five races against the great Glenn Cunningham and Gene Venzke and set a world record. Less MacMitchell, the 1941 winner, was a middle-distance runner from New York University who won the famous Hunter Mile in Boston and tied the world record in the Baxter Mile at Madison Square Garden. Fred Wilt, a two-mile runner, was the top distance runner in the country when he won the award in 1950. Wilt went on to a career with the FBI. The 1952 Sullivan went to Mal Whitfield, the first American to win the Olympic steeplechase. Glenn Davis, the 1958 Sullivan winner, placed first in the 400-meter hurdles in both the 1956 and 1960 Olympics, clocking times of 50.1 and 49.3 seconds, respectively. The 1962 Sullivan hero, Jim Beatty, a student at the University of North Carolina, was the first man to run the indoor mile under four minutes. Under the great Hungarian coach Milhaly Igloi, Beatty soon became the biggest track star in the nation. The Sullivan selection for 1974, Rick Wohlhuter, was a Notre Dame runner who set world records in the 880- and 1000-meter races, set an American record for the 800-meter run, and won the AAU indoor 1000-meter contest.

Field events in track, namely, the shot put, pole vault, and discus, have not been overlooked either. In 1959 a shot putter named Parry O'Brien received the award. Revolutionizing the game with a new technique, in which the thrower turns and thrusts his body in the same direction as the heave, O'Brien dominated the competition and broke the world record that year. Another putter to make it big was Randy Matson. A very large man (in grade school he was over six feet and two hundred pounds) and long-time weight-lifter, Matson won the silver medal in the 1964 Olympics and shortly thereafter shattered the sixty-foot and seventy-foot barriers in the event. He won the Sullivan in 1967.

In the pole vault a young man named John Pennel was reaching great heights. As a boy, he began vaulting in his father's back-yard. Before he knew it, he had twenty-three college scholarships in front of him. He decided on the University of Florida but then transferred to Northeast Louisiana State, where he awed the track world by continually breaking his own records. In 1963 he cleared seventeen feet and won the Sullivan for his efforts. At the trophy presentation, he tried to put it all in perspective: "I'm on top now," he said. "But in track and field there is someone who will come along tomorrow and be better."[4]

Always the best amateur athlete in America, Sullivan award recipients have also, in a few instances, proven to be the greatest in the world. Examples are Rafer Johnson, Bill Toomey, and Bruce Jenner, who won the Olympic decathlon in 1960, 1968, and 1976, respectively.

In high school Rafer Johnson showed much potential to be a great athlete. Though he played the three major sports—football, basketball, and baseball—track was his first love. His idol was Bob Mathias, whose achievement he wanted desperately to repeat. When he finished high school, he won an athletic scholarship to UCLA, where he began his training for the Olympics. About a year before the 1960 games, however, he was involved in an automobile accident. He spent several weeks in the hospital with an injured back. For a long period of time he was unable to train, and his future looked dim. But he eventually came back and made it to the Olympics. At UCLA his best friend and fellow participant in the decathlon was a Chinese student named C. K. Yang. Yang also competed in the 1960 games, but he was a member of China's team. Naturally, the run for the gold came down to a battle between the two. The mile race was the deciding event, and Johnson won it with a big effort down the stretch. "I had to beat my best friend in the track world in the very last event of the long grind to win," he later said. "Yang was tough, but this is something I dreamed about for a long time."[5]

For Toomey and Jenner the battle was just as difficult. When Billy Toomey was just thirteen years old, a friend playfully tossed a glass plate at him. It put a gouge in his wrist, which eventually

Decathlete Bill Toomey, who won an Olympic gold medal, is shown here with the ten events that comprise his Competition. (San Diego Hall of Champions photo)

required six operations to repair. Toomey recovered and later went to the University of Colorado, where he took up the decathlon. In 1964 he tried out for the U.S. Olympic team. He finished fourth at the trials, but, unfortunately, only the top three made the squad. Undaunted, the determined young Toomey was out on the track the very next day. The reason: to get ready for the 1968 trials. When 1968 arrived, Toomey not only made the team, but he won the gold medal at Mexico City. The next year he was awarded the Sullivan.

In 1976 Bruce Jenner won the gold medal in the decathlon at Montreal. He did it with a world record performance, amassing 8,618 points. "Our whole society is based upon specialists," he said. "The decathlon goes against that."[6] Jenner was later declared the winner of the Sullivan. When told of the announcement, he simply replied that he expected it. "This is the perfect way to end my athletic career,"[7] he said.

In 1951 the leading pole vaulter in the nation was a man named Bob Richards. Originally from the University of Illinois, he dominated the event for more than a decade. He won the Millrose Games an unprecedented eleven straight times and became a world record holder and an Olympic hero. What was unusual was that Richards was also an ordained minister. In 1951 "the Vaulting Vicar," as he was called, was given the Sullivan award.

In 1955 a talented hurdler-sprinter hit the track scene. He was Harrison ("Bones") Dillard, a skinny kid from Cleveland whose hero was the great Jesse Owens. Dillard became the first man ever to win both the high hurdles and the 100-meter sprint in the Olympics. At one point in his illustrious career he compiled an amazing eighty-two consecutive victories.

As a boy, Dillard wanted to be a sprinter. The only problem was that the track coach wouldn't let him. One day his idol, Jesse Owens, was working on Cleveland's East Side with some of the kids. He told Bones that he should try to be a hurdler. The rest is history.

Don ("the Iron Man") Lash and Greg ("Little Dynamite") Rice were both very successful distance runners in the late 1930s and early 1940s. As America's first great distance runner, Lash often ran both the mile and two-mile races in the same meet. In 1937 he smashed Paavo Nurmi's two-mile indoor mark. Lash ran his races on the balls of his feet and his toes—a style thought to be unacceptable for distance runners. But he did it and won, and that's all that mattered. Rice, a five-foot, five-inch graduate of Notre Dame, dominated the distance events in the early 1940s. During that period he won sixty-five straight indoor races and set many world records.

Track and field has not been the only sport to have athletes grace the annals of the Sullivan Memorial Trophy. Swimming has also produced many world class athletes. The United States has grown stronger with the years and at present almost dominates the sport. Ann Curtis set the trend back in the 1940s. Winning eighteen U.S. outdoor titles, she was the first great American swimmer after World War II. In 1944 she won the Olympic 400-meter title in London and was later presented with the prestigious Sullivan award.

Twenty years later swimmers became the strong suit of American Summer Olympic teams. With stars such as Don Schollander, Debbie Meyer, John Kinsella, Tim Shaw, Mark Spitz, and John Naber, the United States was turning in some golden performances. Shaw, for example, was only the second man in history to hold the 200-, 400-, and 1500-meter freestyle world records at the same time. At the 1964 games at Tokyo, Schollander, a native of Santa Clara, swam away with four golds. Debbie Meyer, from Sacramento, won three golds at the 1968 Olympics, an achievement never before realized by a woman swimmer.

Probably the greatest of them all was an Indiana University student named Mark Spitz. In the 1968 games at Mexico City the cocky, temperamental young Hoosier predicted that he'd win six golds. No one believed him, and they were right—he failed. Four years later a more mature Spitz en-

tered the games, this time with no bold predictions. He let his swimming do the talking, and he won a record seven gold medals. He later became America's pinup boy, as he made a poster displaying all seven golds on his chest.

Continuing the tradition of fine swimmers were John Naber and Tracy Caulkins. Naber won the Sullivan in 1977 and Caulkins took it in 1978. Naber was a 1976 Olympian, a year in which the U.S. men won twelve gold, ten silver, and five bronze medals in the swimming events. Big John, who won the award in his third attempt, also held some American and world records. For sixteen-year-old Tracy Caulkins, winning the Sullivan was "the biggest thrill of my life."[8] The young Tennessee swimmer had broken or tied twenty-seven world and American records.

Divers have also been able to make a splash on the national sporting scene. Two of them, Sullivan winners, have been especially impressive. They are Sammy Lee and Pat McCormick. Both of them were able to do something about which other athletes only dream: they won gold medals in two straight Olympics. In 1948 Lee won the gold in the highboard and the silver in the springboard. Four years later he repeated the highboard performance.

Record-setting swimmer Tracy Caulkins shown at dinner for gymnast Kurt Thomas. (Indianapolis Convention and Visitors Bureau)

When Lee, a doctor, retired from competitive swimming, he specialized in diseases of the ear, a problem many divers encounter.

McCormick won her double in the 1952 and 1956 games. In 1952 she won the gold in both the highboard and springboard. Coached by her airline pilot husband, she gave birth just five months before the 1956 games in Melbourne. Though her training was severely impeded, she won the gold in both events again. She became the first woman diver ever to repeat such a double. She won the Sullivan and was later the first woman ever elected to the Swimming Hall of Fame.

Records and incredible performances have been a trademark of Sullivan award winners. In 1948 Dick Button won the "grand slam" of ice skating. At the age of sixteen he won the U.S. senior title, and, by the time he finally retired, he had won a total of seven national, three North American, one European, two Olympic, and five world figure skating titles. A powerful skater, he was known for his daring jumps, flying leaps, amazing sit spins, and his famous "flying camel."

In 1973 UCLA's record-setting basketball player Bill Walton won the Sullivan. The six-foot, eleven-inch redhead led the Bruins to eighty-eight straight victories and two NCAA championships. In all three of his varsity seasons he was selected as an all-American and as College Player of the Year.

Other sports also had their representatives in the Sullivan hall of fame. In 1945 West Point's running back—also a winner of The Heisman Memorial Trophy—Felix ("Doc") Blanchard, won the award. Golf's great "grand slam" winner, Bobby Jones, was awarded the Sullivan in 1930 for his tremendous performance. In 1947 Jack Kelly won the Diamond Sculls and Canadian sculling championships and became the first rower ever to win the AAU's prestigious title of Athlete of the Year. His sister was also well-known—she was Princess Grace of Monaco.

Bill Bradley of Princeton University showed that books and basketball can at times work together. In 1964 he played for the U.S. Olympic team that defeated Russia for the gold. He also set a record by scoring fifty-eight points in an NCAA tournament game and was voted MVP of the tourney in his senior year. After he graduated the studious Bradley spent two years at Oxford University in England as a Rhodes scholar. When he finished, Bradley, who was considered the best player in the history of the Ivy League, was drafted by the New York Knicks of the NBA.

In 1980 a young speed skater from Wisconsin staged one of the most incredible performances the

One of college basketball's most dominating players was UCLA center Bill Walton. (San Diego Hall of Champions photo)

sport has ever seen. Competing in the Olympic Games, Eric Heiden raced his way to all five gold medals in the competition. Never before had an Olympic competitor done this. For his efforts, he was awarded the Sullivan trophy. A lifetime devotee of amateur sports, Heiden shunned the lure of professional contracts for the world of amateur bicycle racing.

In keeping with the rich tradition of track superstars, world champion hurdler Edwin Moses won the Sullivan in 1983. The first hurdler to win it since Glenn Davis in 1958, Moses had an outstanding year. He won the U.S. National Championships and then went on to capture the gold medal at the World Games in Helsinki, Finland.

The Sullivan Memorial Trophy is one of the most unusual awards in the world of sports. The winner is often difficult to predict, for there are so many sports to choose from, and no athlete has ever won it twice. According to the AAU, it is the Oscar of the amateur athletic world. "The trophy is presented to the athlete who combines character, sportsmanship, and leadership with outstanding accomplishments in amateur sports."[9]

When an athlete wins the trophy, he is at the top of the sports world. The course he takes to get there is as unique as his personality. When 1943

Speed skater Eric Heiden set the Winter Olympics at Lake Placid on fire with his five gold medal performance. It also earned him the coveted Sullivan Trophy. (UPI photo)

winner Gil Dodds was just a boy, he threw a rock at a passing car. The driver of the car stopped, got out, and gave the boy a good boot. The name of the driver was Lloyd Hahn, a former track star who later helped start Dodds off to his outstanding track career.

For Cornelius ("Dutch") Warmerdam, the 1942 Sullivan winner, success came after he was discovered pole-vaulting as a boy. The person who uncovered his potential was not a track coach or a scout, but a traveling salesman! What's even more unusual is the place in which he was discovered vaulting to great heights—his father's spinach patch!

Sullivan Memorial Trophy Winners

1930	Bobby Jones (golf)
1931	Barney Berlinger (track)
1932	Jim Bausch (track)
1933	Glen Cunningham (track)
1934	Bill Bonthron (track)
1935	Lawson Little (golf)
1936	Glen Morris (track)
1937	Don Budge (tennis)
1938	Don Lash (track)
1939	Joe Burk (rowing)
1940	Greg Rice (track)
1941	Leslie MacMitchell (track)
1942	Cornelius Warmerdam (track)
1942	Gilbert Dodds (track)
1944	Ann Curtis (swimming)
1945	Doc Blanchard (football)
1946	Arnold Tucker (football)
1947	John Kelly, Jr. (rowing)
1948	Robert Mathias (track)
1949	Dick Button (figure skating)
1950	Fred Wilt (track)
1951	Rev. Robert Richards (track)
1952	Horace Ashenfelter (track)
1953	Dr. Sammy Lee (diving)
1954	Mal Whitfield (track)
1955	Harrison Dillard (track)
1956	Patricia McCormick (diving)
1957	Bobby Joe Morrow (track)
1958	Glenn Davis (track)
1959	Parry O'Brien (track)
1960	Rafer Johnson (track)
1961	Wilma Rudolph Ward (track)
1962	James Beatty (track)
1963	John Pennel (track)
1964	Don Schollander (swimming)

1965   Bill Bradley (basketball)
1966   Jim Ryun (track)
1967   Randy Matson (track)
1968   Debbie Meyer (swimming)
1969   Bill Toomey (track)
1970   John Kinsella (swimming)
1971   Mark Spitz (swimming)
1972   Frank Shorter (track)
1973   Bill Walton (basketball)
1974   Rick Wohlhuter (track)

1975   Tim Shaw (swimming)
1976   Bruce Jenner (track)
1977   John Naber (swimming)
1978   Tracy Caulkins (swimming)
1979   Kurt Thomas (gymnastics)
1980   Eric Heiden (speed skating)
1981   Carl Lewis (track)
1982   Mary Decker (track)
1983   Edwin Moses (track)

13
The Borg-Warner Trophy

Drawn by the thrill of high speeds and the excitement of roaring all-out competition, fans from all over the United States flock every year to what many consider to be the pinnacle of auto racing—the Indianapolis 500.

A grueling test of both man and machine, "the Indy 500" has provided some of the most spectacular moments in the history of the sport. Traveling at speeds up to two hundred miles per hour, drivers are constantly faced with the possibility of a failure, either mechanical or human—and the inevitable result. Despite the risk the drivers keep driving and the fans keep coming.

For the competitors it is no wonder. The winner of the 1979 Indy, Rick Mears, brought home over $250,000—earnings that made the event the richest race in the world. But even more important than the financial reward is the prestige that follows. The winner of the Indianapolis 500 is annually presented with the revered Borg-Warner Trophy, a symbol that he is the best there is. Success at the Indy establishes drivers as the top in the world. Future races become easier to find, and recognition is universal.

Along with the Formula I Grand Prix at Monaco and the twenty-four-hour event at Le Mans, the Indy 500 is considered to be one of the premiere events in all the world. To American fans it is the biggest race of the three, and it is the highlight of every racing year.

While winning in the sport of auto racing itself is hard enough, winning at the Indianapolis 500 is an even tougher task. In most auto races there is not much prestige for those who finish in second place or lower. But at Indy, just being in the field brings recognition. To be one of the thirty-two Indy drivers can bring instant popularity. Making the field is not easy, for it is an exclusive club. Out of thousands of racers throughout the world, only a handful qualify for the race.

Established in 1911, the Indy 500 has become a tradition. Since the initial opening flag, the race has been run every year, except during the two world wars. It has become a standard of American culture. Despite depression, bad weather, and domestic troubles the annual running takes place. It has withstood the test of time, and its prestige, popularity, and ceremony remain intact.

The first Indy was won by an Indianapolis pilot named Ray Harroun on 30 May 1911. He drove a Marmon special called the Wasp. The race was held on his home track. From this simple beginning it has grown into what is often called "the greatest spectacle in racing." Harroun won $14,950 for his victory, and since then the pot has steadily grown. His winning time was six hours, forty-two minutes, eight seconds, at an average speed of 74.59 miles per hour. By the early 1970s speeds jumped to an average of over 160 miles per hour and the winner's purse was over a quarter of a mil-

The Borg-Warner Trophy. (Borg-Warner Corp.)

lion dollars. Today, endorsements, appearances, and other rewards can make virtual millionaires of the winning drivers.

In 1912 one of the most memorable races in Indy history took place. Having just over one lap to go, Ralph DePalma led the race by a five-lap margin. Suddenly, the engine on his Mercedes started to die, and the car eventually came to full stop. De-Palma and his riding mechanic were about to give up after driving over six hours. They got out of the car and began to push it along the track. They inched their car toward the finish line, but despite their efforts their victory was not to be. Young Joe Dawson of Indianapolis eventually made up the huge difference and sped by them to win the race. DePalma was bitterly disappointed by the result, but his determination went down as one of the most heroic efforts ever.

Persistence proved to be a virtue for DePalma. In 1915 he won the race and the Borg-Warner Trophy. He was on top of the world, but it didn't last. Bad luck hit him again in 1920. This time he had a two-lap lead on the 187th lap of the race when his car ran out of gas. A man by the name of Gaston Chevrolet (one of three Swiss brothers who started the Chevrolet Motor Company) passed him and went on to win the race. DePalma managed to take fifth place.

The outcome of the race has always been largely

The first Indianapolis 500 was won by Ray Harroun on 30 May 1911. (Indy 500 photo)

influenced by luck, both good and bad. Most drivers experience a little of both. When they experience the bad, it can be fatal. For Chevrolet it was just that: he was tragically killed in a race the same year as his victory. His place on the Frontenac team was filled by a man named Tommy Milton. Milton, who had been born blind in one eye, went on to become the first two-time winner of the 500, winning in 1921 and 1923.

Milton's achievement was later overshadowed by a driver named Louis Meyer. Meyer was very influential in the development of the famous Offenhauser engine, which has ridden to victory on numerous occasions. And on three of those occasions Meyer was in the driver's seat. Winning the race in 1928, 1933, and 1936, he became an Indy immortal.

An amusing aside to the 1933 victory was the way in which a small town in Colorado published the results. The editor of the Walsenberg, Colorado, *World Independent* asked the Associated Press for the results of the race. AP, as was its custom, wired back: "Will Overhead Indianapolis race winner," which simply meant that the result would be sent "overhead" by Western Union. Misinterpreting the message the Colorado editor made up a story about the race, which ran under a page-one banner headline, reading: "Will Overhead Wins Indianapolis Race."

That same 1933 race involved a controversy, which surrounded veteran driver Howdy Wilcox. Wilcox, who had placed second the year before, was given a second physical the morning of the race. A regular on the American Automobile Association driving circuit, he had done well in other races. But the judges, concerned about his physical condition and his diabetes, flunked the veteran this time. The other racers, shocked, threatened to boycott the race. The president of the track, Eddie Rickenbacker, a former Wolrd War I flying ace and Indy driver, stood firm in his decision not to allow Wilcox to race. The situation developed into a standoff. Finally, Rickenbacker threatened to cancel the race and shut down the speedway forever. The drivers were forced to give in, and the race went on as scheduled, without Wilcox.

Taking his place was a rookie named Mauri Rose. He drove a respectable race, running at times as high as fourth place. Rose didn't win, but his day in the sun would come a few years later. In fact he would have three days in the sun. Rose entered an elite club when he won the coveted trophy three times—in 1941, 1947, and 1948.

In 1934 the 500 was won by a popular hometown

By 1935, the starting field along with the onlooking crowds, began to grow. (Indy 500 photo)

boy named Bill Cummings. Lady Luck smiled upon this Indianapolis product, and the victory made him a great hero of the area. Five years later he experienced another kind of luck. Race car owner Mike Boyle reportedly ordered a new Maserati, which he wanted Cummings to drive in the Indy that year. On the day in which the car arrived in the United States, Cummings was driving down a rain-soaked country road some twenty miles outside Indianapolis. As he approached a narrow bridge, an oncoming car skidded out of control and hit Cummings's car head-on. When the smoke cleared and the wreckage was separated, Cummings was found, dead. It was a tragic loss to the sport of auto racing.

From 1937 to 1940 three of the four races were won by the same man. Wilbur Shaw was his name, and his talent on the racetrack soon became widely recognized. His first victory was over Ralph Hepburn by only 2·16 seconds, one of the closest finishes in race history. In 1939 he drove a Maserati to the finish line and repeated that performance the next year. It was the first time a driver had pulled off back-to-back wins at the 500.

The outbreak of World War II almost brought about the death of the famed speedway. In 1909 the old dirt track was paved with 3·2 million bricks. Rickenbacker bought the raceway in 1927. When the Second World War broke out, his interest in the track waned. After many attempts he finally sold the 539-acre facility in 1945. The new owner was an Indiana millionaire named Tony Hulman, who took control of the track under the condition that it wouldn't cost him any money and that he would reinvest the profits into the track. Under his control the speedway became alive once again. Over 250,000 seats were installed, and it became one of the most modern raceways in the world.

After four years of suspended activity, from 1942 to 1945, Hulman used a special promotion to get things back on their feet. Before the war the purse was about $96,000; Hulman raised it to over $115,000, including a whopping $42,500 for the winning driver. Drivers throughout the world took note.

The 500 resumed in 1946 with thirty-three cars starting. Of those, only eight were around at the finish. The winner was George Robinson, who five months later was killed in a race in Atlanta. The next few years belonged to the Blue Crown cars of Mauri Rose and Bill Holland. Rose won in 1947 and 1948, and Holland took the trophy in 1949.

A driver named Bill Vukovich then hit the scene and made his mark. In 1952 Vukovich, competing in just his second Indy, had a large lead after 192

Bill Vukovich (14) edged out Jimmy Bryan (9) for the checkered flag in the 1954 Indy. (Indy 500 photo)

laps of the race when his steering system broke and forced him to drop out. A determined driver, he reappeared the very next year and won the race by a wide margin. A factor that was beginning to take effect was the intense heat on the track. In 1953 eight drivers were forced out of the race because of the temperature, and one, Carl Scarborough, later died of heat exhaustion. The same problem occurred the next year, as twenty-eight relief drivers had to be used. Vukovich, however, was not affected. He won again in 1954, and it seemed that no one could stop him.

No one, that is, except Lady Luck. After 140 miles of the 1955 race a terrible accident occurred. It was one of the biggest multiple-car pileups in the race's history. Rodger Ward (who went on to win the 500 in 1959 and 1962) was heading down the back stretch when the axle on his car broke. Behind him drivers Johnny Boyd and Al Keller hit each other trying to avoid his flipping car. Vukovich tried to race right through the bouncing and careening cars. He didn't make it. After crashing into Boyd, his car bounced wildly across the track, over a wall, and into a crowded parking lot. Two spectators were injured, and Vukovich died instantly of head injuries.

Vukovich's death prompted the American Automobile Association to terminate its association with auto racing and sent fans into an uproar. Bills were introduced into Congress to outlaw racing. But Hulman once again came to the rescue. He started the United States Auto Club to watch over the sport.

The 1958 Indy featured one of the wildest starts that the race has ever seen. From the beginning the lineup was not very well organized. Before a single lap was completed, there was a terrible fifteen-car collision, which resulted in the death of a popular driver, Pat O'Connor. "The accident started," wrote one authority, "when Ed Elisian tried to pass pole position starter Dick Rathmann in what was later considered a dangerous maneuver. They spun, with Elisian taking Rathmann into the wall. Bob Veith hit Jimmy Reece, who spun under O'Connor. O'Connor's car flipped violently. Jerry Unser catapulted over Paul Goldsmith and out of the track."[1] Following the accident, Elisian was barred from further competition by the USAC. He was later reinstated, however, when a judge ruled that he was guilty merely of an error of judgment, for which he could not be penalized.

For any rookie driver at Indy, just making it into the final field is an achievement. Many tried and tested veterans show up year in and year out, keenly aware of what it takes to make the field. But every year, without fail, there is a group of new racers—and some old ones—who show up with one thing in mind—qualifying for the race. They are known as "rookies," which is a deceptive term, for many of them have tried for years but have never made it. Even if they come for five years in a row, they are still rookies until they make the final cut. Despite the stiffness of the competition, many determined rookies trudge on, for the reward at the end of the rainbow is great.

Sometimes, it is a bitter trail searching for that rainbow. Al Loquasto, Jr., of Easton, Pennsylvania, found that out. Loquasto first ventured to the Indy track in 1970. Hard luck hit him right away, as his car had an unfortunate meeting with the wall in the third turn of a practice run. He didn't even have a chance to qualify. Undaunted, he returned in 1971, only to be eliminated by another unfortunate crash. Loquasto then spent many long hours practicing for the 1972 race. He was unable to make a qualifying run, however, and his hopes were dashed again. In 1973 his old friend, the crash, eliminated him from the festivities again. His hard luck continued until 1976, when he finally qualified as a seventh-year rookie. For all his efforts he finished in twenty-fifth place. Loquasto qualified again in 1977 but was forced to drop out early in the race because of mechanical problems. Not to be called a quitter, he qualified once again in 1978. As race day approached, however, he was knocked out of the competition by a car with a faster time.

Some rookies did have some luck at Indy. In fact a few of them combined talent with that luck to capture the Borg-Warner Trophy. To win the 500 in a very first attempt is a rare achievement. Ray Harroun did it in 1911; Jules Goux, in 1913; Rene Thomas, in 1914; Frank Lockhart, in 1926; George Souders, in 1927; and Graham Hill, in 1966. A rookie winning at the Indianapolis 500 is like the United States winning a gold medal in ice hockey at the Olympics. But then, that happens every once in a while too.

A third class of first-year drivers are the rookies who never really know that they are rookies. The president of this small club was a young driver named Billy Arnold. He appeared at the track one day in 1930. Veteran driver Harry Hartz, always a top runner at Indy, had just realized that he was no longer able to qualify a car for the 500. What really annoyed him was that he and mechanic Jean Marcenac had spent all winter building a powerful car that they knew would do well in the race. All week, during the time trials, Arnold hung around the pits to try to get Hartz's permission to drive the racer. Finally, out of desperation, Hartz told him to get in the car and start it up. The rest is history. Arnold gained the pole position by qualifying with the fastest speed and went on to win the race, leading the field the entire way.

Hartz and Arnold returned to the speedway the following year and continued to amaze people. Once again, Arnold pulled away from the field gaining, at times, a five-lap lead. But Arnold, known to have a heavy foot on the gas pedal, soon ran into trouble. Hartz, seeing how big a lead his car had, thought that the young driver was pushing it too hard. He continually held up pit signs telling Arnold to slow down, but the enthusiastic racer would just nod, wave, and keep right on going. Then, on the 162d lap, the rear axle on the car broke, and the car crashed into a racer driven by Luther Johnson. Arnold's car flew over the wall and landed in a burst of flames, and the driver barely escaped. Meanwhile, one of Arnold's huge tires had bounced out of the raceway, careened down the street for over a quarter of a mile, and finally struck and killed a young boy.

In 1932 Arnold and Hartz returned to the speedway with a new racer and a determination to make up for the previous year. After just two laps, the young daredevil had built a big lead and, while trying to pass a slower car, lost control and smashed into the wall. The car was destroyed and Arnold was injured. After he recovered, Arnold decided to retire. The sport will never be the same.

In 1960 a classic battle took place at the speedway. The lead changed hands a record twenty-nine times, as Jim Rathmann and Rodger Ward fought for the title and the trophy. Neither racer was able to establish control until the 197th lap. That's when Ward's right front tire started to wear down. Rathmann passed him, kept the lead, and raced home for a tight twelve-second victory.

Another incredibly close race occurred the next year. This time it was between A. J. Foyt, a rookie in the 1958 Indy, and Eddie Sachs. It came down to a battle of the pit crews, as both Foyt and Sachs seemed to have the race won at various points. After the third and supposedly final pit stop, Foyt suddenly left the track again to check the amount of fuel in his tank. Because his refueling nozzle stuck on his third stop, he hadn't gotten totally refueled. Seventeen seconds after his fourth pit stop, he headed back onto the track after Sachs. There were just two laps to go, and it looked good for Sachs. But then he too was forced into the pits to repair a shredded right rear tire. Twenty-three seconds later Sachs roared back onto the raceway, but Foyt was too far ahead to catch. The Texan won the race.

An interesting statistic is that in four pit stops, Sachs's crew took a total of 99 seconds, while Foyt's took 91·7. The time difference of 7·3 seconds doesn't seem to be much until it is realized that Foyt won the race by just 8·3 seconds! The same fate befell Sachs the following year. His crew took twenty seconds longer than the crew of winner Rodger Ward, and Ward beat Sachs by, yes, twenty seconds.

Parnelli Jones won the 500 in 1963, but once again Sachs was near the center of attention. During the race the tank on Jones's car developed a leak and began throwing oil. Despite the problem Jones continued. Sachs publicly criticized the winner for his dangerous actions, and the day after the race the two had a well-publicized fight.

The 1964 race brought about another tragic accident, and once again the man in the middle was Eddie Sachs. A pack of cars was making the fourth turn on the second lap when Dave MacDonald's slid into the inside wall. Upon impact the car burst into flames and bounced back across the track in front of the oncoming drivers. As it slid towards the outside wall, Sachs crashed head-on into the burning car, and there was a horrifying explosion. Flames shot high into the air, and a black cloud hung over the racetrack. Both Sachs and MacDonald were killed and many other racers were burned. For the first time in history, the race was stopped. When it did resume, it was eventually won by A. J. Foyt.

Another hectic start took place in 1966, when sixteen cars crashed into each other. Though there were no injuries, eleven cars were unable to continue. By the time the 500 was completed, there were only seven cars left on the track. A rookie by the name of Graham Hill won in what was considered a shallow victory.

In 1971 Al Unser captured his second of three eventual Borg-Warner Trophies. (Indy 500 photo)

Winning his third Indy in 1967, Foyt was considered by many to be the greatest American racer ever. In that 1967 race he trailed Parnelli Jones until the 197th lap, when Jones had a mechanical failure. Foyt sped away to victory. Opportunity didn't knock too often for Foyt after that, however, as that coveted fourth Indy championship eluded him.

The famous Unser family then began to make its mark at Indianapolis. Bobby Unser won the race in 1968 and 1975, and his brother Al took it in 1970, 1971, and 1978.

In 1973 another tragedy made the news at the 500. During the month before the race, competitors spend long hours practicing on the track. The morning of pole-position qualifications, driver Art Pollard was killed. Then, on race day, shortly after it started, officials were forced to stop the race because of a thirteen-car crash. The car of Salt Walther bounced into the air and crashed into the fence. His tank was torn open, and eighty gallons of gasoline were released onto the track. The fuel then ignited, and pieces of the car flew into the crowd, burning numerous spectators. Walther's auto then flipped back onto the raceway, crashing into the other cars on the track. Flames and debris spread over the area, but, surprisingly, no one was killed. Although badly burned, Walther did recover and went on to continue his racing career.

Black clouds hung ominously over the track, it began to rain heavily and the race was postponed. The next day, as the cars lined up to start, another downpour caused the race to be postponed again. On the third day officials were determined to get the race underway. Again the weather was threatening, and the drivers and their teams were

The start of the 1980 Indy shows just how big an event the race has become, as thousands of people line the famed Indianapolis Motor Speedway track. (Indy 500 photo)

lax about their preparations. Then, suddenly, the officials announced that the race would start in twenty minutes. Unprepared, the drivers frantically readied their vehicles, and the race began. After about 100 miles the car of Swede Savage hit the inside wall on the fourth turn. His car bounced back across the track. While the injured Savage tried to pull himself away from the fiery debris, a fire truck rushed to the scene and in the process struck and killed one of Savage's teammates, Armando Teran. Firemen, doctors, and volunteers rushed to the scene to aid the helpless driver. But it was too late—Swede Savage had died.

After a delay officials restarted the race, only to have it postponed sixty miles later due to rain. Gordon Johncock, who was in the lead at the time, was declared the winner. He collected over $225,000 for the victory.

In response to criticism regarding the safety of the race, improvements were made in 1974. A classic battle was then staged between Foyt and Johnny Rutherford. A broken oil pump forced Foyt out of the competition in the latter stages, and Rutherford cruised home to victory. Proving that his victory was no fluke, Rutherford went on to win the prestigious trophy once again in 1976.

In 1977 something remarkable happened. Ten years after his last victory, the amazing A. J. Foyt won his fourth Indianapolis 500. He had served notice in 1976, when he finished second, so it was just a matter of time. With the victory Foyt undoubtedly placed his name in the record books as the greatest racer ever to leave rubber on the famed track. It was a spectacular achievement for a spectacular driver.

One of the most controversial and eventful races in 500 history occurred in 1981. Disasters characterized the sixty-fifth running, which saw five crashes, numerous fires, eight men hospitalized, and no less than eleven caution periods. It was a day filled with bad luck for many. Rick Mears was

Johnny Rutherford went on to win the 1980 Indianapolis 500. (Indy 500 photo)

one of them. After fifty-seven laps he was leading the race and decided to pull in for a pit stop. Suddenly, his car burst into flames, and the fire enveloped both him and a crew member. The pit crew quickly extinguished the flames, but Mears and the crewmen suffered serious burns.

At the end of the day Bobby Unser crossed the finish line at the checkered flag with one of the slowest winning times (139·084 miles per hour) since the early 1960s. But on a day when the unexpected became the expected, questions soon arose as to whether Unser really won. Mario Andretti filed a protest, claiming that Unser had illegally passed eight or nine cars during a caution period. The next day the Stewards of the Indianapolis Motor Speedway, after reviewing films of the race, declared that Unser had committed an infraction and penalized him one lap. This made Andretti the winner. Unser protested and the decision was later reversed—giving him the trophy.

In its seventy-year history the Indianapolis 500 has been marked by spectacular events. Not all of them are good, for some end in tragedy. More so than most sports, auto racing is representative of life itself. There are risks—grave ones—and there is uncertainty. But the reward is so great that no driver would dare pass it up. Maybe that's why millions of fans follow this one event so religiously. It is not just a race between machines or a race between drivers. It is a race between life and death, prestige and failure. And when a driver steps up to the winner's circle to receive the Borg-Warner Trophy, millions of people are standing right there with him.

Borg-Warner Trophy Winners

1911	Ray Harroun
1912	Joe Dawson
1913	Jules Goux
1914	Rene Thomas
1915	Ralph DePalma
1916	Dario Resta
1919	Howdy Wicox
1920	Gaston Chevrolet
1921	Tommy Milton
1922	Jimmy Murphy
1923	Tommy Milton
1924	L. L. Corum, Joe Boyer
1925	Peter DePaolo
1926	Frank Lockhart
1927	George Souders
1928	Louis Meyer
1929	Ray Keech
1930	Billy Arnold
1931	Louis Schneider
1932	Fred Frame
1933	Louis Meyer
1934	Bill Cummings
1935	Kelly Petillo
1936	Louis Meyer
1937	Wilbur Shaw
1938	Floyd Roberts
1939	Wilbur Shaw
1940	Wilbur Shaw
1941	Floyd Davis, Mauri Rose
1946	George Robson
1947	Mauri Rose
1948	Mauri Rose
1949	Bill Holland
1950	Johnnie Parsons
1951	Lee Wallard
1952	Troy Ruttman
1953	Bill Vukovich
1954	Bill Vukovich
1955	Bob Sweikert
1956	Pat Flaherty
1957	Sam Hanks
1958	Jimmy Bryan
1959	Rodger Ward
1960	Jim Rathmann
1961	AJ Foyt
1962	Rodger Ward
1963	Parnelli Jones
1964	AJ Foyt
1965	Jim Clark
1966	Graham Hill
1967	AJ Foyt
1968	Bobby Unser
1969	Mario Andretti
1970	Al Unser

1971	Al Unser	1978	Al Unser
1972	Mark Donohue	1979	Rick Mears
1973	Gordon Johncock	1980	Johnny Rutherford
1974	John Rutherford	1981	Bobby Unser
1975	Bobby Unser	1982	Gordon Johncock
1976	John Rutherford	1983	Tom Sneva
1977	AJ Foyt		

14
The Walker Cup

"The award that never was"—that's almost what the Walker Cup, the esteemed trophy of American and British amateur golf, came to be known as.

The brainchild and gift of George Herbert Walker, the president of the United States Golf Association (USGA), the Walker Cup represented an attempt to promote a worldwide competition of amateur golfers. When Walker presented his idea to the USGA in 1920, it was enthusiastically accepted, and invitations were sent out to nations all over the world to compete for the cup, originally called the International Challenge Trophy. The Americans sat back and waited. Nobody came. The British, who were at that time considered the best and most enthusiastic golfers in the world, did not reply.

The Americans refused to be discouraged. That same year, at the invitation of the Royal Ancient Club at St. Andrews, Walker and other USGA officials traveled to Great Britain to discuss possible modifications in the playing code. One outcome of the meeting was a match between the countries the following year. The match was set up at Hoylake, the place of the 1921 British Amateur Championship. The talented group of American golfers, led by Bill Fownes, thoroughly trounced their astonished English opponents, 9–3. Impressed, the British golf hierarchy finally decided to accept the USGA's invitation. Thus was born one of golf's most prestigious competitions.

It was no small achievement for a group of brash young Americans to go in and beat the best in the world on their own course. For the sport of golf in Great Britain is steeped with tradition. Those who participate are surrounded by glory, honor, recognition, and a reverent sense of history.

Though a modern game, golf is thought to have roots as far back as ancient Rome. The Romans played a game called *paganica*, which involved hitting a feathered ball with a crooked stick. It is believed that Roman soldiers brought the game to the British Isles and Europe, and that it was fairly well established by the fourth century, when they withdrew from these areas.

In the Middle Ages "kolf" was played in the low countries on ice. Players hit a ball with a crooked stick at a pole, strategically placed in the ice. From this practice, it is believed, emerged golf, as well as croquet, curling, and other sports.

The game continued to grow. By 1500 it had become developed and refined. The Scots are given credit for that achievement. Using clubs, they hit leather balls into holes. Though officially banned in 1457 because it kept men from their all-important archery practice, the game was so popular that the law was never really enforced.

The first golf match ever recorded was between the Prince of Wales and two English noblemen. A large bet was made, and the prince, along with an Edinburgh cobbler, won the contest.

The Walker Cup, donated in 1920 by George Herbert Walker, President of the United States Golf Association. (USGA photo)

Not surprisingly, then, when George Walker donated a cup and sent out invitations for a challenge, the British were somewhat amused. World War I was coming to an end, and an era known as "the Golden Twenties" of the golf world was being ushered in. Because of the war and the traveling it involved, people had become more familiar with other areas of the globe. This helped set the stage for worldwide sports competition, and the Walker Cup became one of its offshoots.

The idea to stage matches between amateur golfers from the United States and Great Britain had surfaced many years earlier. The Americans had already been involved in similar matches with their northern neighbor, Canada. In 1919 The Royal Canadian Golf Association invited the USGA to send a team to Canada. The USGA accepted and sent a team which, captained by Fownes, included Bobby Jones, Chick Evans, Jr., Bob Gardner, Oswald Kirkby, Max Marston, Francis Ouimet, George Ormiston, Jerome Travers, John Anderson, and Eben Byers. The match was played at the Hamilton Golf Club in Ontario on 25 July. There were five foursomes in the morning and ten individual matches in the afternoon. The United States won, 12–3.

In 1920 a return match was played at the Engineers Country Club in Roslyn, New York. Once again, the Americans were successful, this time by an equally impressive 10–4 score. They now felt ready to challenge anybody. A clash between the U.S. and Great Britain seemed almost inevitable. Ouimet had already beaten England's renowned twosome, Harry Vardon and Ted Ray, in the 1913 U.S. Open. They were ready to make a new challenge. When the British came to America to play in some of the tournaments, they took an enthusiastic interest in the U.S.-Canada matches. They wanted to initiate similar competition. The Americans were more than willing to accommodate them.

Despite its initial failures, the Walker Cup eventually caught on. It came to symbolize one of the biggest golf events in history. After the American amateurs trounced the British, 9–3, in 1921, the cup matches got into full swing. The first Walker Cup match was played at the National Links at Southampton on Long Island. The president of the USGA at that time, Howard Whitney, worked out the final details with the Royal and Ancient Club members. Each country was to select eight players, and the matches were to consist of four foursomes and eight singles. It was to be a thirty-six-hole event, played over a two-day period.

The United States fielded much the same team as they did the year before at Hoylake. Fownes was captain, and Jones, Evans, Guilford, and Ouimet headed his lineup. Ouimet had won the hearts of golf fans all over the world with his incredible victory over his British opponents in the 1913 U.S. Open. He was just twenty years old at the time, and nobody gave him a shot at even being competitive in the tournament. He was known as "the gardener's son, who lived across the street from the Country Club."[1] A birdie on the seventeenth hole of regulation play gave him a tie for the lead and set up a play-off with the two wily veterans. He won it the next day with a seventy-two, and headlines all over the world told of the shocking upset.

When the Americans headed into that first Walker Cup match, Ouimet was much older and wiser. He was joined by other golfers, such as Guilford and Jones, and by some less experienced players, including Bob Gardner, Max Marston, Jess Sweetser, and Rudolf Knepper. The British also fielded a strong team, captained by Bob Harris and including Cyril Tolley, Roger Wethered, and Colin Aylmer. The Americans knew that they'd have their hands full. The Americans won three of the four foursome matches and five of the eight singles. Their 8–4 victory over the British once again proved their superiority.

An important development of the first Walker Cup match was the decision to rule out extra-hole play-offs. Before the decision was made, C. V. L. Hooman of Great Britain had beaten Sweetser in a sudden-death play-off in order to break a tie.

The next year the British were bent on revenge. The match was played on their home course. They jumped out fast, taking three of the four foursome matches on the first day. Their hot play continued the next day. At one point they led the singles by twenty-four holes. But then the Americans, led by Ouimet, George Rotan, Marston, and Fred Wright, bounced back to tie the score, 5–5. The deciding match was played between America's O. F. Willing and Britain's William Murray. Willing won the thirty-fourth and thirty-fifth holes to win the match and secure the cup for America.

The trend for the competition had been set. In 1924 the United States won at the Garden City Golf Club by a 9–3 margin. It was then decided to schedule the matches every two years instead of every year.

Led by the amazing Bobby Jones, the Americans swept to victories in 1926, 1928, and 1930. Jones was once hailed as "an amateur golfer in the purest sense." A child prodigy, he could hit the ball two hundred fifty yards when he was just fourteen years old. It was news whenever or wherever he went out to play. He led the Walker Cup team to many impressive victories. And in 1930 he did the impossible—he captured the "grand slam" of golf by winning the U.S. Open, U.S. Amateur, British Open, and British Amateur championships.

Despite Jones's amazing achievements, golf wasn't his whole life. He studied mechanical engineering at Georgia Tech, earned a degree in English Literature at Harvard, became involved in real estate, entered law school at Emory University, and eventually passed the state bar examinations. He worked his way into shape for the 1930 competition by playing a game that he called "Doug" in an abandoned Atlanta theater. Devised by his friend Douglas Fairbanks, it was a cross between paddle tennis and badminton. Mobs of people would follow Jones wherever he went on the golf course. In fact some of his celebrity friends, such as Fairbanks and Maurice Chevalier, would watch him compete. Winning the Walker Cup and then following it up with the "grand slam" made him a hero when he returned to the States. In New York, he was greeted with a ticker-tape parade down Broadway.

At the age of twenty-eight, Bobby Jones decided to retire from golf. During his membership on the Walker Cup team, he had reigned supreme. But even his retirement couldn't stop the momentum that the Americans had built up. With Lawson Little, Johnny Goodman, John Fischer, Charley Yates, and Sweetser leading the way, they won by impressive 8–1, 9–2, and 9–0 scores in the next three Walker Cup matches.

Many of the American golfers also asserted themselves in other international amateur tournaments. Sweetser, for example, won the British Amateur Championship in 1926. In the process, however, he almost killed himself. He traveled to England by boat, and somewhere along the way he picked up a bad case of influenza. After staggering through his matches, he suffered a series of serious hemorrhages in the lungs. Though he won the tournament, it took him over a year to recover from it.

From 1922 to 1936 the Americans won nine straight matches before the British were able to stop their domination. Captained by John Beck, the British battled an overconfident group of Americans at the St. Andrews course in 1938. They were a determined team who refused to succomb, and when it was all said and done, they came away with a 7–4 decision and their first Walker Cup win.

The United States Walker Cup squad. (USGA photo)

World War II suspended the competition for the next eight years. When play was resumed in 1947, the Americans reasserted themselves. The results were the same, only the names had changed. Willie Turnesa, Skee Riegal, Frank Stranahan, and Bud Ward orchestrated an impressive 8–4 victory for the United States. A new winning streak had begun.

Fielding very strong teams, the Americans continued to sink the British like six-inch putts. Many of the Americans subsequently turned professional, but as soon as they did, a new amateur came along to fill their shoes. They came from all over the country, and some stayed longer than others. Some were less familiar than others—Charley Coe of Oklahoma City, Jim McHale of Philadelphia, Sam Urzetta of Rochester, and Bill Campbell of West Virginia. Campbell, a Princeton student, was a very popular and successful member of the team who eventually became its captain. There were also big-name players who temporarily graced the team with their magnificent play. Gene Littler, Ken Venturi, Tommy Aaron, and Jack Nicklaus all went on to outstanding pro careers before their brief stints on the Walker Cup team.

Known as "the Golden Bear," Nicklaus spearheaded a 9–3 victory over the British at Muirfield in 1959. At the time, he was thought to be "representative of this new breed of home run sluggers on the golf tour. . . . He drove the ball higher, straighter, and farther with more consistency than any [other] player who had ever lived. He was a superb putter—exasperatingly slow but remarkably sure. He was a cold and calculating competitor." Nicklaus's domination of the game continued through the sixties and seventies. In 1978, at the age of thirty-eight, *Sports Illustrated* selected him as Sportsman of the Year.

Other Walker Cuppers—such as Coe, Bill Hyndman, Dean Beman, and Billy Joe Patton—were not lured into the pro ranks and remained in amateur play. Patton, it was said, "swung at the ball like a drunk at a driving range."[3] He was a runner-up in the 1954 Masters Tournament. The Americans continued to rack up victories until 1965, when the British managed a 12–12 tie. In 1963 the rules of the matches were changed to require eight foursomes and sixteen singles, played over eighteen holes instead of thirty-six.

The most amazing comeback in cup play occurred in that 1965 tie. Led by veteran Ed Tutwiler, the United States, trailing 10–5, staged a furious rally to tie the score. It took a 34-foot putt on the final hole by Britain's twenty-year-old Clive Clark to preserve the tie.

Many great professionals, such as Gene Littler, got their start in Walker Cup play. (San Diego Hall of Champions photo)

The British turned in another creditable performance in 1971, when they pulled out a 13–11 victory. Their success was short-lived, however, as the United States swept up four more wins in the seventies. In 1979 many of the top amateur golfers in America were forced to miss the match because of a schedule conflict. The National Collegiate Athletic Association staged its golf championship on the same week as the Walker Cup match was to be played. Some of the collegians, including Doug Clarke of Stanford, Griff Moody of Georgia, Hal Sutton of Centenary, and Mike Gove of Weber State, opted to play on the Walker Cup team. They went on to post a 15½–8½ win over the British.

Throughout the years the Walker Cup has shown the abundance of talent that exists among American amateur golfers. But it is not the only cup awarded in the sport. In fact there are more cups in golf than there are in a football team's locker room. There is the Curtis Cup for American and British women amateurs; there is the Ryder Cup for American and British professionals; and the World Cup (formerly called the Canada Cup and not to be confused with the soccer trophy) for international two-man teams. There are also hundreds of other tournaments held each year, both on the professional and amateur

One of the main reasons the United States was able to dominate their foes from Great Britain was the presence of the great Jack Nicklaus. (San Diego Hall of Champions photo)

circuits. One of the most rapidly growing sports in the world, golf is played in over sixty nations. The United States leads the way with over twelve million participants. The game is quickly taking root in the Orient.

"Golf has been called 'the most human of games' and 'a reflection of life,' said Bobby Jones. "One reason that we enjoy it and that it challenges us is that it enables us to run the entire gamut of human emotions, not only in a brief space of time, but

likewise without measurable damage either to ourselves or to others."[4]

There is not a sports event more exciting or traditional than the biennial Walker Cup match. Jack Nicklaus described it best: "I have never stopped looking back to it. Not only because the matches changed me from a good junior golfer to a good golfer, but also because that whole week at Muirfield—the preparation for the matches as well as the matches themselves—was an experience I'll never forget."[5]

Walker Cup Results

1922	U.S. 8, G.B. 4
1923	U.S. 6½, G.B. 4½
1924	U.S. 9, G.B. 3
1925	U.S. 6½, G.B. 4½
1928	U.S. 11, G.B. 1
1930	U.S. 10, G.B. 2
1932	U.S. 9½, G.B. 2½
1934	U.S. 9½, G.B. 2½
1936	U.S. 10½, G.B. 1½
1938	G.B. 7½, U.S. 4½
1947	U.S. 8, G.B. 4
1949	U.S. 10, G.B. 2
1951	U.S. 7½, G.B. 4½
1953	U.S. 9, G.B. 3
1955	U.S. 10, G.B. 2
1957	U.S. 8½, G.B. 3½
1959	U.S. 9, G.B. 3
1961	U.S. 11, G.B. 1
1963	U.S. 14, G.B. 10
1965	G.B. 12, U.S. 12
1967	U.S. 15, G.B. 9
1969	U.S. 13, G.B. 11
1971	G.B. 13, U.S. 11
1973	U.S. 14, G.B. 10
1975	U.S. 15½, G.B. 8½
1977	U.S. 16, G.B. 8
1979	U.S. 15½, G.B.-Ireland 8½
1981	U.S. 15, G.B.-Ireland 9
1983	U.S. 13½, G.B.-Ireland 10½

15
The Boston Marathon Medal

By modern standards, it isn't much. As trophies and medals go, it's small. Some people might even mistake it for some type of currency. But that doesn't matter, at least not to the people who know what it's all about. And what it's all about is pain, endurance, mental anxiety, and 26 miles, 385 yards of the toughest running in the world.

The Boston Marathon is the premiere event in the United States for long-distance runners. A test not only of speed and endurance, it is for many a test of survival. For the winner, at the end of it all, there is satisfaction, a sense of achievement, recognition, and the winner's medal. To some it may appear small, but to those who know, it represents a gigantic accomplishment.

Sponsored by the Boston Athletic Association, the marathon is held every year on the third Monday in April. Running in America has become a national obsession, and over two hundred fifty thousand spectators line the famed course to observe "the Boston." Observes one national magazine: "Marathon running had blossomed from the highly select pastime of a few competitive oddballs of seemingly seperhuman stamina into a mass movement of seriously trained amateurs, who find the distance of 26·2 miles manageable, even though it is a test of the flesh and spirit which can't be found in any other sport."[1] From its humble beginnings in 1897 with only fifteen participants, the marathon has grown into a national event with over fifteen hundred runners taking part.

Tradition is as much a part of the mystique of the Boston Marathon as anything else. From the beginning the Boston Athletic Association wanted the event to be nonprofessional, nonpolitical, and noncommercial. That's exactly the way it began, and the way it has been maintained through over eighty years of competition. The biggest and oldest marathon in the United States, it was the first race to attract runners from throughout the world.

The race starts in Hopkinton, halfway between Boston and Worcester, and ends in Boston. Thousands of runners struggle painfully just to make it to the finish line in the downtown area. For most, it is a fantasy just to complete it, but for a group of well-trained, top-notch competitors it is a fight-to-the-finish battle for the winner's medal.

When that first runner crosses the tape, physically and emotionally sapped of every ounce of strength he possesses, he receives a hero's welcome, the first-place medal, and an overdose of muscular cramps and exhaustion. The following thirty-four finishers receive either a small trophy or bronze medal and a congratulations for their strength and endurance.

Runners who participate in the Boston come from all callings in life. There are college students, businessmen, housewives, doctors, priests, and

Thousands of runners jam the streets and head out over the 26 mile, 385 yard course to downtown Boston. (UPI photo)

even handicapped people. In 1970 a twenty-four-year-old Marine crossed the finish line seven hours after he started. Having lost both his legs in Vietnam, he completed the race in a wheelchair. In 1969 a sixty-two-year-old mill worker named Alfred Ventrillo finished in about four and a half hours. he was blind.

Outlining the history of the Boston Marathon is similar to retracing the course of distance running in America. It started out very slowly in 1897, went through a period of rapid growth, experienced an influx of foreign competitors, was forced to deal with publicity hounds and thrill seekers, finally admitted female participants, and grew to such proportions that restrictions had to be placed on it.

The first Boston Marathon was won by John McDermott of New York. Battling his own fatigue, he finished the race in just under three hours. There were fifteen runners in the original race, which was run on some dusty, unpaved roads that severely hampered their efforts. The distance was 24 miles, 1,232 yards. It was a slow start, but it was a start.

Foreign runners didn't wait long to make their presence felt. In 1900 two Canadians, James Caffrey and Bill Sherring, finished first and second, respectively, and the trend was set. A countryman of theirs, Indian Tom Longboat, won the race in 1907, but it wasn't without its obstacles. He and second-place finisher Bob Fowler were the only runners who weren't stopped and delayed for a long period of time by a passing freight train.

Weather has always been a key factor in the endurance of the competitors in their trek to Boston. In 1909 the biggest field of runners up to that point, 164 in all, was greeted by an unbearable 97-degree day. Henri Renaud proved too hot to handle as he ran away to an impressive win, after ninety-nine of the runners dropped out.

The following year was marked by the appearance of a man who proved to be the most memorable runner in the history of the race. His name was Clarence DeMar, and his efforts and successes in the Boston Marathon immortalized him in the sport.

A native of Boston, DeMar was born with a curvature of the spine and consequently had an unnatural walk. He began running at a young age and developed a severe infection on his ankle and foot. Doctors considered amputating it, but the condition improved before this drastic step became necessary.

DeMar then began running again. When he was a student at the University of Vermont, he undertook two jobs and ran to and from each of them. The distance totalled about eight miles, and his endurance grew. Having gained self-confidence, he tried out for the school's track team. Despite his awkward running style he was accepted by the coach, mainly because of his enthusiasm and determination. He soon became a better runner and learned more efficient techniques. He was forced to quit the team, however, to help support his family.

DeMar took a job in Boston, and once again his mode of transportation was his feet. He ran to and from work every day for a total of fourteen miles. The idea of entering a marathon entered his mind, and he began to train for it. He analyzed the course of the Boston and worked hard trying to conquer it.

On 19 April 1910 DeMar entered the race, along with twenty other aspiring marathoners. He stayed near the front of the pack as the race progressed and utilized his training to the utmost. As he climbed his way up famous Heartbreak Hill, he realized he had been making decisive progress. As the runners headed into the city, he suddenly realized he was in fourth place and moving fast. It was a matter of minutes before he was in second and racing for the finish line. Although Freddie Cameron, who was too far ahead to catch, won the race, DeMar finished second, only one minute behind.

In the prerace physical the next near, DeMar was discovered to have a heart murmur and told he shouldn't race. After pleading with the doctor, he finally was allowed to run, but only on the condition that he would drop out if he experienced any problems. The only problems that popped up during the race were those that the other runners experienced trying to keep up with DeMar. He went on to win the marathon in a record time of two hours, twenty-one minutes, thirty-nine seconds. Quite an accomplishment for a man with a twisted spine and a heart murmur.

DeMar was then picked for the United States Olympic team. The coaches recommended that he change his running style, and in the 1912 games in Sweden he finished in a dismal eleventh place. DeMar served in World War I, but kept right on training, often running in his army boots. When he returned to the United States from France, he continued where he had left off. He won the 1922 Boston Marathon, and despite illness just a month before the race, won again in 1923 and again in 1924. He was the first runner ever to win the event four times.

Even though he was thirty-six years old at the time, DeMar continued to run successfully. He competed in other marathons with the same result. He finished third in the 1924 Olympics and twenty-seventh in 1928. He became known as "the Old Man of Marathoning." The Boston run continued to be his favorite as he went on for a record seven wins, a truly remarkable achievement.

In 1934, at the age of sixty-six, Clarence DeMar ran in his thirty-fourth Boston Marathon. He finished seventy-eighth out of one hundred thirty-three starters. His last race was three years later, at the age of sixty-nine. The next year he died, and the world of running lost a true hero. During his life DeMar competed in over one thousand long-distance races!

Other runners had a big impact on the race, although none matched DeMar. In 1924 the race was finally lengthened to the standard international distance, 26 miles, 385 yards. Persistence proved to be a rewarding virtue for James Henigan. In his tenth attempt, at the age of thirty-eight, he won the marathon. The amazing part of his story is that he dropped out of the race in eight of his first nine tries. In 1941 thirty-six-year-old Les Pawson won his third Boston with his fastest time ever.

Following World War II, the race was dominated by foreign runners. Stylianos Kyriakides, a Greek, set the trend with his victory in 1946. In 1948 Gerard Cote of Canada won his fourth race, but it wasn't without its intense moments. He and second-place finisher Ted Vogel almost came to blows as they ran alongside each other in what is considered one of the low points in the race's history.

Johnny Kelley was one of the most durable runners the Boston has ever known. (UPI photo)

Two years later, Korean runners swept the first three places, with Kee Yong Ham taking the winner's medal. In 1957 Johnny Kelley of Connecticut became the first American to win the title in eleven years. He established a new course record with a time of 2:20:05.

Kelley made his way into the headlines four years later, in 1961, but this time it was for a different reason. A light snow filled the air and a thirty-eight-degree temperature chilled the runners as they prepared for the big race that year. The marathon began, and two men asserted themselves right away. They were John Kelley and Eino Oksanen of Finland. The two headed out across the course and successfully fought off every challenger who approached them. Well, almost every challenger. For fourteen miles a dog followed along at their heels, darting back and forth across the road, eluding state troopers, and occasionally nipping at the heels of the runners.

A thirty-nine-year-old British coal miner named Fred Norris came up on the two front-runners. There were only ten miles to go when, suddenly, the dog lunged out from the crowd right into the runners. Oksanen jumped to avoid him, but Kelley, unable to maneuver, was hit squarely in the side of the legs. He crashed violently to the ground, his body scraping along the pavement. The press bus, traveling alongside the runners, almost drove right over him. His legs, arms, and face were badly cut as he lay there, dazed. Norris ran by and yelled at Kelley to get up. He didn't respond so Norris stopped, picked him up, and snapped him out of it.

Re-entering the race, Kelley tried once again to catch Oksanen. Norris, meanwhile, developed a pain in his side and began to slow down. The runners headed up the hills and toward the city when Kelley, to everyone's amazement, passed Oksanen. But Oksanen stayed right behind him, using him as a windbreak. Then, with only about one thousand yards to go, Oksanen passed the American with a great surge. Kelley desperately tried to catch him but couldn't. The detective from Finland won the race in a time of 2:23:29. Kelley finished second, just twenty-five seconds behind him. It was one of the closest finishes in Boston Marathon history. The real hero of the day was Fred Norris, who came rolling in to take third place in a race that really went to the dogs.

Despite the mishaps the race continued to grow and become immensely popular. In 1964 the field grew to over three hundred, and by 1967 it had balloned past six hundred. Foreign runners also continued to assert their influence during this period. Japanese marathoners were especially suc-

cessful. Led by the talented Morio Shigematsu, they took five of the top six places (all except fourth) in 1965. The next year they did it again, sweeping the top four spots.

Finally, the explosive growth of the race got out of hand. Over eleven hundred fifty runners participated in 1969. The next year the Boston Athletic Association imposed a new rule that disallowed participation by anyone who had not finished under four hours in a previous marathon. This succeeded in lowering the number to 1,011. In 1971 the association knocked the time limit down further—to 3½ hours. This achieved better results—the field contained only 887 runners that year.

In 1972 the historic Boston Marathon finally caught up with the times. Up until that year female runners were forbidden to participate. But that didn't mean that some ambitious women hadn't tried. In 1966 Roberta Gibb Bingay devised a plan to get into the race unofficially. Having trained with her husband, she came to love the sport and tried to enter the Boston that year along with him. She soon learned of the ban, but she was still determined. After hiding in some bushes near the starting line, Roberta jumped out into the pack as the race got underway. Because of her hooded sweatsuit, her identity went undetected. When the heat became a factor, however, she was forced to take off the sweat clothes and divulge her true identity—in a bathing suit and shorts! Out of 416 competitors she finished a very respectable 124th. Officials refused to recognize the achievement, however, and her placement was not acknowledged.

Roberta entered again the next year, but this time she was not alone. A young Syracuse University coed named Kathy Switzer also decided to give it a try. She was even more clever than Roberta. She obtained an official number by putting "K. Switzer" on her application. Race officials approved the form without realizing what they had done. On race day, however, they soon found out, as they observed her striding along the course. One of the race directors, Jock Semple, spotted her and jumped out on the course to try to take away her number. But Kathy was well prepared; her huge, hammer-throwing boyfriend, who was also in the race gave Semple a body block, which sent him reeling. After the race the Amateur Atheletic Union specifically banned Kathy from further competition. In 1972 the ban on female runners was lifted. Since then, many have competed in the prestigious event.

In 1975 a certain American runner made his presence immediately felt. His name was Bill Rodgers, and he won the Boston four times (1975, 1978, 1979, 1980). Winning during this period was

There is always one man to beat, when four-time winner Bill Rodgers is in the race. (UPI photo)

no small achievement. In 1977 the field of runners numbered 2,933, and the following year estimates had it exploding over the forty-seven-hundred mark. A three-hour time limit was imposed but proved to be no barrier at all, especially to Rodgers. He was soon becoming the premiere marathoner of his time, and his blazing speeds were a barometer. In 1975 he set a course record, winning in a time of 2:09:55. A member of the Greater Boston Track Club, Rodgers was successful in many other races. He competed for the United States in the 1976 Olympic Games and has compiled numerous victories in other prestigious races, such as the New York Marathon and the Fukuoka Marathon in Japan. In 1978 he was runner-up in the balloting for the Sullivan Memorial Trophy, given every year to the nation's top amateur athlete.

Runners, such as Rodgers, who win the marathon soon become heroes of the running world. They are placed on a pedestal as an example for amateurs everywhere. While each winner is a champion in his own right, there are some who stand above the rest. For example, there is the immortal Clarence DeMar, a seven-time winner, his final victory coming at the age of forty-two. Then there were the two Johnny Kelleys. "Old John" won his first Boston in 1935 and followed it up with another win and seven second-place finishes. He ran in forty straight marathons before being forced out of the race at the age of sixty due

to ill health. "Young John" followed the same pattern at Boston. Like Old John he was known for his hard luck. He won the race in 1958 after five second-place finishes. The 1961 dog incident hurt his chances of winning, and at the age of 39 he cracked his ribs while training. The odd part was that he was trying to avoid a charging bull!

It's not just the heroes that make the headlines at the Boston. Unusual happenings and strange similarities often outlive their time. For example, the fans at the marathon, no ordinary lot, often try to become a part of the race. In 1971 the partisan spectators cheered wildly as hometown Irishman Pat McMahon battled Alvaro Mejia of Colombia. After 26 miles, 235 yards the two were in a virtual dead heat. But the enthusiasm of the crowd was not enough to help McMahon overcome severe blisters, and Mejia pulled away for the victory. It was one of the closest races in history, and the story lives on.

With its reputation for attracting the world's best runners, the Boston Marathon has also been called "the Graveyard of Olympic Champions." Runners who have won the marathon in the Olympic Games have perennially experienced bad luck in the Boston. For example, Tom Hicks, the 1904 Olympic champion, failed in four attempts to win the Boston. Other examples include Johnny Hayes, the 1908 champion; Hannes Kolchmainen, the 1920 champion; Albin Stenroos, the 1924 champion; Delfo Cabrera, the 1948 champion; Abebe Bikila, the 1960 and 1964 champion; and Mamo Wolde, the 1968 champion. All of them were considered the best in their field at the time, but all of them failed when they made their run at the Boston Marathon.

As much a tradition as the great runners at Boston is the infamous Heartbreak Hill. Many a runner has had his dream shattered on this merciless incline. Strategically stationed at the twenty-mile mark, it challenges runners when they are already emotionally and physically drained. Says physician George Sheehan, himself a marathoner: "Heartbreak is fourth and longest and steepest of a series of long, steep grades, which begin at seventeen miles. Heartbreak is not only fearsome in itself, but it comes at the very moment when the body reaches the physiological (and probably psychological) make-or-break point. Here is, if it is anywhere, the moment of truth."

Once a runner has made it over this overwhelming obstacle, he is on his way to finishing one of the greatest races in the world. He is on his way to capturing, or attempting to capture, the Boston Marathon medal. "There are, you see, over one

1980 Boston Marathon winner Toshihiko Seko shows the joy and pain of winning. (UPI photo)

thousand Boston Marathons," says Dr. Sheehan, "one for each entrant, each alone in his own world, making his own decision, knowing that the result is clearly his to live with and no one else's, knowing also that his goal is to fulfill his potential, to complete himself as a human being."[2]

Boston Marathon Champions

1897	John McDermott
1898	Ronald McDonald
1899	Lawrence Brignolia
1900	James Caffrey
1901	James Caffrey
1902	Sammy Mellor
1903	John Lorden
1904	Michael Spring
1905	Fred Lorz
1906	Timothy Ford
1907	Tom Longboat
1908	Thomas Morrisey
1909	Henri Renaud
1910	Fred Cameron
1911	Clarence DeMar
1912	Mike Ryan
1913	Fritz Carlson
1914	James Duffy
1915	Edouard Fabre
1916	Arthur Roth
1917	Bill Kennedy
1919	Carl Linder
1920	Peter Trivoulidas
1921	Frank Zuna
1922	Clarence DeMar
1923	Clarence DeMar
1924	Clarence DeMar
1925	Charles Mellor
1926	John Miles
1927	Clarence DeMar
1928	Clarence DeMar
1929	John Miles
1930	Clarence DeMar
1931	James Henigan
1932	Paul de Bruyn
1933	Leslie Pawson
1934	Dave Komonen
1935	John A. Kelley
1936	Ellison Brown
1937	Walter Young
1938	Leslie Pawson
1939	Elison Brown
1940	Gerard Cote
1941	Leslie Pawson
1942	Joseph Smith
1943	Gerard Cote
1944	Gerard Cote
1945	John A. Kelley
1946	Stylianos Kyriakides
1947	Yun Bok Suh
1948	Gerard Cote
1949	Gosta Leandersson
1950	Kee Yong Ham
1951	Shigeki Tanaka
1952	Doroteo Flores
1953	Keizo Yamada
1954	Veikko Karvonen
1955	Hideo Hamamura
1956	Antti Viskari
1957	John J. Kelley
1958	Franjo Mihalic
1959	Eino Oksanen
1960	Paavo Kotila
1961	Eino Oksanen
1962	Eino Oksanen
1964	Aurele Vandendriessche
1965	Aurele Vandendriessche
1966	Kenji Kimihara
1967	Dave McKenzie
1968	Amby Burfoot
1969	Yoshiaki Unetani
1970	Ron Hill
1971	Alvaro Mejia
1972	Olavi Suomalainen

1973	Jon Anderson		1979	Bill Rodgers
1974	Neil Cusack		1980	Bill Rodgers
1975	Bill Rodgers		1981	Toshihiko Seko
1976	Jack Fultz		1982	Alberto Salazar
1977	Jerome Drayton		1983	Greg Meyer
1978	Bill Rodgers			

16
The Bowler of the Year Award

Somewhere in Germay around the third or fourth century A.D. a religious ceremony is about to take place. A young man enters the church and is informed that he must take a test to prove his faith. Standing at the back end of the church aisle, he is prepared. Meanwhile, at the front of the same aisle, a *heide* is set down. The young man is then handed a stone. He slowly rolls it back and forth from one hand to the other, contemplating what he is about to do. He is ready. Leaning back with the stone firmly in his hand, he aims and rolls it cautiously down the aisle toward the *heide*.

If the stone were to go down the aisle and knock down the *heide*, it would be concluded that the young man is leading a good, clean life and that he is capable of overcoming evil. If he were to miss, he would have shown that his faith is not strong enough and that he thus has a need to attend church more often in order to strengthen it. For, by missing the *heide*, which means "heathen," he would have shown that he is incapable of overcoming evil. After the ceremony, a dinner is prepared to honor the successful *kegelers*.

What seemed at the time to be nothing more than a simple religious ceremony turned out to be much more than that. What began as an exercise in faith turned into the seedling of one of the most popular of modern sports. Such is the generally accepted origin of tenpin, or "bowling," as it is commonly called.

The roots of the game, however, go much farther back. Historians claim to have proof of a similar activity seven thousand years ago. In the Stone Age the practice of throwing rocks at different objects resulted in the game called duck-on-the-rocks, which could very well have been an ancestor of bowling. There is evidence that the ancient Egyptians played a game similar to tenpin. The grave of an Egyptian child, estimated to have been built around 5200 B.C., contains artifacts of what is believed to be the oldest known form of bowling.

In the South Seas a game called *ula maika* was played by the ancient Polynesians. It entailed rolling a polished stone along a path and knocking down objects of various kinds. Various derivations of the game were eventually found in other cultures throughout the globe. These included Italian boccie, English skittles, Basque quilles, and lawn bowls. Though the rules and style of play often differed, the basis was the same.

Around the third or fourth century A.D., the game crystallized in the form of the German religious ceremony. The word *kegel* means "to bowl," and *kegelers* the people that were able to successfully knock down the *heide*. Clergymen began to take a special liking to the game. They often put more than one pin together and practice "bowling" at them. Around the fifteenth century, the game found an avid player in Martin Luther. The famous German clergyman even built a bowling lane for his family.

As the religious aspect eventually disappeared,

bowling became more of a pastime of the people. The Dutch and Swiss engaged in various forms of the sport. There were no definite rules, and the number of pins often varied. In Scotland, a game called curling was played. Some referred to it as "bowling on ice."

The practice of betting on the sport began as early as 1325. Soon thereafter it became against the law even to play the game in such cities as Berlin and Cologne. Throughout much of the land, however, it continued to be a popular pastime during festivals, feasts, and parties. In 1455 the first indoor bowling lane was built in London. During the sixteenth century ninepin became the accepted version, although a variation in arrangement was apparent.

The United States got its first taste of bowling in 1623, when the Dutch imported lawn bowling. This game was played in New York City in an area known as Bowling Green. It is believed that bowling at pins soon followed, but the exact date of its arrival in America is not known. By 1820, an indoor version of tenpin had become popular in New York. As in the past, gambling soon began to take hold of the sport. As a result, legal attempts were made to ban the game. In 1841, for example, the Connecticut state legislature passed a statute prohibiting participation in bowling. In 1875 enthusiasts of the sport got together to try to regulate and control it. Representatives from nine bowling clubs in New York and Brooklyn met and established a standard set of rules, attempting to limit the gambling and illegal aspect. Out of this gathering was formed the National Bowling Association, the official organization for the sport as it is now played. Unfortunately, the gambling was still difficult to control. Fifteen years later another association, the American Amateur Bowling Union, sprang up, but it didn't last very long.

On 9 September 1895 bowling took a big step forward. A large group of enthusiasts met in New York at Beethoven Hall. Known as the American Bowling Congress (ABC), it became a federation of bowling clubs. Rules were once again set up as to how the game should be played and how it should be controlled. The ABC soon became the governing body for over five million bowlers in the United States, Canada, and several other nations.

The first ABC national tournament was held in 1901 in Chicago. Forty-one five-man teams entered. The tourney has been held annually ever since (except during World War II). Today, it is still the major tournament of the year for professional bowlers. It became so popular that in 1961 the ABC split it into two divisions—Regular, for league bowlers from all over the country, and Classic, for tournament professionals.

By 1958 bowling had become so big that further organization was necessary. The Profesional Bowlers Association (PBA) was then born. Its duty was to set up and organize the tour for the pros. It experienced very rapid growth, and the purses began to swell. In 1960, two years after the inception of the PBA, total prize money for the three-tournament year was $49,500. By 1975 bowler Earl Anthony alone collected over a hundred thousand dollars on the tour.

Other nations soon became interested in the game. As a result, the Federation Internationale des Quilleurs (FIQ) was formed as a worldwide governing body. With over fifty members on its rolls, it stages its own Olympics every four years. The initial competition took place in Mexico in 1963. The United States and Japan were the only nations with professionals, and the Americans dominated the event. To stimulate interest, bowlers from other countries were allowed to compete, no matter what their level of competence. Attempts have also been made to make bowling a part of the Olympic Games. Thus far, it has only been played as a demonstration at the competition.

Since the development of the PBA and a regular, sustained tour, many talented professionals have struck it rich. To recognize the greatest among them, the Bowler of the Year Award was instituted in 1942. As the highest recognition that a bowler can receive, it is given to the year's most outstanding performer by the Bowling Writers' Association.

The first man to win the Bowler of the Year Award was Johnny Crimmins of Detroit, Michigan. Following in his footsteps were such stars as Ned Day (who averaged 200 for twenty-eight years in a row), Steve Nagy (who averaged 208 during a ten-year period), Bob Lillard (a Texan who became the first bowler in history to win five ABC titles), and Eddie Lubanski (who quit a promising minor-league baseball career to go into bowling). All of these men were very talented professionals who made a contribution to the sport. But, then there is another group of men who did more than that. With their singular performances, they actually made the sport into what it is today. When the names of Andy Varipapa, Don Carter, Dick Weber, Don Johnson, and Earl Anthony are mentioned, the word *superstar* is usually somewhere nearby.

The first man to bring bowling into the national spotlight was the great Andy Varipapa. The sport was still in its infancy when he came along, and during his career he helped mature it greatly. He was the first bowler to make a living from the game,

One of the greatest showmen the sport of bowling has ever known, Andy Varipapa was the first man to bring it into the big-time national spotlight. (American Bowling Congress photo)

er." In 1946 and 1947 he lived up to his idea of himself by winning the National All-Star Tournament. The next season he was selected Bowler of the Year. Varipapa became the greatest showman that the game has ever known. Crowds were constantly dazzled by his trick shots during exhibitions, which he staged until he was over eighty years old. He gave much to the sport, but as he himself said, "The Great Varipapa won't work for peanuts."[1]

The next great bowler to come along was a man named Don Carter. Considered by many to be the greatest bowler of all time, he was as talented as Varipapa was flamboyant. From 1950 to 1964 he captured every major championship, was the leading money winner, and generally dominated the sport. He was also named Bowler of the Year six times.

After graduating from high school in St. Louis, Missouri, Carter signed a baseball contract with the Philadelphia Athletics. But after one minor league season, he called it quits and turned to bowling. In 1953 he was asked to join the prestigious Anheuser-Busch team. He helped make the team one of the most successful in the nation. Despite his unorthodox style, he continued to be the biggest star that the sport had known. He rolled twenty-three perfect games during his career, and in 1970 he was a unanimous choice for the ABC Hall of Fame.

Besides a very talented bowler, Carter was a

mainly through his widely publicized match games, tournaments, and exhibitions. Born in Italy in 1891, Varipapa's initial association with bowling came through the game of boccie. After becoming familiar with the American game, he moved to the United States because he wanted a faster life-style. He worked as a toolmaker in Brooklyn and participated in bowling as much as possible on the side. His expertise and ability soon grew, and in a 1930 tournament he astounded local enthusiasts by rolling three straight games of 279 and averaging 260 overall.

But what Varipapa will mainly be remembered for is his competitive flair and his love of the limelight. He often billed himself as "the Great Varipapa" and "the World's Most Sensational Bowl-

From 1950 to 1964 Don Carter captured every major championship, was the leading money winner and generally dominated the bowling world. (ABC photo)

Dick Weber helped lead the Budweiser team to the national crown his first year and also combined with Ray Bluth to win the first of their four national doubles titles. (ABC photo)

very good judge of talent. In the 1954 All-Star Tournament in Chicago, he took note of a very talented young bowler in the next lane. At the conclusion of the tourney, Carter approached him and inquired if he would be interested in joining the Budweiser squad. To be asked to join the Buds is like being asked to join the Pittsburgh Steelers in football. The young man, Dick Weber, quickly accepted, and the career of bowling's next big superstar had begun.

Prior to Weber's exposure to Carter, his talents were little known. At the time of that 1954 tourney, he was working as a mail sorter, and his career in bowling had been uneventful. But once he joined the Budweisers, the country kid made his presence felt immediately. In his first year he helped lead them to the national team crown and, in combination with Ray Bluth, won the first of their four national doubles titles. Individually, Weber also made his mark. During the 1961 and 1962 seasons he won seven of nine PBA tournaments. The ensuing years were just as successful for him and in 1961, 1963, and 1965 he was selected Bowler of the Year. Not bad for a twenty-five year old mail sorter from Indianapolis, Indiana.

Down the road, another Indiana country boy was making a name for himself in bowling. Known as

"the Kokomo Kid," Don Johnson started out much the same way as Weber did. As a boy, he worked hard on his father's farm and spent his off-hours learning how to bowl. His first year on the pro tour, 1962, was not a great one—he earned only $900. Then in 1964, he won his first tournament in Denver and things began to turn around. In 1971 he won six PBA championships and earned over $80,000. At the Firestone Tournament of Champions the year before, Johnson almost pulled off an incredible feat. He was on his last frame, and all he needed was one more strike to throw a perfect game. Unfortunately, on that last throw he left a single pin standing—one that cost him $10,000 and a spot in bowling immortality. He still went on to win the tourney and prove without a doubt that he was one of bowling's greatest performers. In 1971 and 1972 Johnson, for his efforts, was selected Bowler of the Year. He continued his successes until the late seventies, when, at one point he moved up into second place among all-time tournament winners. The man in front of him—Earl Anthony.

In 1970 Anthony joined the tour as a 32-year old rookie. He immediately made his presence felt—if not because of his crewcut and softspoken manner, then certainly because of his ability to collect strikes. In 1975 he became the first bowler in history to earn over $100,000 in one year. He set a

Known as the "Kokomo Kid," Don Johnson won the Bowler of the Year Award in 1971 and 1972. (ABC photo)

In 1975 Earl Anthony became the first bowler in history to win over $100,000 during the year. (ABC photo)

PBA record for most tournament victories in one year (seven), won the national championship three straight years, bowled four 300 games in one year (1974), and won more PBA titles than any other man. To top it off he was selected Bowler of the Year three times—in 1974, 1975, and 1976. Earl Anthony's contributions to the game will never be doubted.

As a boy, Anthony took a special liking to the sport of baseball. He went on to become a very proficient pitcher. In 1960 he attended training camp with Vancouver of the Pacific Coast League and received a contract offer from the Baltimore Orioles. He turned it down, saying that it wasn't enough money. For a twenty-two-year old he was very intelligent; after all how many minor league baseball players ever earn over $100,000 a year?

In the United States the sport of bowling has been constantly on the rise. Referred to as "the family sport," it has come to be played and viewed by people of all ages. The women's tour has brought fame to female bowlers, and the game continues to grow. As with any sport, the struggling apprentice almost invariably models himself after the athletes he considers to be the superstars. In bowling, all they need do is look up the Bowler of the Year.

Bowler of the Year Award

1942	Johnny Crimmins
1943	Ned Day
1944	Ned Day
1945	Buddy Bomar
1946	Joseph Wilman
1947	Buddy Bomar
1948	Andy Varipapa
1949	Connie Schwoegler
1950	Junie McMahon
1951	Lee Jouglard
1952	Steve Nagy
1953	Don Carter
1954	Don Carter
1955	Steve Nagy
1956	Bob Lillard
1957	Don Carter
1958	Don Carter
1959	Ed Lubanski
1960	Don Carter
1961	Dick Weber
1962	Don Carter

1963	Dick Weber		1974	Earl Anthony
1964	Billy Hardwick		1975	Earl Anthony
1965	Dick Weber		1976	Earl Anthony
1966	Wayne Zahn		1977	Mark Roth
1967	Dave Davis		1978	Mark Roth
1968	Jim Stefanich		1979	Mark Roth
1969	Billy Hardwick		1980	Wayne Webb
1970	Nelson Burton, Jr.		1981	Earl Anthony
1971	Don Johnson		1982	Earl Anthony
1972	Don Johnson		1983	Earl Anthony
1973	Don McCune			

17
The Kentucky Derby Trophy

It lasts only a few minutes, but for pageantry, sheer excitement, and tradition, it is hard to match. Thousands of tourists, fans, and experts of the sport descend on the city of Louisville every year for this party of parties, this event of events. Millions of dollars are exchanged as predictions and counter-predictions flood the air.

When the race is completed and the victor trots over to the winner's circle, it is evident that there is nothing else like it. For enthusiasts of the sport of horse racing, there is undoubtedly no equal to the Kentucky Derby. It is America's most exciting and glamorous horse racing event, and its history has provided some colorful and controversial moments.

The Kentucky Derby is a race of finely tuned and polished thoroughbreds. Their development is controlled and maintained through methodical training; and when Derby Week arrives, they are as prepared as an Indianapolis 500 race car. The Churchill Downs racetrack is the home for the mile-and-a-quarter race, but through television and other media, the Derby is closely followed by millions of fans throughout the country. Certain restrictions are set as to what type of horse may enter. They must be three years old. Colts and geldings must weigh 126 pounds; and fillies, 121 pounds.

The week before the race, up to race day itself, is one big party in the city of Louisville. Owners and breeders hold exclusive bashes at their mansions outside the city while tourists and townfolk engage in their merrymaking closer to the track. Betting abounds, and monetary loss becomes inconsequential. The people are there to take part in the festivities, and the amount of money they spend really doesn't matter. Every year millions of dollars are wagered on that first Saturday in May in an attempt to determine who is king of the thoroughbreds.

The first Derby was organized in 1875. The race was modeled after some prestigious English races, and the track was 1½ miles long. In 1896 it was changed to its current length, and it took on a character all its own. The winner of the first race was Aristides, "the Little Red Horse." Vagrant won the second Derby in 1876 and was followed by Baden Baden the next year. The list of winners is nothing less than an enumeration of the greatest horses in the sport. There was Exterminator in 1918, Reigh Count in 1928, Twenty Grand in 1931, Swaps in 1955, Carry Back in 1961, and Cannonade in 1974. The mere mention of these names to an avid race fan will conjure up fond memories of the great champions that they were.

A victory in the Kentucky Derby is a great achievement, but there is something that is even more spectacular. In the weeks following the Derby there are two other races of major importance. They are the Preakness and the Belmont Stakes. Though not very prestigious by themselves,

The Kentucky Derby Trophy. (photo courtesy of Churchill Downs)

when they are combined with the mighty Kentucky Derby, quite a threesome results. To win all three races in a single year is a very great achievement for a horse. Not many have done it. When they do, they are placed in a class above the rest. They become royalty, a symbol of excellence. The first horse to win the Triple Crown was Sir Barton in 1919. Eleven years later Gallant Fox won it, and Omaha did it in 1935. The six other horses to achieve the feat are War Admiral (1937), Whirlaway (1941), Count Fleet (1943), Assault (1946), Citation (1948), and Secretariat (1973). They will be forever honored.

In a sport as highly competitive as racing horses, it is no easy task to win three such difficult events. When Secretariat won it in 1973, she broke a twenty-year span in which no horse had been able to accomplish the remarkable triple. The reasons for this are numerous. As the popularity of the races have grown, so have the number of prospective entrants. With the number of competing horses on the rise, the level of performance has also been forced to go up. Such stiff competition and high standards have made it nearly impossible for a horse to win two, let alone all three, of the races. No ordinary horse can do it.

But then Secretariat was no ordinary horse. Owned by Penny Tweedy and trained by Lucien Laurin, Secretariat had shown throughout her development that she was a promising thoroughbred. Two weeks before the Kentucky Derby, however, she struggled to a third-place finish in the Wood Memorial at New York's Aqueduct Track. The performance raised many questions as to whether she would be able to live up to her big billing.

Some impressive trial runs at Churchill Downs prior to the race relieved many of the worries of her handlers. Still, there was that uncertainty. Derby Day arrived, and jockey Ron Turcotte planned his strategy. He decided that he would sit back in the pack for much of the race, and then let her go flat out at the end. It seemed like a sound idea. At the clubhouse turn, Secretariat sat back in eleventh place and moved up to sixth down the backstretch. When the far turn came around, she put it in high gear and passed all the other horses as if they were nailed to the ground. The bid red colt went on to win in a Derby record time of 1:59.4. Secretariat proved that the victory was no fluke by following it up with similarly impressive victories in the Preakness and Belmont. She became only the ninth horse in history to win the Triple Crown.

Sir Barton, the first to win all three races, had a different recipe for success. He preferred to be a front-runner, or at least to hang alongside the leader and win by setting hard, fast paces. The small colt was owned by Commander J. K. L. Ross.

In 1919 the Derby was won by Sir Barton, who was also the first horse to win the Triple Crown. (photo courtesy of Churchill Downs)

Ross entered another horse in the Derby in the same year. It was Billy Kelly. Months before the big race, Ross was in a New York restaurant having a discussion with a man named Arnold Rothstein. The subject of the upcoming Derby soon entered the conversation. Rothstein, known as a big gambler, was a supporter of a Derby entrant named Eternal. Ross bet Rothstein a "fifty" that Billy Kelly would finish ahead of Eternal. Rothstein took the bet, but Ross later discovered, to his shock, that Rothstein interpreted it as a fifty-thousand dollar bet, not a fifty-dollar wager.

Sir Barton won the race for Ross, but that had no bearing on his "Mississippi gambler" move with Rothstein. Eternal finished in tenth place. Billy Kelly ran hard and impressively, taking second place and a big weight off his owner's shoulders. Rothstein paid Ross the money in what is considered one of the most incredible bets in Derby history.

William Woodward's Gallant Fox was the second horse to win the Triple Crown. Unlike Sir Barton, Gallant Fox preferred to run farther back with the rest of the horses and then to pour it on near the end of the race. It proved to be a successful strategy, and after winning the Big Three, his jockey, Earl Sande, proclaimed, "You could ride him backwards and still win."[1] An exaggeration, but not by much. Gallant Fox was also the only Derby winner whose offspring repeated the achievement. His colt, Omaha, won all three races in 1935. Both animals were trained by Jim Fitzsimmons.

In 1937 another Triple Crown winner, War Admiral, came along. His sire, the famous Kentucky horse Man O'War, never raced in the Derby. War Admiral, a smaller colt, liked to run away from the field. Owned by Sam Riddle of Glen Riddle Farm, he was run by jockey Charlie Kurtsinger in the Derby. And run he did. War Admiral took the lead early in the race and coasted home to victory.

A year later War Admiral was involved in a match race that stirred up quite a bit of publicity.

The first turn at Churchill Downs has become one of the most famous in the world of horse racing. (photo courtesy of Churchill Downs)

Positioning was a key facter to many a Derby finish. The 1931 race proved to be a money run, at least for eventual winner, Twenty Grand. (photo courtesy of Churchill Downs)

The opponent was a well-known California horse named Seabiscuit. The race took place at Pimlico, and the result was memorable. Seabiscuit ran impressively and defeated the Triple Crown winner by four lengths. The two horses did have something in common, though. Seabiscuit, ironically, was a grandson of Man O'War.

In 1941 a popular horse named Whirlaway appeared on the scene. Nicknames such as "Mr. Long Tail" and "Whacky Whirly" were soon pinned on him because of his appearance and his often unpredictable behavior on the track. Owned by Calumet Farms and trained by six-time Derby winner Ben Jones, Whirlaway soon became a favorite of the crowds. Once he was disciplined and his talent was allowed to show through, he became a formidable opponent. Jockeyed by Eddie Arcaro in the Derby, Whirlaway made his move on the far turn and went on to win by eight lengths.

Two years later another Kentucky Derby winner took the horse racing world by storm. He was appropriately named Count Fleet. The property of Mrs. John Hertz, the Count was another famous front-runner. At Churchill Downs he raced wire-to-wire for a three-length victory and followed it up with wins of eight lengths in the Preakness and an incredible twenty-five lengths at Belmont Park. He was certainly a horse on which his owner could count! But he was also known as somewhat of a romantic. In a Belmont race in 1942 a young filly named Askmenow caught his eye. In fact he was so impressed with her that he stayed right behind her all the way down the stretch run. When the final results were in, Occupation won the race, Askmenow took second, and, yes, Count Fleet was right behind her in third place.

The Derby of 1946 was won by a horse named Assault. What he did to the rest of the field was considered criminal—winning by eight lengths. When he was just a yearling, he stepped on something that went right through his hoof and left him deformed. Nicknames such as "Clubfoot" arose. But Assault was a powerful horse, and when he assaulted the competition in the Preakness and the Belmont to take the Triple Crown, there was no doubt that he was a champion.

In 1948 Ben Jones brought in another horse that ran his way into national prominence. This time it was Citation, and when he won the Derby that year, he became one of eight horses to capture it for Calumet Farms. With Eddie Arcaro aboard, he swept through the Triple Crown races, the second such achievement for a Jones horse. Before the Belmont Stakes, Jones and Arcaro were a confident duo. Arcaro went so far as to claim that the only way Citation wouldn't win would be if he fell off his mount. And that's what almost happened. At the start of the race Citation stumbled as he left the gate, and Arcaro almost went tumbling to the ground. Luckily, he held on. The rest is history.

In 1981 another horse with big potential hit the scene. Trained by New Yorker Johnny Campo, Pleasant Colony was picked to be the class of the field in the Derby. Two minutes, two seconds after the famed race began, the colt thundered home three-quarters of a length ahead of second-place finisher, Woodchopper. Thoughts in the racing world now turned to the possibility of another Triple Crown winner, and when Pleasant Colony won the Preakness in Baltimore just two weeks later, it appeared inevitable. But like many dreams, it was not to be. By winning the Belmont, a determined colt named Summing burst Campo's bubble and thwarted Pleasant Colony's bid.

Monetary reward is certainly an important part of Kentucky Derby competition. Owners of thoroughbred horses spend a great deal of money breeding, training, and racing their thoroughbreds in hopes that someday it will pay off. For some it does, while for others it is a losing proposition. The Kentucky Derby's purse for the winning horse alone makes it very worhwhile, and, coupled with the national recognition that follows, it becomes a lucrative venture. While winning the Kentucky Derby is a very profitable accomplishment, winning the Triple Crown is far more profitable. Of the Triple Crown winners, two have brought in over a million dollars in earnings to their owners. The mention of their names immediately stirs up debate as to who truly is the greatest horse of all time. As in any other sport, greatness in horse racing is measured by success, both on the field of competition and in the pocketbook. And in both categories Citation and Secretariat are unparalleled.

Some experts say that Secretariat was the greatest of them all. Evidence can be found to support that claim. His thirty-one-length victory at Bel-

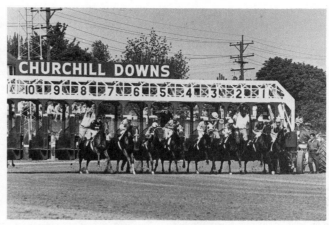

All eight horses break from the gate in the start of the 1969 Derby. (photo courtesy of Churchill Downs)

mont made a believer out of many. His grace, beauty, and seemingly effortless style made believers of others. But, undoubtedly, his overwhelming success on the track is the most impressive credential of this majestic champion.

Throughout the history of the Derby there have been many wild and controversial moments. In 1957, for example, Iron Leige of Calumet Farms was involved in a neck-to-neck battle with Gallant Man. The horses were charging toward the finish line when jockey Willie Shoemaker on Gallant Man misjudged where he was on the track. When the horses hit the sixteenth post, Shoemaker stood up in his irons for a moment not realizing that he wasn't at the finish line. It was a small mistake, but Iron Leige took full advantage by scooting past the confused Shoemaker for the victory. Iron Leige won by less than a foot, or—should we say—by a shoe!

In 1968 Dancer's Image crossed the finish line first for an apparent Derby victory. But the track chemist found traces of pain killers in the horse's blood, and the win was taken away. The second-place finisher, Forward Pass, also of Calumet Farms, was declared the winner. After a long court battle a Kentucky Court ruled that the decision should stand, and Forward Pass remained the winner.

Another controversial race took place in 1933. This time it was between two horses named Head Play and Brokers Tip. Actually, it would be more accurate to say that it was between their jockeys. Don Meade was riding Brokers Tip, and Herb Fisher was aboard Head Play. Fisher had the lead as the horses headed down the stretch run. Brokers Tip was moving up fast and shot through the inside. Fisher decided that it would be wise to close in on

Cannonade sprints for the finish line in 1974. (photo courtesy of Churchill Downs)

the onrushing horse and force him to the inside. Seeing the horse coming at him and fearing that he would be bumped through the fence, Meade grabbed Fisher on the arm. The result was a series of grabs, pushes, holds, and pulls as the two horses rushed for the finish.

In those days Derby judges did not have the benefit of the techonology available today. There were no sophisticated cameras that could reproduce the finish in exact detail. The existing cameras, however, did manage to capture the two jockeys in a wrestler's lock on one another. The judges had to make a decision, so they declared Brokers Tip to be the winner by a nose. After the race, in the jockey's room, Fisher lunged at Meade with his fists flying. Shouting and claiming that he had been robbed by his opponent, he went after him violently. Luckily, the fight was quickly broken up by spectators.

There have also been many upsets at the Downs. In 1940 Gallahadion beat highly favored Bimilech in a real surprise. In 1918 Exterminator, originally a workhorse for another Derby prospective, Sun

Briar, went on to win by a length. The biggest payoff in Derby history came in 1913 when Donerail returned $184.90 for a $2.00 mutuel. Throughout the years the Derby has consistently risen in value. In 1875 the winner's purse was $2,850; when Cannonade won in 1974, the winnings for owner John Olin were in excess of $274,000.

In many sports events, money is a primary concern to both the participants and the observers. Horse racing creates large fan participation through its legalized gambling on the outcome of the various races. The Kentucky Derby has been no exception. But there is something about the Derby that makes it stand out above the rest. That something is tradition. It has a history of being the single most important race of the year. Possession of the coveted Kentucky Derby Trophy is the most prized possession that an owner can attain. It symbolizes the greatness usually reserved for nobility, and in this case the horses that achieve it are considered nobility. For one year, until the next Kentucky Derby is run and a new king is crowned, one horse and one owner stand atop the world of horse racing.

Kentucky Derby Trophy Winners

1875	Aristides	1928	Reigh Count
1876	Vagrant	1929	Clyde Van Dusen
1877	Baden Baden	1930	Gallant Fox
1878	Day Star	1931	Twenty Grand
1879	Lord Murphy	1932	Burgoo King
1880	Fonso	1933	Brokers Tip
1881	Hindoo	1934	Cavalcade
1882	Apollo	1935	Omaha
1883	Leonatus	1936	Bold Venture
1884	Buchanan	1937	War Admiral
1885	Joe Cotton	1938	Lawrin
1886	Ben Ali	1939	Johnstown
1887	Montrose	1940	Gallahadion
1888	Macbeth II	1941	Whirlaway
1889	Spokane	1942	Shut Out
1890	Riley	1943	Count Fleet
1891	Kingman	1944	Pensive
1892	Azra	1945	Hoop, Jr.
1893	Lookout	1946	Assault
1894	Chant	1947	Jet Pilot
1895	Halma	1948	Citation
1896	Ben Brush	1949	Ponder
1897	Typhoon II	1950	Middleground
1898	Plaudit	1951	Count Turf
1899	Manuel	1952	Hill Gail
1900	Lieutenant Gibson	1953	Dark Star
1901	His Eminence	1954	Determine
1902	Alan-a-Dale	1955	Swaps
1903	Judge Himes	1956	Needles
1904	Elwood	1957	Iron Leige
1905	Agile	1958	Tim Tam
1906	Sir Huon	1959	Tomy Lee
1907	Pink Star	1960	Venetian
1908	Stone Street	1961	Carry Back
1909	Wintergreen	1962	Decidedly
1910	Donau	1963	Chateaugay
1911	Meridian	1964	Northern Dancer
1912	Worth	1965	Lucky Debonair
1913	Donerail	1966	Kauai King
1914	Old Rosebud	1967	Proud Clarion
1915	Regret	1968	Forward Pass
1916	George Smith	1969	Majestic Prince
1917	Omar Khayyam	1970	Dust Commander
1918	Exterminator	1971	Canonero II
1919	Sir Barton	1972	Riva Ridge
1920	Paul Jones	1973	Secretariat
1921	Behave Yourself	1974	Cannonade
1922	Morvich	1975	Foolish Pleasure
1923	Zev	1976	Bold Forbes
1924	Black Gold	1977	Seattle Slew
1925	Flying Ebony	1978	Affirmed
1926	Bubbling Over	1979	Spectacular Bid
1927	Whiskery	1980	Genuine Risk
		1981	Pleasant Colony
		1982	Gato del Sol
		1983	Sunny's Halo

18
The World Champion Cowboy Award

Throughout history heroes have played a vital role in the development of cultures. For the Greeks, life would have been stagnant without the great philosophers to stimulate their minds. The Romans emulated their mighty warriors. And for the English, the great kings and queens were objects of veneration. In America the hero has been just as prevalent. Back in the days of the Wild West, the cowboy emerged as one of the legendary figures of his time.

The cowboy came to the West from virtually every part of the nation, bringing with him little more than an insatiable thirst for adventure and a daring not possessed by the average man. He was one who didn't fit in with the well-mannered, families or the sedate life-style of the East. He needed freedom—the ability to do anything he wanted at any time and at any place. There was only one place in which he could realize this freedom—the untamed lands west of the Mississippi.

Contrary to popular opinion the West was much more than a geographical location on the map. The West was a life-style, a culture in itself. Law and order was often determined by who had the quickest gun or the fastest horse. Uncertainty was a way of life, for towns often rose and fell with the sun. As one writer on the subject puts it:

The West has a distinctive look and smell and feel. There is about it an inexplicable sense of something big, something outsized and exaggerated—except it is also subtle, which is equally inexplicable. You might find it in something as simple as the way tall buffalo grass gradually gives way to sage, the sage to cactus, cactus to sand; or feel it in those dry chiseling winds that send tall clouds kiting across a sky as wide as Wyoming; or see it in the thin comb of rain hanging on some distant horizon."[1]

The West was an environment in which the cow-

The old spirit of the West and the untamed lifestyle of the cowboy are still very much a part of the modern rodeo. (photo by Rich DeFrancesco)

boy thrived and which, for the most part, he relished. He grittily welcomed the challenge from nature, whether it was a Texas windstorm or a fierce wild animal. To overcome the climate and environment, he built ranches and worked the land until it was his. Up at dawn and working until dusk, his life was not an easy one. To defeat the wild animals of the area, he set about to tame them. They were not just a threat to his survival; they were a threat to his ego. It was as if the wild bronc undermined his claim to be the freest spirit roaming the land. It was a contest of who could be controlled—the animal or the cowboy. And the cowboy was not about to let an animal usurp his status.

It was this battle of wills that spawned the seed of the sport of rodeo. Many Western towns have claimed to be the birthplace of rodeo, but the accuracy of these claims is nearly impossible to ascertain. "Rodeo started right out in the middle of nowhere, in the dirt and brush," says one authority. "No one can say when. Any man around in those times was lucky to know the year, let alone the day. If he cared."[2]

Originally, riding bucking broncs was part of the everyday work of the cowboy. After finishing a long, hard day, he looked for some form of entertainment. Many cowboys maintain that rodeo began as a contest between man and animal, specifically, a man and his horse. There was always a crazed and wild bronc that nobody could ride. These battles between cowboys and notorious horses soon attracted the townsfolk, who gathered to observe them.

It was quite a confrontation. The cowboy was a breed of man unlike any other, and the horse could be a very wild and unpredictable creature. Wildly entertaining battles ensued. Soon impromptu competitions in riding, roping, shooting, and broncobusting were popping up everywhere.

The word *rodeo* comes from the Spanish word meaning "cattle market." In 1882 Buffalo Bill Cody was asked to help put on a Fourth of July celebration in North Platte, Nebraska. As part of his Old Glory Blowout, he staged some "rodeo" events. Many claimed this to be the origin of the sport.

The people of the town of Prescott, Arizona, are of a different opinion. In 1888 the cow town decided to try to formalize some form of competition. A grandstand was built, tickets were sold, and, according to natives, the first "real" rodeo was held. The winning cowboys were awarded silver belt buckles and other prizes. Other towns soon jumped on the bandwagon, and the idea took off.

In the beginning, rodeo wasn't a very serious competition. The objective was primarily entertainment and fun. Eventually, as the events were

formalized, it took shape as a sport. Cowboys began to take the competition very seriously and trained for it. Money became an important part of the rodeo. Many cowboys tried to make a living from competing and became professionals. And spectators soon came flocking in to watch them perform. In 1897 the famous Cheyenne Frontier Days celebration was held before very large crowds.

It was not until 1936 that the sport acquired a truly professional organization. At the famed Boston Garden in Boston, Massachusetts, the cowboys had gone on strike in order to get more purse money. They got together, formed the Cowboys Turtle Association, and drew up some rules and regulations for the sport. In 1945 the association was reorganized into the Rodeo Cowboys Association (RCA). Formed as an organization of contestants, it steadily grew and became the governing body for the sport. Many responsibilities soon fell into its saddle. Today, it is the chief supervising and sanctioning body for professional rodeo competition in the United States and Canada.

The RCA has on its listings over three thousand licensed rodeo cowboys, and there are more than six hundred sanctioned rodeos every year. Some are small, but others have become big-time events, which annually dole out over five million dollars in prize money. A full-time competitor may enter more than one hundred rodeos a year. Staged in almost every state of the Union, they draw over twelve million fans each year.

A significant event in rodeo history took place in 1959 in Dallas, Texas. The first National Finals Rodeo (NFR) was staged and a "World Champion Cowboy" was crowned. As the Super Bowl of rodeo, the NFR admits only the world's top fifteen cowboys in each event. The top cowboys are determined by the amount of money they earned during

Women's events, such as barrel racing (shown here), have become a big part of rodeo competition. (photo by Rich De-Francesco)

the previous year. The "World Champion Cowboy" is the cowboy who wins the most money during the season. There is one catch—he has to place in two or more events during the nine-day National Finals Rodeo competition. Since 1965, this new world championship of rodeo has been held at a permanent site in Oklahoma City. By that time the purses had shot up to over the hundred-thousand-dollar mark. Rodeo had become big time.

Despite its climb to national prestige, rodeo has often been compared to a circus. There are bands, judges, wildly dressed officials, and crazy clowns. But even the clowns serve a vital function. They are there to protect the cowboys. Their job is to lure the crashing bull or bucking horse away from the fallen rider in order to keep him from getting trampled or seriously injured.

Most rodeos are made up of five major events—bareback riding, bull riding, saddle-bronc riding, calf roping, and steer wrestling. Steer roping and team roping are also often included. In Canada, steer decorating is another sanctioned event. For the cowgirls, there is the barrel race and, for amusement, wild cow milking and a wild horse race.

In the riding events—bareback, bull, and saddle-bronc—the cowboy must stay on the mount for a specific amount of time, usually eight to ten seconds, to get the maximum points. Judging is subjective, and the quality of the animal, as well as the ride, are taken into account. An "easy" horse or bull is harder to score well on. In bronc-riding contests the rider must not touch the horse or anything else with his free hand and, in the saddle competition, the rider's feet must stay in the stirrups. A foul can bring about disqualification.

A calf roper's most valuable asset is his horse. In this event a calf is released into the arena from a

Considered one of the toughest events in a rodeo is the bull riding competition. (photo by Rich DeFrancesco)

chute. When it crosses the "scoreline," a mounted cowboy bursts from another chute in hot pursuit. He then catches the calf, ropes it, dismounts, throws the calf down, and ties its feet together. The horse plays a vital function in this process. While the cowboy is busily involved, the horse must face the calf and keep the rope tight by backing away and pulling out any slack in the rope. The cowboy with the fastest time is declared the winner. "Calf roping is an art," says world champion calf roper Ernie Taylor. "The name of the game is speed. The fastest time always wins. The secret of success is getting your time and your moves down to perfection."[3]

Started by a black cowboy named Bill Pickett, steer wrestling is one of the most dangerous events of the rodeo. Also known as "bulldogging," it combines the speed of the roping events with the ferocity of the bucking competition. A steer is released from a chute, with a "hazer" riding alongside it to keep it in a straight path. The competing cowboy rides up on the other side, jumps from his horse, and grabs the steer by its horns. He then tries to stop it as quickly as possible and bring it to the ground by twisting its neck.

A brutal event, steer wrestling is naturally often dominated by the bigger cowboys. But that is not always the case. Tom Ferguson and Phil Lyne, both World Champion cowboys, are not big men, but both have done well in the event. "As small as I am, I like to drop as much of my weight on the steer's head as possible,"[4] says Lyne. Utilizing such a reckless style can often result in injury for the cowboy. Veteran steer wrestler Frank Shepperson has witnessed such mishaps. "My father had a horn run completely through him. I've seen people have their spleens and a lot of other organs punctured with horns. It just takes a slip—anything can go wrong. The steer can slip and come down on you."[5]

Steers are not the only rodeo animals known to cut short a cowboy's career. Injuries are a part of the sport. Every cowboy learns to live with the danger, but when they get up on that bronc or bull, they find it very hard to accept. The animal on which they are sitting is no ordinary house pet. "Bulls are the meanest, rankest creatures on earth," says six-time World Champion Cowboy Larry Mahan. "Horses don't want to step on you when they throw you off. They don't want to trip. Bulls love to step on you, or whip your face into the back of their skull and break your nose and knock out your teeth."[6]

Mahan should know. In the history of rodeo competition he has been one of the most injured—and most successful—cowboys ever to ride off into the sunset. Born in Salem, Oregon, Mahan got his first taste of rodeo by breaking in wild colts at the state fairground. When he was just thirteen years old, he entered his first junior rodeo at Canby, Oregon. Mahan soon developed into a talented cowboy and in 1962, upon finishing high school, he won the state all-around championship. In 1963 Mahan joined the Rodeo Cowboys Association. During the next few years fans across the nation began noticing his fine performances more and more. His winnings had grown to over $40,000 when, in 1966, he won the all-around championship and was declared World Champion Cowboy. He followed it up by winning the title for the next five years and then again in 1973. His achievements put him in a class by himself in the sport of rodeo.

Larry Mahan was truly a driving force for the sport of rodeo. When he put together his incredible string of championships, the nation began to take notice. The National Finals Rodeo was developing into a prestigious event, and its success was due largely to cowboys like Mahan and the great Jim Shoulders of the 1950s.

Like many sports, rodeo has gone through stages of transition. From 1929 to 1944 the Rodeo Association of America named the champion cowboy. The sport was still in its growing stages, and many of the winners—such as Earl Thode, Everett Bowman, John Bowman, and Louis Brooks—kept it going with their lively performances. From 1947 to 1958 the season's top money winner was declared champion. Bill Linderman won the title twice (1950 and 1953) as did another talented competitor, Casey Tibbs (1951 and 1955). But the biggest occurrence of this period was the emergence of a stubborn, never-say-die cowboy named Jim Shoulders.

A native of Tulsa, Oklahoma, Shoulders was the top money winner in 1949, 1956, 1957, and 1958. Known for his bareback and bull riding, he became the best all-around competitor on the circuit. For a long period of time he reigned as king of the rodeo. "One reason for Shoulders' long reign as champion all-around cowboy," explains one sports writer, "was his toughness. He often kept on riding in spite of injuries. Every competition cowboy gets hurt from time to time. But Jim Shoulders could stand the pain and take the abuse and keep on riding. Once in 1957, in Lewiston, Idaho, while he was bareback riding, he tore his collarbone loose from his shoulder. He came back the next day and won on two horses and two bulls."[7]

The first true hero of rodeo, Shoulders set a standard that many would try to duplicate. He was the winner of the first National Finals Rodeo competition in 1959, the last of his world championships.

With the establishment of the National Finals Rodeo competition, rodeo found an identity and a

In 1951 Casey Tibb's all-around performance earned him the title "World Champion Cowboy." (National Cowboy Hall of Fame photo)

One of the greatest cowboys ever, Jim Shoulders won the award an incredible five times. (National Cowboy Hall of Fame photo)

sense of stability. The first three championships, held in Dallas, Texas, were won by Shoulders, Harry Thompkins, and Benny Reynolds, respectively. In 1962 the NFR made another three-year stint, this time on the West Coast, in Los Angeles. It was marked by the appearance of a talented young man named Dean Oliver, who won three straight titles. Finally, in 1965 the National Finals Rodeo found its permanent home—Oklahoma City.

Then the great Larry Mahan took control. From 1966 to 1973 he was named World Champion Cowboy five out of seven times. Only Phil Lyne managed to break up his string of victories—in 1971 and 1972. Following Mahan's reign, other cowboys took aim, but it was only the special ones, such as Tom Ferguson and Leo Camarillo, who made it.

To become king of the mountain in rodeo, a cowboy must possess a certain reckless disregard for life itself. One man who possesses this quality is Denny Flynn. In July 1975 Flynn competed in a rodeo in Salt Lake City, Utah. The twenty-four-year-old from Arkansas was entered in the bull-riding competition. As his turn to ride came, he entered the chute, positioned himself on the bull, and readied himself. Then the buzzer sounded and he was off. Near the end of the ride Flynn decided to loosen the rope that held his hand to the back of the animal so that he could get off on the fence. Just as he was doing this, the bull gave a wild leap, stabbing at the air with its horns. Flynn reached for the fence as he went up into the air. But he was unable to grasp it, and when he came down, the bull hooked him.

"You get grazed or hit by the horn all the time, usually in a glancing way," Flynn later said, "but this felt a little different when it happened. I reached down and felt something in my shirt. It wasn't blood."[8] Flynn crashed to the ground, got up and staggered hurriedly over the fence. As one observer recalled, "The bull's horn had shot up under Denny's rib cage, splitting his liver and stopping only a few inches from his heart. When the horn was jerked back out, as quickly as it had gone in, some of his intestines came with it." As Flynn was rushed to the hospital, there was doubt that he would even live. Six days later he was out of the hospital and back home. Later that year Flynn qualified for the NFR, because, just three months after his near-fatal accident, he was back on the circuit competing.

The story of Denny Flynn is an amazing one, but there are others just like it in the world of rodeo. Not many have come as close to death, but they have tried. From the time they compete as "little britches" to their first big-time competition, the danger, as well as the excitement, is there. For much of the rodeo season the cowboy lives on the road, bouncing from one competition to the next— as many as four or five in a single week. It is a painful, sleepless, and often thankless life-style. But it is one that few of them would wish to relinquish and that many of them greatly desire. Perhaps Larry Mahan speaks for them all when he says:

Most of the guys are out here because they love to be around animals, love to compete, love the life. They don't want to be stuck in some town all their lives at some dull job. The adrenaline flows pretty fast out here. Plenty of guys get hurt, but you worry about a good ride more than about your safety. I figure if I ride three more years, I'll be up on fifteen hundred more head of bucking stock. Now, it's not reasonable to think you can ride fifteen hundred head of bucking stock without going to the hospital, so you just put that idea out of your mind and think about riding and winning and loving the life. I love it more every day."[10]

World Champion Cowboy Award

1929	Earl Thode
1930	Clay Carr
1931	John Schneider
1932	Donald Nesbitt
1933	Clay Carr
1934	Leonard Ward
1935	Everett Bowman
1936	John Bowman
1937	Everett Bowman
1938	Burel Mulkey
1939	Paul Carney
1940	Fritz Truan
1941	Homer Pettigrew
1942	Gerald Roberts
1943	Louis Brooks
1944	Louis Brooks
1947	Todd Whatley
1948	Gerald Roberts
1949	Jim Shoulders
1950	Bill Linderman
1951	Casey Tibbs
1952	Harry Tompkins
1953	Bill Linderman
1954	Buck Rutherford
1955	Casey Tibbs
1956	Jim Shoulders
1957	Jim Shoulders
1958	Jim Shoulders
1959	Jim Shoulders
1960	Harry Tompkins
1961	Benny Reynolds

1962	Tom Nesmith	1973	Larry Mahan
1963	Dean Oliver	1974	Tom Ferguson
1964	Dean Oliver	1975	Tom Fergusson, Leo Camarillo
1965	Dean Oliver	1976	Tom Ferguson
1966	Larry Mahan	1977	Tom Ferguson
1967	Larry Mahan	1978	Tom Ferguson
1968	Larry Mahan	1979	Tom Ferguson
1969	Larry Mahan	1980	Paul Tierney
1970	Larry Mahan	1981	Jimmie Cooper
1971	Phil Lyne	1982	Chris Lybbert
1972	Phil Lyne	1983	**Roy Cooper**

19
The Special Olympics Medal

Special. To different people this word means different things. In the world of sports it has become a trite expression. Games are said to have special importance, players are said to have special performances, and results are said to have special significance. It has reached the point where almost everything falls into this category, and it is no longer enough to be just "special."

Despite the overuse the term can still be justifiably applied to certain things. The birth of a baby is a special moment. Watching a beautiful sunset can be a special experience. And winning a hundred-yard dash can be a very special achievement.

Somehow, the last reference seems a bit misplaced. To most people, running a hundred yards in a straight line is so easy that it's laughable. How could this be special? What if the person running it has braces on both legs, was once told that he would never walk, and has been handicapped all his life. Then, it is truly special.

In sports many things are taken for granted. Who would doubt that every year the Pittsburgh Steelers will be in the play-offs for the Super Bowl; or that the New York Yankees will be in contention for the World Series; or that the Montreal Canadiens will have their names etched on the Stanley Cup? But to those who take part every year in the Special Olympics competition, not even the next step forward is a sure thing.

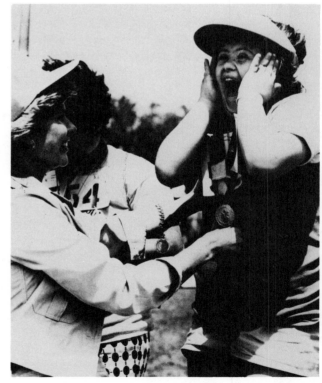

"You *can* do it!" is the spirit of Special Olympics. And the thrill that comes with being brave in the attempt is mirrored in the joy of a million smiling faces. (Special Olympics photo)

According to Daniel Webster, *special* stands for anything "pertaining to something distinct or differing from others." In this context it is indeed very special to take part in or observe a competition such as this. It is special, not to see what athletes win and what athletes lose, but just that they are there. More than any other tournament or play-off in existence, the Special Olympics embody the true meaning of athletic competition. Participants bask in the joy of just participating. It matters little in what place they finish in or what time they record; the victory is already theirs.

Though the event itself originated in 1968 the idea popped up years earlier. In 1963 the Joseph P. Kennedy, Jr., Foundation and the American Association for Health, Physical Education and Recreation developed a physical fitness program for mentally retarded individuals. From this simple beginning grew a reality that became international in scope and attracted thousands of spectators and participants.

Five years after this initial program developed, the first International Special Olympics competition was held in Chicago. Ted Kennedy announced the establishment of the Special Olympics, Inc., and the concept took off. Entries from France and Canada were received within just two years, all fifty states of the Union developed Special Olympics organizations, and over fifty thousand athletes participated. The competition has included track-and-field events, swimming, diving, gymnastics, bowling, basketball, soccer, volleyball, and certain wheelchair events. There have been both individual and team competitions.

By 1974 the number of participants ballooned to over four hundred thousand. Programs were started in other countries, including Honduras, the Bahamas, and Puerto Rico, and donations to support the games became more abundant. The fourth International Special Olympics took place the next year, in 1975, at Central Michigan University, with thirty-two hundred young athletes taking part.

Progress was unbelievable. Through the hard work and determination of the founder and president, Eunice Shriver, seven hundred thousand people, representing nineteen nations, were participating by 1977. The concept became so popular that it was expanded to include winter events. The "Winter Special Olympics were held in Steamboat Springs, Colorado, with skiing and skating among the events.

What has been responsible for this enormous growth? It is difficult to put a finger on it. Anyone who has involved himself with the games has been drawn back time and time again. Eunice Shriver tried to describe why: "In Special Olympics it is not

Corinne Scruggs, of Florida who at seventy was the oldest participant in the Fourth International Games, held in Mount Pleasant, Michigan in August 1975, took the bronze medal in the twenty-five-yard wheelchair event. (Special Olympics photo)

the strongest body or the most dazzling mind that counts. It is the invincible spirit which overcomes all handicaps. For without this spirit winning medals is empty. But with it, there is no defeat."[1]

Can that be it? Can it be that, no matter who wins the race or contest, everybody comes away as the winner? A unique idea, especially in the world of sports, but it seems to be right. Gold, silver, and bronze medals are awarded, but they really don't matter. The inscription on the back of these medals sums up this "invincible spirit:"

"In a close 400-meter race one Special Olympian was about to cross the finish line. At the very moment of victory she saw that a friend, also in the race, had fallen. Without hesitation, she turned, ran back, and helped up her fallen friend. Hand in hand they crossed the finish line together. This is the Spirit of the Special Olympics."[2]

Nowhere did the popularity of the games become more evident than at the campus of the State University of New York at Brockport. That's where the Special Olympics took place in 1979. Every state was represented. There were participants from twenty-four foreign countries. The number of people filling the stadium was incredible—fifteen hundred coaches and chaperones, five thousand volunteers, over six hundred journalists, and more than twenty thousand spectators. Sports celebrities present included boxer Muhammad Ali, Olympian Rafer Johnson, high jumper Dick Fosbury, body builder Arnold Schwarzenegger, swimmer John Naber, and baseball's Hammerin' Hank Aaron.

The reason they were there: to see people like Audie Rewis compete. A jack-of-all-trades, Audie won a bronze medal for the standing broad jump (six feet) and a gold medal in the softball throw (150 feet). But his expertise doesn't end there. He also eagerly participates in football, baseball, and wrestling, and has his eye on gymnastics. "You've got to practice a lot," Audie warned. "You've got to have teachers to spot you on what you are doing wrong. . . . When I get up in the morning I just get up, get dressed, and get ready to go. By then I feel better and I get out there. . . . I think life's pretty good."[3]

Then, there is the story of fourteen-year-old Raymond Snyder. In the 1980 games, held in San Francisco, he entered four events—bowling, swimming, gymnastics, and track. Raymond is paralyzed from the waist down. Like many other Special Olympians, that isn't enough to keep him from taking part. In the swimming competition he is aided by a floatation device; in bowling he uses an angled ramp to assist him with his aims; and in track, he enters the fifty-meter wheelchair dash. In the 1979 State Special Olympics, held at the University of California at Los Angeles (UCLA), Raymond showed his expertise by rolling away with three gold medals.

Another honored Special Olympian is young Melvin Hoover of Tulsa, Oklahoma. When he first joined the games, he had many obstacles to overcome. Unable to walk, Melvin spent the previous year sitting at home and having to be carried around. Once he became an Olympian, he developed into champion material quickly. Bowling was his first event, and he made his mark. Crawling up to the line on his hands and knees, he lunged forward, pushed the ball toward the pins, and landed face down in spread-eagle fashion on the lane. This unusual style proved to be successful— he went on to take first place in his division. Melvin has not stopped with his success at the games, however. He still has one goal that is very important to him: "I want to walk," he says.

Throughout the history of the Special Olympics, donations have played a vital role. Realizing the importance and value of the games, professional athletes have provided support in many ways. Soc-

The Special Olympics Flame of Hope is part of every Opening Ceremony. (Special Olympics photo)

cer's Kyle Rote, Jr., and football's O. J. Simpson each donated five thousand dollars of his first-prize money from the American Broadcasting Company's superstars competition. The National Basketball Association became a major sponsor when it donated twenty-five thousand dollars, which helped send 125 competitors to the 1979 Summer Special Olympics. One of the biggest shows of support came from the American Legion, which gave a whopping seven hundred eighty-five thousand dollars the same year. Through the vehicles of donation and volunteer work, the Special Olympics have survived and flourished.

For many people it is difficult to know what a competition for the handicapped is like and why so many become involved. On 9 December 1978 Dave Kindred wrote a story for the *Washington Post* that outlined the special feeling that surrounds such circumstances. The following is part of that story:

"Until Travis was 1½ or 2 years old, when he cried, he never uttered a sound. We could tell

Special Olympics has attracted some of America's greatest superstars in sports, communications and show business. Champions like Olympic gold medalists Rafer Johnson and Bill Toomey, sports stars like U.S. heavyweight champion George Foreman, Rosie Grier and Arthus Ashe, and entertainers like Arte Johnson, David Cassidy and Sally Struthers of "All In The Family" fame (pictured here) visit local and state meets, present awards, assist in promotion, and give their support to Special Olympics activities everywhere. (Special Olympics photo)

the pain he was in from his face, but no sound came from his throat. We all felt tears because he had no power of speech."

This is a love story, Ron Guidry telling it. He's the Yankee pitcher who has the world at the end of his fastball. He won twenty-seven games last season, won the Cy Young Award, was second in the Most Valuable Player voting and, darkly handsome enough to pass as, say, a French balladeer, now is engaged in selling his fame: endorsements and appearances, agreements and banquets.

For love, not money, Guidry is in Washington. He's here to help out the Special Olympics,

a program of athletic competition for the mentally retarded. If some sports stars take for granted their extraordinary blessings of body and mind, Ron Guidry is not among them. He remembers how wonderful it felt to hear his mentally retarded brother, Travis, first cry out loud.

"And now Travis can form sentences in conjunction with what is going on around him." Guidry said. "He's eleven years old, and the last six years he's been in a special school. Maybe I shouldn't say this, but he has progressed more than the other kids. I am amazed by him." . . .

Now Guidry shares his life with Travis. They play basketball together, football. They run together. Ron has taught Travis to play the drum and shoot a rifle safely. They talk about the Yankees. . . .

"I treat him very, very rough at times and he likes it," Ron said. "Boys can be treated with all kinds of love, constant love, but deep down they need the roughness. When you were young, guys bigger than you chased you. Boys like Travis miss that feeling and they need it, too. They need feeling to chase and be chased.

"So I tackle him and he tackles me, and I run after him and he runs after me.

"He laughs and I laugh." . . .

"The thing that tickles me," said Ron, who throws a baseball nearly one hundred miles per hour, "is that Travis, in a race, is usually faster than everybody else—but once he gets ahead, he'll stop and wait for everybody to catch up.

"To him, it means nothing to win the race. Other boys understand and they run right past Travis.

"But when he finally crosses that finish line—last—there's a big grin on his face."[4]

Herein lies the meaning of "special" in the Special Olympics. Ralph B. Potter, Professor of Social Ethics, Harvard Divinity School, sums it up:

The excellence and the drama which reveal the meaning of sport to those who share in Special Olympics do not rest in the exhibition of physical superiority or in the clever promotion of new variations on the theme of "the thrill of victory and the agony of defeat." The impact of Special Olympics upon us seems, rather, to reside in our capacity to identify with the competitors' striving against their limits and limitations; in our ability to apply to our own lives the example of their hope, and will, and courage to overcome."[5]

Notes

Introduction

1. Oxford Dictionary of the English Language, p. 399.
2. Ibid., p. 399.
3. Ibid., p. 399.
4. *New York Sunday News,*5 January 1969.

Chapter 1: The Stanley Cup

1. Henry Roxborough, *The Stanley Cup Story*, p. 12.
2. Ibid., p. 98.

Chapter 2: The Heisman Memorial Trophy

1. John Cappelletti, "Acceptance Speech for 1973 Heisman Trophy," p. 1.
2. *New York Times,* December 1956, (Sec. 5) p. 1.
3. Ibid., (Sec. 5) p. 1.
4. *New York Times,* 12 December 1957, (Sec 5) p. 1.
5. Ibid., (Sec. 5) p. 1.
6. Ibid., (Sec. 5) p. 1.
7. Ibid., 12 December 1957, (sports) p. 1.
8. *Sports Illustrated,* 12 January 1963, p. 16–21.
9. *New York Times,* 25 November 1963, (Sec. 5) p. 1.
10. *Los Angeles Times,* 25 November 1964, (Sports) p. 1.
11. *Los Angeles Herald Examiner,* 31 January 1968, p. 1-C, 3-C (Sports).
12. Ibid., 24 November 1965, p. B1-3.
13. *Los Angeles Times,* (Sports) p. 1, 6.
14. Ibid., (Sports) p. 1, 6.
15. *Reader's Digest,* January 1970 p. 80.

Chapter 3: The World Series Trophy

1. Daniel Okrent, *The Ultimate Baseball Book*, p. 81.
2. John Devaney, *The World Series*, p. 13.

3. Ibid., p. 29.
4. Ibid., p. 137.
5. Ibid., p. 195.

Chapter 4: The Olympic Medals

1. John Durant, *Highlights of the Olympics*, p. 8.
2. Ibid., p. 18.
3. *San Francisco Chronicle*, 25 February 1980, p. 47, 49.

Chapter 5: The Heavyweight Championship Belt

1. John Grombach, *The Saga of the Fist*, p. 43.
2. Ibid., p. 49.
3. Ibid., p. 58.

Chapter 6: The Davis Cup

1. *Los Angeles Times*, 17 December 1979.
2. Ibid.
3. Will Grimsley, *Tennis—It's History, People and Events*, p. 214.
4. Lord Aberdare, *The Story of Tennis*, p. 132.
5. Allison Danzig, *The Fireside Book of Tennis*, p. 39.
6. Ibid., p. 530.
7. Ibid., p. 606.
8. Ibid., p. 336.
9. Ibid., p. 762.
10. Ibid., p. 453.
11. *Sports Illustrated*, 31 December 1979.
12. Danzig, *Fireside Book of Tennis*, p. 764.

Chapter 7: The Lombardi Trophy

1. John Wiebusch, *Lombardi*, p. 49.
2. Ibid., p. 49.

3. Tom Bennett, et al., *The NFL's Official Encyclopedic History of Pro Football*, p. 320.

4. *Sports Illustrated*, 21 January 1980, p. 5.

5. Tom Bennett, et al., *The NFL's Official Encyclopedic History of Pro Football*, p. 322.

6. *Sports Illustrated*, 21 January 1980, p. 6.

7. Ibid., p. 6.

8. Tom Bennett, et al., *The NFL's Official Encyclopedic History of Pro Football*, p. 324.

9. *Sports Illustrated*, 21 January 1980, p. 8.

10. Ibid., p. 11.

11. Tom Bennett, et al., *The NFL's Official Encyclopedic History of Pro Football*, p. 326.

12. *Sports Illustrated*, 21 January 1980, p. 14.

13. Tom Bennett, et al., p. 328.

14. Ibid., p. 330.

15. Ibid., p. 330.

16. Ibid., p. 330.

17. Ibid., p. 332.

18. Ibid., p. 334.

19. Ibid., p. 334.

20. Ibid. p. 340.

21. Ibid., p.. 340.

22. *Sports* Illustrated, 21 January 1980, p. 29.

23. *Los Angeles Times*, 16 January 1980.

24. *Sports Illustrated*, 28 January 1980, p. 12.

25. *Sports Illustrated*, 21 January 1980, p. 5.

Chapter 8: The Podoloff Cup

1. Zander Hollander, *The Modern Encyclopaedia of Basketball*, p. 347.

2. Sports Resouces Co., *Lincoln Library of Sports Champions*, (Vol. 15) p. 337.

3. Ibid., p. 127.

4. Ibid., p. 126.

5. Ibid., p. 58.

6. Ibid., p. 54.

7. Hollander, *Modern Encyclopaedia of Basketball*, p. 349–50.

8. Gloria Cummins and Jim Cummins, *Basketball by the Pros*, p. 68.

9. Sports Resources Co., *Lincoln Library of Sports Champions*, (vol. 15) p. 27.

10. Hollander, *Modern Encyclopaedia of Basketball*, p. 329.

11. Sports Resources Co., *Lincoln Library of Sports Champions*, (vol. 1) p. 32.

12. Ibid., (vol. 4) p. 73.

13. Gloria Cummins and Jim Cummins, *Basketball by the Pros*, p. 65.

14. Sports Resources, (vol. 11) p. 46.

15. Ibid., *Lincoln Library of Sports Champions*, *(vol. 11)* p. 48.

16. Ibid., (vol. 11) p. 46.

17. Ibid., (vol. 18) p. 109.

18. Ibid., (vol. 18) p. 104.

19. Gloria Cummins and Jim Cummins, *Basketball by the Pros*, p. 58.

20. *Sports Illustrated*, 19 February 1979, p. 66.

Chapter 9: The World Cup

1. Derek Conrad, et. al., *World Cup '78—The Game of the Century*, p. 15.

2. Jared Lebow, *All about Soccer*, p. 54.

3. Ibid., p. 80.

Chapter 10: The America's Cup

1. F. W. Lipscomb, *A Hundred Years of the America's Cup*, p. 1.

2. Herbert Stone, et al., *The America's Cup Races*, p. 21–22.

Chapter 11: The Cy Young Award

1. Sports Resources Co., *The Lincoln Library of Sports Champions*, p. 103–4.

2. Ibid., p. 103.

3. Ibid., p. 16.

4. Ibid., p. 12.

5. *Santa Barbara News Press*, 20 October 1979, p. A-9.

6. Sports Resources Co., *The Lincoln Library of Sports Champions*, vol-3 p. 81.

7. Daniel Oksent, *The Ultimate Baseball Book*, p. 29.

Chapter 12: The Sullivan Memorial Trophy

1. Mac Davis, *Pacemakers in Track and Field*, p. 93.

2. Wally Donovan, *A History of Indoor Track and Field*, p. 29.

3. Ibid., p. 1.

4. Davis, *Pacemakers in Track and Field*, p. 81.

5. Ibid., p. 70.

6. Sports Resources Co., *The Lincoln Library of Sports Champions*, (vol. 9) p. 14.

7. Amateur Athletic Union, *Amateur Athlete Yearbook, 1976*, p. 82.

8. Ibid., 1977, p. 104.

9. Amateur Athletic Union, *Amateur Athlete Yearbook, 1976*, p. 3.

Chapter 13: The Borg-Warner Trophy

1. Associated Press, *A Century of Champions*, p. 231.

Chapter 14: The Walker Cup

1. Charles Price, *The World of Golf*, p. 28.

2. Will Grimsley, *Golf: Its History, People and Events*, p. 132.

3. Charles Price, *The World of Golf*, p. 127.

4. Ibid., p. 135.

5. *Golf Magazine*, January 1980, p. 56.

Chapter 15: The Boston Marathon Medal

1. *The New Yorker*, 29 May 1978, p. 78.

2. *Runners' Monthly Booklet No. 10*, p. 26.

Chapter 16: The Bowler of the Year Award

1. Sports Resources Co., *Lincoln Library of Sports Champions*, (vol. 18) p. 82.

Chapter 17: The Kentucky Derby Trophy

1. Associated Press, *A Century of Champions*, p. 196.

Chapter 18: The World Champion Cowboy Award

1. Douglas Kent Hall, *Rodeo,* p. 9–10.
2. Ibid., p. 8.
3. Ibid., p. 86.
4. Ibid., p. 112.
5. Ibid., p. 115.
6. *Sports Illustrated,* 3 December 1973, p. 43.
7. Sports Resources Co., *The Lincoln Library of Sports Champions,* (vol. 16) p. 108.
8. Bob St. John, *On Down the Road,* p. 209.
9. Ibid., p. 210.
10. *Sports Illustrated,* 3 December 1973, p. 43.

Chapter 19: The Special Olympics Medal

1. *Special Olympics Salutes "Superman," the Movie,* p. 2.
2. Ibid., p. 2.
3. *Special Olympics Newsletter,* November 1979, p. 6.
4. *Washington Post,* 9 December 1978.
5. Ralph Potter, "Special Olympics: What's So Special?" *Special Olympics Salutes "Superman," the Movie,* p. 3.

Bibliography

Introduction

Heisler, Mark. "Athletes Check Their Trophies with $ in Their Eyes." *Los Angeles Times*, 7 March 1980, p. 1, 10.

Pepe, Phil. "A Trophy Arrives Safely." New York: *Sunday News*, 5 January 1969.

Southern California Trophy Co., Inc. *Trophy Thesaurus*, Los Angeles: Southern California Trophy Co. 1979. p. 1–48.

Chapter 1: The Stanley Cup

Roxborough, Henry. *The Stanley Cup Story*. Toronto: Ryerson Press, 1964.

Wigge, Larry (ed.) *"Pro and Amateur Hockey Guide."* *Sporting News*, 1980–81.

Styer, Robert. *The Encyclopaedia of Hockey*. New York: A. S. Barnes & Co., 1970.

Chapter 2: The Heisman Memorial Trophy

"Statue of Limitations." *Reader's Digest*, January 1970, p. 80.

Associated Press. "Irish QB Huarte Wins Heisman Trophy." *Los Angeles Times*, 25 November 1964, Sports Section p–1.

Bisheff, Steve. "Beban Faces Heisman Jinx." *Los Angeles Herald Examiner*. 31 January 1968, Sports Section p. 1-c, 3-c.

Blunk, Frank. "Cassady of Ohio State Eleven Receives Heisman Trophy." *New York Times*, 9 December 1955, Sports Section p. 2.

Bradley, Hugh. "Hornung, Heisman Winner, Lauds Brennan, ND Spirit." *New York Times* 9 December 1956.

Cody, Steve. "Staubach Wears Laurels Well." *New York Times*. 25 November 1963, Sports Section p–1.

Cappelletti, John. "Acceptance Speech for 1973 Heisman Trophy." Presentation given at Downtown Athletic Club, New York, 13 December 1973. Mimeographed.

Daley, Arthur. "As the Crow Flies in the Southwest." *New York Times*, 12 December 1957, Sports Section p–1.

Dickey, Glenn. "An NFL Expert Evaluates Charles White." *San Francisco Chronicle*, 2 January 1980, p. 53.

Downtown Athletic Club, "Heisman—'80." *Downtown Athletic Club Journal*, December 1980, p. 1–76.

Hoffer, Richard. "White Runs Away from Everybody One More Time." *Los Angeles Times*, 4 December 1979, Sports Section p–1, 6.

Parker, Raymond. "Heisman Memorial Trophy Award Brings Nationwide Prominence." *Downtown Athletic Club Journal*, October 1950, p. 40–45.

Sheehan, Joseph. "John Crow Gets Heisman Trophy." *New York Times*, 12 December 1957, Sports Section p–1.

———. "Cannon Gets a Salute from Nixon." *New York Times*, 13 December 1959, Sports Section p. 1.

Tinkham, Harley. "Garrett's Year." *Los Angeles Herald Examiner*, 24 November 1965, p. B1–3.

Ward, Gene. "Crow Hit Peak the Hard Way." *New York Times*, 12 December 1957, Sports Section p. 1.

Wright, Alfred. "Sportsman of the Year: Terry Baker." *Sports Illustrated*, 12 January 1963, p. 16–21.

Chapter 3: The World Series Trophy

Associated Press. *A Century of Champions*. Edited by Ben Olan. 1976.

Devaney, John, and Goldblatt, Burt. *The World Series: A Complete Pictorial History*. New York: Rand McNally & Co., 1972.

Lewine, Harris, and Okrent, Daniel. *The Ultimate Baseball Book*. Boston:Houghton Mifflin Co., 1979.

Seymour, Harold. *The Golden Age of Baseball*. New York: Oxford University Press, 1971.

Chapter 4: The Olympic Medals

Amdur, Neil. "He Beat the Clock." *Los Angeles Herald Examiner*, 17 February 1980, p. D–1.

Olan, Ben (ed.) and the AP Sports Staff, *A Century of Champions*, Associated Press, 1976.

Associated Press and United Press International. "U.S. Completes Its Sweep to Hockey Gold Medal." *San Francisco Chronicle*, 25 February 1980, p. 47, 49.

Benagh, Jim. *Incredible Olympic Feats*. New York: McGraw-Hill, 1976.

Cohn, Lowell. "Memories of Black Protest." *San Francisco Chronicle*, 8 February 1980, p. 68.

Durant, John. *Highlights of the Olympics*. New York: Hastings House Publishers, 1969.

Graham, Peter. *The Modern Olympics*. Edited by Horst Uberhorst. Cornwall, N.Y.: Leisure Press, 1978.

"Heiden Skates to First U.S. Gold." *San Francisco Chronicle*, 16 February 1980, p. 41–42.

Jacobson, Steve. "The U.S.'s Most Memorable Gold Medal." *San Francisco Chronicle* 14 February 1980, p. 71.

Lochner, Bob. "Squaw Valley's Miracle of 1960." *Los Angeles Times*, 7 February 1980, Sports Section p–1.

Chapter 5: The Heavyweight Championship Belt

Olan, Ben (ed.) and the AP Sports Staff. *A Century of Champions*, Associated Press, 1976.

Dribble, R. F. *John L. Sullivan*. Boston: Little, Brown & Co., 1925.

Eskin, Lew. "Ali-Holmes: the 'Last Hurrah.'" *Boxing Illustrated*. (Montreal), December 1980, p. 16.

_____."Heavyweight Showdown—Round Two." *Boxing Illustrated* (Montreal), December 1980, p. 20.

Grombach, John. *The Sage of the Fist*. New York: A. S. Barnes & Co., 1977.

Lardner, Rex. *The Legendary Champions*. New York: American Heritage Press, 1972.

Chapter 6: The Davis Cup

Aberdare, Lord. *The Story of Tennis*. London: Stanley Paul & Co., 1959.

Danzig, Allison. *The Fireside Book of Tennis*. Edited by Petr Schwed. New York: Simon and Schuster, 1972.

Greenberg, Alan. "McEnroe Stars in Court Comedy." *Los Angeles Times*, 17 December 1979.

Grimsley, Will. *Tennis—Its History, People, and Events*. Englewood Cliffs, N. J.: Prentice-Hall, 1971.

Kirkpatrick, Curry. "The Italians Get the Boot." *Sports Illustrated*, 31 December 1979, p. 75.

Chapter 7: The Lombardi Trophy

Bennett, Tom; Boss, David; Campbell, Jim; Siwoff, Seymour; Smith, Rick; and Wiebusch, John. *The NFL's Official Encyclopedic History of Professional Football*. New York: Macmillan Co., 1977.

Heisler, Mark. "France Chides Ram Fans: Super Bowl 'Not Theirs.'" *Los Angeles Times*, 16 January 1980.

Smith, Robert. *Illustrated History of Pro Football*, New York: Grosset and Dunlap, 1972.

"The Super Bowl." *Sports Illustrated*, 21 January 1980, p. 1–40. (supplement.)

Wiebusch, John. *Lombardi*. Chicago: Follett Publishing Co., 1971.

Zimmerman, Paul. "Super Bowl XIV." *Sports Illustrated*, 28 January 1980, p. 12.

Chapter 8: The Podoloff Cup

Olan, Ben (ed.) and the Associated Press Sports Staff, *A Century of Champions*, Associated Press, 1976.

Cummins, Gloria, and Cummins, Jim. *Basketball by the Pros*. New York: Mason-Charter, 1977.

Deford, Frank. "Bounding into Prominence." *Sports Illustrated*, 19 February 1979, p. 60.

Fox, Larry. *Illustrated History of Basketball*. New York: Grosset and Dunlap, 1974.

Hollander, Zander. *The Modern Encyclopaedia of Basketball*. New York: Four Winds Press, 1973.

Sports Resources Co., *Lincoln Library of Sports Champions*, Columbus, Ohio: Frontier Press, 1978.

Newman, Bruce. "NBA Play-offs." *Sports Illustrated*, 5 May 1980, p. 16.

White, Dick. *Los Angeles Lakers Illustrated*. Los Angeles: Jaffe Printers: Los Angeles, 1973.

Chapter 9: The World Cup

Archer, Michael; Arnold, Peter; Davis, Christopher; Gardner, Paul; and Tyler, Martin. *The International Book of Soccer*. New York: A & W Publishers, 1977.

Batty, Eric, ed. *International Football Book*. London: Souvenir Press, 1977.

Conrad, Derek; Sidaway, Robert; and Wilson, Bob. *World Cup '78: The Game of the Century*. London: William Collins Sons & Co., 1978.

Lebow, Jared. *All about Soccer*. New York: Newsweek Books, 1978.

Signy, Dennis. *A Pictorial History of Soccer*. New York: Spring Books, 1968.

Soar, Phil. *World Cup '78*. London: Marshall Cavendish Editions, 1978.

Chapter 10: The America's Cup

Olan, Ben (ed.) and the AP Sports Staff, *A Century of Champions*. Associated Press, 1976.

Distel, Dave. "America's Yachtsman?" *Los Angeles Times*, 7 February 1980; p. 1, 6, 12 (sports section.).

Lipscomb, F. W. "A Hundred Years of the America's Cup". *New York Graphic Society Ltd*, October 1972.

Livingston, Kimball. "The Distant Sail for the America's Cup." *San Francisco Chronicle*, 10 January 1980, p. 49, 53.

Satchell, Michael. "Ted Turner Puts His Money Where His Mouth Is." *Parade*, 2 March 1980, p. 10–12.

Stone, Herbert; Taylor, Williams; and Robinson, William. The America's Cup Races & W. W. Norton and Co., Inc.

Chapter 11: The Cy Young Award

Olan, Ben, (ed.), and the AP Sports Staff, *A Century of Champions*, The Associated Press, 1976.

Associated Press. "Mike Flanagan Wins Cy Young." *Santa Barbara News Press*, 1979. p. A-90

Hawkins, Burton. "A Chat with Cy Young." *Baseball Digest*, New York: Rand McNally and Co., p. 20.

Okrent, Daniel. *The Ultimate Baseball Book*. Edited by Harris Lewine. Boston: Houghton-Mifflin Co., 1979.

Sports Resources Co. *The Lincoln Library of Sports Champions*. Columbus, Ohio: Frontier Press. 1978.

Vass, George. "Tom Seaver: The Game I'll Never Forget." *Baseball Digest*, New York: Rand McNally & Co., p. 181–82.

Chapter 12: The Sullivan Memorial Trophy

Amateur Athletic Union. "The Sullivan Award." In *Amateur Athlete Yearbook, 1978*. Indianapolis: Amateur Athletic Union, 1978, p. 104–5.

———. "The Sullivan Award." In *Amateur Athlete yearbook, 1977*. Indianapolis: Amateur Atheltic Union, 1977, p. 94–95.

Besford, Pat. *Encyclopaedia of Swimming*. New York: St. Martin's Press, 1976.

Davis, Mac. *Pacemakers in Track and Field*. World Publishing Co., 1968.

Donovan, Wally. *A History of Indoor Track and Field*. El Cajon, Calif.: Edward Jules Co., 1976.

Sports Resources Co., *The Lincoln Library of Sports Champions*. Columbus, Ohio: Frontier Press, 1978.

Chapter 13: The Borg-Warner Trophy

Olan, Ben (ed) and the Associated Press Sports Staff, *A Century of Champions*, Associated Press, 1976.

Bloemaker, Al. *Five Hundred Miles to Go*. New York: Coward-McCann, 1961.

Devaney, John, and Devaney Barbara. *The Indianapolis 500*. New York: Rand McNally Co., 1976.

"The Indy 500," *Sports Illustrated* (supplement), 26 May 1980.

Olney, Ross. *Great Moments in Speed*. Englewood Cliffs, N.J.: Prentice-Hall, 1970.

Stambler, Irwin. *Great Moments in Auto Racing*. New York: Four Winds Press, 1968.

Chapter 14: The Walker Cup

Grimsley, Will. *Golf: Its History, People, and Events*, Englewood Cliffs, N.J.: Prentice-Hall, 1966.

Hickok, Ralph. *New Encyclopedia of Sports*, New York: McGraw-Hill, 1977.

Menke, Frank, and Treat, Suzanne. *The Encyclopedia of Sports*. New York: A. S. Barnes & Co., 1975.

Peper, George, ed. "Jack at 40," *Golf Magazine*, January 1980, p. 56.

Price, Charles. *The World of Golf*. New York: Random House, 1972.

Chapter 15: The Boston Marathon Medal

"The Boston Marathon." In *Runners' Monthly Booklet No. 10*. Mountain View, Calif.: World Publication, 1974, p. 1.

Woodley, Richard. "The Miracle of Marathoning." *Sport*, May 1979, p. 53.

Chapter 16: The Bowler of the Year Award

Benagh, Jim and Pratt, John Lowell. *The Official Ency-*

clopedia of Sports. New York: Franklin-Watts Inc., 1964.

Hickok, Ralph. *New Encyclopedia of Sports*. New York: McGraw-Hill Co., 1977.

Sports Resources Co., *The Lincoln Library of Sports Champions*. Columbus, Ohio: Frontier Press. 1978.

Chapter 17: The Kentucky Derby Trophy

Olan, Ben (ed.), and the Associated Press Sports Staff, *A Century of Champions*, Associated Press, 1976

Chapter 18: The World Champion Cowboy Award

Anderson, Bob, ed. *Sportsource*. Mountain View, Cal.: World Publications, 1975.

Benagh, Jim, and Penzler, Otto. *ABC's Wide World of Sports Encyclopedia*. New York: Stadia Sports, 1973.

Hall, Douglas Kent. *Rodeo*. New York: Ballantine Books, 1976.

Hickok, Ralph. *New Encyclopedia of Sports*, New York: McGraw-Hill, 1977.

St. John, Bob. *On down the Road: The World of the Rodeo Cowboy*. Englewood Cliffs, N.J.: Prentice-Hall, 1977.

Savitt, Sam. *Rodeo*. New York: Doubleday & Co., 1963.

Shrake, Edwin. "Horsing Around with Bull." *Sports Illustrated*, 3 December 1973, p. 43.

Sports Resources Co. *The Lincoln Library of Sports Champions*. Columbus, Ohio: Frontier Press, 1978.

Chapter 19: The Special Olympic Medal

Kindred, Dave. "First Cry Brings Tears to Older Brother Guidry." *Washington Post*, 9 December 1978.

Potter, Ralph B. "Special Olympics: What's So Special?" In *Special Olympics Salutes "Superman," the Movie*. Washington, D.C.: Special Olympics, Inc., 19 December 1978, p. 3.

Rosenbaum, Art. "The Best Olympics of All." *San Francisco Chronicle*, 14 April 1980.

Special Olympics, Inc. *Special Olympics Newsletter*. November 1979.

Index